# Herbs:
# Medicinal, Magical, Marvelous!

# Herbs:
# Medicinal, Magical, Marvelous!

Deborah J. Martin, MH

BOOKS

Winchester, UK
Washington, USA

First published by O-Books, 2010
O Books is an imprint of John Hunt Publishing Ltd., The Bothy, Deershot Lodge, Park Lane, Ropley,
Hants, SO24 0BE, UK
office1@o-books.net
www.o-books.com

For distributor details and how to order please visit the 'Ordering' section on our website.

Text copyright: Deborah J. Martin 2009

ISBN: 978 1 84694 372 0

Design: Stuart Davies

The information contained herein is not intended to take the place of diagnosis and treatment
by a qualified medical practitioner or naturopath. Any recommendations are for educational
purposes only and are believed to be effective. No expressed or implied guarantee as to the
effectiveness of this information can be given nor liability taken.

Printed in the UK by CPI Antony Rowe

We operate a distinctive and ethical publishing philosophy in all
areas of our business, from our global network of authors to
production and worldwide distribution.

# CONTENTS

*The study of herbs can at first appear overwhelming. This book however demystifies the practice, and presents the material in a humorous yet authoritative manner. The author explains the structure behind the Latin names, which otherwise can often confuse the beginner, and gives details on the differences between synthetic drugs and natural alternatives. She also details how to work with herbs safely, and references to astrological correspondences whilst also giving a simple ailment list which enables the reader to quickly find a cure for their problem, magically and medicinally. Many books on herbs will tell you what to do, but not how to do it; this book explains in simple terms how to use herbal preparations, and the cheat sheets make for simple referencing, giving the reader a concise overview of each herbs' use and the safety precautions.*

**Vikki Bramshaw**, Author, *Craft of the Wise*

*Genuinely magical and marvelous, Herbs, Deborah J. Martin's herbal, is an excellent resource for anyone interested in plants, spell casting or traditional healing. Martin points out an extremely significant fact: when it comes to botanicals, it is not always easy or even possible to separate metaphysical and therapeutic properties. Herbs: Medicinal, Magical, Marvelous! is that rare book that focuses simultaneously on different aspects of plant powers, not just one. Herbs is well organized, detailed, fun, and highly recommended. Keep a copy beside the herbal medicine chest and your Book of Shadows.*

**Judika Illes**, Author, *The Encyclopedia of 5000 Spells, Pure Magic*

*If you're searching for a thorough and accurate herbal resource that combines the medicinal and magical aspects of plants, look no further than Herbs: Medicinal, Magical, Marvelous! Deborah Martin's years of knowledge and experience with witchcraft and herbs translate seamlessly into a cohesive source of information that can function both as detailed reference and written journal. All green witches, from novice to adept, will find this book to be invaluable in their day-to-day craft!*

**Cairelle Perilloux**, Proprietress, Witchy Living

# Preface

Every witch I know, without exception, is interested in the use of herbs, not only from a magical perspective but also for medicinal purposes. Like all my friends, I spent hours scouring books and the Internet for the information I needed, whether it's what a particular herb is good for, or which herb to use in a particular application. There are sources that have medicinal uses or magical uses but none I could find that combined the two. This compilation is the accumulation of research for my own purposes. I hope you will find it as useful as I do.

# Introduction

*Herbs work on the physical, emotional, mental and spiritual levels of existence.*
~ Matthew Wood

Like many herbalists, I have a difficult time separating the physical effect of herbs from the spiritual, or magical, effect. I am joined in this by herbalists going back centuries. Some of the oldest books on medicine were written by Babylonians as early as 2000 BCE, using both herbs and incantations to cure illness. What little we know of life before the arrival of Christianity suggests that herbs were used in rituals on a regular basis, not just in Britain but all over the world. Tribal medicine men and shamans from diverse cultures in Siberia, North and South America, India and Africa have used plants and incantations to heal the sick for over 4,000 years. It has been forgotten by many that plants are living beings who can add their energies to ours, not only on the physical level but on the spiritual level as well.

Scientifically-speaking, Man has been using herbs probably since the first time someone observed an animal eating a plant, put a piece of that same plant in their mouth, discovered it didn't taste *too* bad and filled the belly at the same time. Over the centuries, observation and experimentation have given us knowledge of plants' uses in many different applications: some for food, medicine, and clothing; others for fuel; and yet others for magic.

Or, if you believe in animism (everything in Nature has a consciousness), plants have told us of their wonderful properties. It's not difficult to imagine some prehistoric hunter walking along, feeling rather poorly when he hears, "if you eat a few of my leaves, I can help you feel better". He followed the instructions of the voice and lo and behold, felt better! Just in case he got the same sickness, he took one of the plants back to his cave and planted it there so he'd have it nearby the next time. The same thing happened to many people in many different situations and word spread.

Whichever way you think, our society is trying to come full circle: science took us from herbal medicine to synthetic medicine and from living with the land to living with technology. I see signs today that many are now interested in reclaiming their "natural" heritage, not necessarily to reject science and technology but to try to blend everything into a harmonious life. Herbs can and should play a large part in our "natural" lives.

The dictionary defines an herb as a non-woody, seed-producing plant, like peppermint. An herbalist's definition includes not only that non-woody, seed-producing plant but seaweeds, ferns, fungi, mosses, trees and the resins exuded from trees. Fruits and vegetables are also included as they, too, have therapeutic and magical properties.

If you're interested in herbs, no matter the application, I encourage you to start learning the Latin binomial names of plants. They are unique identifiers given to individual plants and if you use them, you won't confuse yourself or anyone else. Binomial means "two names". The first is the Genus – the "parent" name, like *Lavandula* for lavender. The second name is the Species, which identifies the individual plant like *officinalis* or *angustifolia* (two different plants, but *Lavandula officinalis* and *Lavandula angustifolia* are both lavender). Many herbs have the same common name and it's easy to confuse one with the other. For example, *Melissa officinalis* and *Monarda fistulosa* are both commonly known in different parts of the world as Balm. They do share some of the same properties, but not all, and are not in the same botanical family. Using the Latin binomial means you'll be getting the exact plant you want and it's therapeutic or magical properties. To help you in this task, the herbs in the appendices are listed by Latin binomial, although I've included a cheat sheet which has the common name I know the herbs by. You can easily create your own using any computer's spreadsheet program. This will allow you to sort, and then re-sort as you add herbs.

Getting herbs today is really easy. Your grocery store will carry many fresh herbs in the produce department, or the baking aisle has row upon row of little tins and jars. There are many other stores, both brick-and-mortar and virtual, which sell herbs. I do advocate the use of Certified Organic herbs but governmental regulations have made that rather expensive. So, be sure what you're buying is at least pesticide- and fungicide-free and hasn't been irradiated. You want the plant in as close to its natural state as possible. Be careful if you're buying dried herbs. Little pieces of green leaf or brown bark can look the same. Dried herbs don't necessarily smell the same as fresh so you can't always trust your nose. Reputable herb dealers will give you the Latin binomial name of the plant they're selling you. If at all possible, the best herbs to use are the ones you or your neighbors grow in a garden; or in pots on a deck, patio or window ledge. If the herb grows in the same environment you live in yourself, it will interact with your body more easily.

As you familiarize yourself with herbs you'll notice many are what landscapers and others refer to as "weeds". A weed is simply a plant growing where it's not wanted. I have a lot of uses for the perfectly-kept-lawn suburbanite's banes: dandelion and plantain. Many wildflowers that grow alongside rural fields are also very useful. So, keep your eyes peeled for "weeds" you can use, too. Just be sure that you harvest them *at least* 50 feet away from the road (to lessen the toxic chemicals picked up from car exhaust) and that you have permission from the land owner to harvest it.

If you harvest from the wild, *be sure of the plant.* Many plants look the same and you can accidentally pick the wrong one, or even something that's harmful. Take along a good field guide and be sure of your identification. If you're not entirely certain of the plant, don't use it! And, if you harvest from the wild, *do not take it all.* My rule is one-third of any one stand of plants in a given area. That way there will be more not only the next time you need it but also for future generations of herb users.

Also be sure to consult books regarding the best time to harvest. As a general rule if you're collecting the above-ground part of the plant, get it just before it flowers unless you're using the flowers themselves. If you want the flowers, harvest as the flower opens. Roots should be collected either in the early Spring or late Fall but not while the plant is in its growing stage. The "good stuff" will collect in the roots when the plant is dormant. For any type of plant, harvest it in the morning just after the dew has dried to get the highest concentration of volatile oils and other chemicals.

There are many methods of drying herbs. For leafy herbs the best thing to do is to separate the leaf from the stalk and spread them out on a screen, away from sunlight but with plenty of air circulation, to dry. (And old window screen laid across the top of an open box works great, or make a frame of lumber and staple screen material to it.) If the best part to use is the "aerial" (above-ground) part of the plant, bunch three to five stalks together with twine or a rubber band and hang them from a ceiling somewhere warm and dry. To collect seeds as they dry, hang bunches of stalks from the ceiling with a paper bag tied around the seed heads, tapping the stalks every day or two to loosen the seeds. To dry roots, wash them thoroughly, and then split them at least in half with a sharp knife. Spread out on a screen. Depending on your climate, most herbs will dry in two or three weeks but roots can take a month or more to dry thoroughly. Leafy herbs spread on a cookie sheet in a warm oven (no higher than 200° F) will dry to a crisp in a couple of hours.

Now that you've got them, you need to keep them somewhere. If you have fresh herbs, put them in the vegetable bin in your refrigerator with the setting for that bin on low humidity. Dried herbs need to be stored in an airtight container in a cool, dark, dry place.

Some other things you may want to collect before starting on your exploration of herbs:

- Colored highlighting pens. Use them to highlight edges of pages of books where you've recorded or found useful information and also the information on that page ... whether in your notebook or a published work. Color-code your information so when you're looking for something magical related to health, for example, just look for the red edges. Or if you're researching how to get rid of the flu, you might use a blue highlighter. This gets rid of all the sticky notes popping out of the tops of books and makes everything fit onto the bookshelf. The highlighters also won't lose their adhesion and fall out.

- A mortar & pestle is needed to break up herbs. No matter your preparation, you want to crush the herb(s) a bit to release the oils and make it easier for the liquid to seep into the pores of the herb to get all the goodness out. (As an aside, if you're making a cup of tea from a commercial tea bag, try squeezing the bag slightly before putting it in the water. I think you'll find your tea much more flavorful.) Be sure your mortar & pestle are of a non-woody substance like stone or ceramic. Wood will absorb the oils from the plants as you crush them and those oils will mix with a subsequent plant being worked on. I also recommend that if you're working with toxic plants that you have two sets. Use one set for the non-toxic plants and the other for toxic. This will avoid *any* chance of mixing one with the other. Be sure everything is cleaned thoroughly after each use, using isopropyl (rubbing) alcohol prior to washing if you're working with resins. That said, using a mortar & pestle to powder roots, barks and resins can be nearly impossible unless you're built like Charles Atlas. An electric coffee grinder, blender or food processor will make the process much easier. If you use an electric appliance, be sure you don't grind your herbs too fine unless you really do want a powder. Using a powder in a liquid preparation will result in a paste that is nearly impossible to strain. Like the mortar & pestle, be sure your appliance is cleaned thoroughly prior to using it again.

- Heatproof container(s). For burning raw incense and candles, a heatproof container is an absolute must. You can go all-out and get a fancy incense burner (a censer) or use a drain saucer from a clay flower pot with about an inch of sand in the bottom. I wouldn't recommend using a glass or plastic ashtray. They're not meant to have heat directly applied for long periods and could shatter. I've seen ashtrays made of cast iron (they look like a miniature frying pan) which will combine the need for a heatproof container *and* the power of iron[*]. Whatever your choice, ensure it has some sort of a rim so if your candle overflows or you burn it all the way out, the resulting puddle of wax won't flow over the edge and onto things it shouldn't.

- Charcoal tablets will be needed if you're going to burn raw or granular incense. These are just like the charcoal you use in your barbeque grill but are smaller, round and have an indentation in the center to hold the incense as you sprinkle it on. Be sure to get the self-igniting ones. Regular charcoal takes a very long time to catch.

- Cloth bags or scraps of material. You probably know someone who still sews, although that's getting to be a lost art. With your friend's permission, raid their scrap bag for small pieces of cotton or linen cloth you can make into sachets or ask your friend to sew up some small bags for you. The squares sold by fabric stores already cut for quilting are a good size for a small sachet. If you need to make a sachet it's easier to have the supplies on hand than to drive to the fabric store to get a quarter-yard of material. Should the spell call for a particular color fabric and you don't happen to have that color in stock at the moment, I've found it works just as well to use fabric paint to paint a design in the appropriate color on plain muslin. (So maybe you should keep some fabric paint on hand, too.)

- Opaque jars. Dried herbs will keep longer if stored away from light in an airtight container. Old vitamin or pain reliever jars (normally plastic or a dark-colored glass) washed with soap and hot water or run through the dishwasher and thoroughly air dried work great. If you want to remove the old paper labels, soak the bottle in white

---

[*] The use of iron in a magical sense goes back centuries. Because it isn't found in its pure state on Earth, it was considered a gift of the gods when a meteorite fell. Iron provides power and protection. It will keep malevolent spirits (and intentions) at bay. It is an element of healing (surgical instruments of old) but can also harm or kill (knives and guns).

vinegar for 10-15 minutes before washing to soften the adhesive. Most labels will come off easily after this period of time but some require a longer soak. Re-label with the contents and, in the case of herbs, the date purchased or harvested. You can also use the *glass* jars for your bath salts (salt and plastic don't like each other). If you're going to store a lot of herbs and don't have that many jars around, get yourself some canning jars. A half-pint or pint jar will hold more than an ounce of most herbs or several ounces of a salt mixture. For storing herbs, once you've screwed the lid on, put the jar in a brown paper bag, like a lunch bag, and then use a twist-tie to close the bag. Label the bag with the contents and the date you purchased or harvested it. If you keep them in a cool, dark, dry place (like a kitchen cupboard away from the stove or better yet, in your basement if you have one), most herbs stored this way will last up to two years. Check your stock occasionally for freshness. If you open the jar, take a whiff and don't get a hint of what's inside or get a musty smell, it's time to recycle and replace that herb.

- Smaller bottles, jars and vials. Travel-sized shampoo, mouthwash or lotion bottles, once washed thoroughly, are just about the right size for storing your 1/8 cup base oil/essential oil mixture. Perfume sample vials are great for holding mixtures of essential oils only. The more expensive brands of perfume usually use a glass vial with a small plastic applicator. These you will need to rinse with isopropyl alcohol prior to washing to get all the perfume out. They hold 10 to 20 drops of essential oil. Cosmetic jars can be quite small and hold ointments or powders nicely.

- Labels. You can get a small package at the office supply store for a minimal amount of money. Use these to label your re-used jars and bottles.

- Cheesecloth, old pantyhose, old T-shirts, coffee filters. If you're making a tea, infused oil, ointment or tincture with loose herbs, you'll need to strain the herb out. The T-shirts and pantyhose can be washed and re-used and have a finer weave than an aluminum strainer or cheesecloth. Don't use fabric softener when washing these items – it will leave a residue that is great if you're going to have a shirt next to your skin but you don't want that combining with your herbal mixture. Coffee filters can be used to get the "dregs" out which can spoil and make your mixture go bad faster. I've found that the flour-sacking dish towels Mom used are wonderful for a first-strain. They are thinner than T-shirts and the weave is generally tighter than cheesecloth. They're still available from a couple of Internet sources. (Hint: dampen any cloth or filter before starting to strain. This will prevent the liquid from "wicking" up and makes the straining go faster.) You can also stretch cheese-cloth or pantyhose on a frame (pull a wire coat hanger square) and use it to dry herbs. Place the frame on top of an open box so air will circulate.

- A notebook or binder. You'll want to keep a diary of your experiments with herbs. In the back of this book are templates I designed for myself. You're welcome to copy them if you find them useful.

I'd like to advocate that once used, you recycle your herbs back to the Earth. Allow them to nourish a new plant. If you can, start a compost pile. If you live somewhere that's not allowed or practical, ask if you can bury them in a flower bed, or mix them with the dirt in the pots on your patio or deck.

# Herbs as Medicine

*Most science is only high falutin' nature studies.*

~ Stephen Strauss

I am always amused when I hear herbal medicine (and other traditions) referred to as "alternative" medicine. It's *original* medicine! Traditional Chinese Medicine is a system that goes back nearly 5,000 years. Indian Ayurvedic medicine is just about as old and still in use today. Both systems are very effective. If they weren't, they would have died out years ago.

For most peoples and for most of our history, there hasn't been a clear line between food and medicine. Archaeological sites in Iraq show the Neanderthals used herbs more than 60,000 years ago. Excavations of Neolithic villages in England and Switzerland have shown that our ancestors in those areas used herbs as well. A prehistoric man found frozen in the Italian Alps carried pieces of a fungus that we know would cure his intestinal parasites. It is estimated he died 5,300 years ago. Hippocrates (ca. 460 BCE – ca. 370 BCE) is generally considered the "Father of Medicine" and he advocated the use of herbs for healing.

Before about the 1930's in our Western world, Man principally relied on herbs to heal what ailed him. (We won't go into the use of leeches.) People didn't generally travel very far and UPS certainly didn't deliver door-to-door, so folks relied on what they had growing in their garden, what they could harvest along the sides of fields or roads or what they could trade for.

When the Industrial Revolution hit Europe and people flocked to the cities for jobs, they no long had access to those gardens or fields and had to rely on doctors and apothecaries with shops in the city. Many of these were charlatans and most were too expensive for the average Joe to afford. Families were fragmented and knowledge wasn't always handed down from generation to generation as it had been in the past.

Most books written on medicine were in Greek or Latin, something most people didn't read – if they could read at all.

Nicholas Culpeper was one of the first to write an herbal in English with an emphasis on English plants that could be locally obtained without importation. If you read his herbal, first published in 1649, you'll notice that he includes astrology in his description of the plants. While he was ridiculed by many for including astrology, magic and folklore, his book was, and continues to be a best-seller. Magically-speaking, astrology still plays a large part in the use of herbs.

Today's Western herbalism is an accumulation of everything that has been handed down through the centuries, not just from the Greeks and Romans, but from the Arabs and local folk traditions as well. When Europeans discovered the New World, they added to their repertoire what the indigenous peoples used. Seeds have traveled across the world's waters, so what was found in the Americas is now grown in Europe and Asia and vice versa.

Before scientific experimentation on plants started in the 1800's, herbalists *did* try to make a science of it by developing and relying on the Doctrine of Signatures. This meant that the plant's appearance was an indication of what it would help. It wasn't very exact: it was thought that a fungus found growing on a dead tree would revive a deceased person. However, sometimes they were right. Take Eyebright as an example. Its leaves are very mottled and look something like bloodshot eyes. Therefore, it would be good for treating sore eyes. Science has since proven that it really is good for sore eyes but not because of the way it looks but because of the chemical constituents of the plant.

Science has made great strides in understanding why herbs work the way they do. From the flower Foxglove, they synthesized the active ingredient and made digitalis for heart problems. From the Willow tree and the herb Meadowsweet they synthesized the active ingredient and made what we now know as aspirin. While I will not argue that synthesizing some of these chemicals has saved some plants from extinction, herbs are much more than their main active ingredient. They are made up of everything they touch; from the vibrations of the sun, moon and air on their leaves; to the trace minerals in the soil their roots touch; and the life-giving qualities of the water they drink. If we isolate the main active chemical from the whole plant, we interrupt the plant's harmony, which is where the secret of health and healing lies. The Indian herb Rauwolfia has been used for centuries *in its entirety* with great success to treat hypertension. Scientists synthesized the main active ingredient and although effective, that drug has some rather unpleasant side effects.

Synthetic drugs also have only one therapeutic action ... they work on one invader in the body, be it a bacterium, virus or fungus. Herbs on the other hand generally have more than one therapeutic action. Lavender is widely known as a calming herb. It is *also* antiseptic and healing. The next time you burn yourself, put a couple of drops of Lavender essential oil on the burn, feel it start to get rid of the pain and smell the aroma to calm your racing heartbeat. You'll notice the burn will heal faster, too.

Today there's another problem with synthetic drugs: antibiotics. Not only are they 'way over-prescribed but they are used on our food animals and found in our water supply as well. Bacteria have the ability to adapt their own immune systems very quickly to one chemical hitting them and science can't develop antibiotics fast enough to keep up with ever-more-resistant bacteria. Herbs, on the other hand, have many chemicals in them. Bacteria can't adapt themselves to so many chemicals bombarding them at one time and thus die. Penicillin has one chemical: penicillin. Garlic, on the other hand, has been found to contain 33 sulfur compounds, 17 amino acids and a host of other chemicals. Because of this, Garlic is one of the best all-round healing herbs.

Herbal medicine sounds complicated, doesn't it? Requires specialized knowledge, huh? *Nope.* Unless your problem is a serious one, you can and should use herbs on your own both as preventive measure and to treat minor illnesses. Start small, like with a cut on your finger, a tension headache or a minor bout of the flu. Do some research and then some experimentation. Often your doctor will give you a prescription and tell you, "try this. If it doesn't work, call me and we'll try something else." Herbs are the same. Because your body is unique, it may take a bit to find out what herbs work for you in a given situation but believe me, they will. Be sure to keep a diary: what you took, how you prepared it, how much and how often you took it and what the results were. This way you'll build up not only your knowledge of herbs but also a list of favorites.

Favorites? Yes, favorites. As of this writing there are approximately 50,000 plants on this Earth used for medicinal purposes. In the 1950's a well-known botanist named Richard Evans Schultes documented the medicinal qualities of more than 2,000 plants in the Amazon jungle. Experts think he touched on just 1% of what's available in that small corner of the world. No one can know (or get) all of them and your reaction to a particular herb may not be the same as mine, so you'll get to know which herb available to *you* works for the particular problem *you* have.

Allow me to reiterate: do your research. Some herbs can interact with each other and/or with prescription drugs – sometimes unfavorably. Dosages for babies, children, the elderly and the frail can be much more critical. If you have allergies, practice some caution. For example, if you have a ragweed allergy, be careful using Feverfew or Calendula. All three are in the same botanical family and if you're allergic to one, you may be allergic to all. If you're pregnant, are planning on becoming pregnant or are nursing be sure to speak with your doctor first. Remember that what you take will make its way into your baby's body. And always remember: more isn't better. Start with small doses and work your way up.

You also need to know that not all herbs are safe. It's widely thought that Vincent Van Gogh cut off his ear while under the influence of absinthe, an alcoholic drink made from Wormwood. Wormwood is hallucinogenic in even moderate quantities and, although he probably had some psychological issues, I understand he drank a lot of the stuff. Many plants have what is known as a "low therapeutic margin". That means that a correct dose can help, anything over that can harm or even kill. If you're unsure of anything herbal, please be sure to consult a qualified naturopathic physician or herbalist.

# Herbs in Magic

*The unnatural – that too is natural.*
~ Goethe

Why do we use herbs in our magical spells? The true answer to that question lies hidden behind the veil of antiquity.

In the 1960's, a polygraph (lie detector) expert did some experiments with plants and found out that they were sentient. The book *The Secret Life of Plants* details the results of those experiments. (If you don't remember, this is what set the whole world to talking to plants. Those of us that know better were doing it long before then.) It has been scientifically proven that plants are aware of their surroundings and respond to human communication.

Perhaps someone at some time discovered this prior to the advent of scientific experimentation. Like that prehistoric hunter eating a plant to cure his illness, a plant told someone they could help protect the cave from the nasty next-cave neighbor. I have always believed plants have their own spirits and energies and if you ask them nicely, they will add their energies to yours. The more positive energy you have working for you, the easier it is to accomplish your aims.

Does herb magic work? You bet. As long as your expectations are reasonable, you should expect to see positive results. If you think you're going to lose 50 pounds overnight, think again. That is not a reasonable expectation (and not very healthy, either). But if you're looking to lose 50 pounds over the next six months to a year, herb magic can help.

The Universe also helps those who help themselves. If you want to lose weight, you're going to have to pay attention to your diet and start exercising. If you need to pay off your bills, stop buying every frivolous thing that catches your eye and live within a budget. Magic, herbal or otherwise, is simply a tool and will *assist* you in your efforts. It won't do anything on its' own.

# Preparations

Interestingly enough, many types of herbal preparations are useful in both a medicinal *and* magical context. As you're doing your research, you'll find out which types of preparations work best in a given situation. Be sure to record these in your diary.

In this section I'm going to always use dried herbs unless otherwise noted. Be aware that for the most part, dried herbs are twice as strong as fresh so if you're using fresh, double the amount in your recipe. Also be sure you slightly crush your herbs as mentioned before.

The easiest method to use herbs is in **food**. You have to eat, so why not? You can make a very healthful meal using fruits and vegetables and adding some herbs. Or, you can make your meal a truly magical one by reciting your spell as you're cooking.

The most widely used preparation is a **tea** or tisane. (Actually, Tea is an herb. Its Latin binomial is *Camellia sinensis*.) Medicinally it's called an infusion or decoction. Magically, it's usually called a brew, potion or philter. To make a tea of a leaf or flower (an infusion) put one teaspoon herb in one cup just-boiled water. The water should be still steaming but not bubbling. Cover the cup to prevent the steam from escaping and allow it to steep for about ten minutes. Strain before use or use a tea bag or ball. To make a tea of a root or bark (a decoction), put one teaspoon herb in one and a half cups *cold* water. Bring the water to a boil, reduce the heat and allow it to simmer until your liquid is reduced to one cup. Again, strain before use.

I'm sure you know you can drink the tea (but be sure the herb is safe to ingest, first). A tea is used to make a **fomentation**. Prepare a strong infusion or decoction (double the amount of herb you use) and then soak a cloth in it. Bind the cloth around the area of the body you want to affect and cover with another cloth. This is very useful not only medicinally but in magical health workings targeted to a specific part of the body. You can also use a tea in skin preparations; as a wash, whether for yourself, your house or your magical items; or swish it into your bath water.

A **Poultice** is used in the same way as a fomentation to affect a part of the body. In this case, make a mash of herb(s) and warm water and apply directly to the skin. Cover with a warm cloth. Do not use a poultice if the skin is broken or inflamed. Use a fomentation instead.

**Tinctures** or **Simples** are an alcoholic extract of a single herb. They are a great way to use herbs medicinally, especially if you're taking or using more than one. A tincture is much more portable than trying to haul all the accoutrements for making tea. In addition, it's a lot easier to get down if the herb tastes bad (and many do). The folk method of making a tincture is to put one ounce herb into one pint good-quality vodka or brandy and let it steep for about 2 weeks, shaking it once a day. If the herb absorbs the liquid (many will), add more vodka or brandy until the level is about one-quarter inch above the herb. Strain well (use a coffee filter to get all the dregs), bottle and store in a cool, dark place. The alcohol acts as a preserving agent and tinctures will last for up to four years. Medicinally, put drops of the tincture (usually fifteen to thirty) into a glass of water or juice to drink, or dilute it further for a skin preparation. Magically, tinctures are used in the same way as a tea and can also charge paper used for written work. Soak the paper in the tincture and let it dry before using.

If you're averse to the use of alcohol in any form, you can make tinctures from apple cider vinegar or vegetable glycerin. Just be aware that your preparation won't be as potent. Also, if you make a vinegar tincture, be sure to use a jar *without* a metal lid. The fumes from the vinegar will corrode the metal.

**Herbal Wine** is a tasty way of taking your medicine. A cup of wine can be drunk as part of a magical working, too. To make an herbal wine, use the same method as a tincture, substituting either red or white wine for the brandy or vodka (red will be more medicinally-potent). Or, go all-out and make your own wine from virtually any berry.

Pure **Essential Oils** are the best-smelling way to use herbs. They are the "volatile oil" component of a plant and are extracted through a distillation process. They are also *strong* and can be toxic. Lavender,

Tea Tree and in some instances, Clove are the only ones you can apply directly on your skin without worrying about overdosing. Never use any other essential oil directly on the skin without first diluting it in a base oil (see infused oils for a partial list). And, *never* ingest an essential oil unless you're under the guidance of a certified aromatherapist. Because they are so strong, it only takes about ten drops to one-eighth cup (one ounce) of base oil. To mix your oils, put the essential oils in the bottle first, then add the base oil. Cap and turn the bottle up and down in your hand ten times before using. Be aware of the difference between an "essential oil" and a "fragrance oil". Fragrance oils are usually synthetic and, if they have any therapeutic actions or magical energies at all, they're not the same ones as true essential oils. Also be aware that there is a difference in qualities of essential oils. The purer the oil, the better. Again, as close to the natural plant as possible. You'll pay for the good stuff but it's worth it. You can use essential oils in your skin care preparations, swish a few drops into your bath or put a few drops into a steam vaporizer and inhale the fumes. Magically, dab the oil onto your pulse points, put a few drops onto a handkerchief to carry with you, rub it into candles or burn it in an oil warmer or on charcoal. If you choose to burn the oil on charcoal, be aware that the aroma won't last longer than a few seconds. Again, if you're going to come into skin contact, be sure to dilute the essential oil first. Essential oils will keep for two to five years. As a general rule, the thicker the oil, the longer it will keep. Be sure to keep the bottle tightly capped as air will destroy the oil faster.

**Hydrosols** or **Flower Waters** are a by-product when essential oils are obtained by a steam distillation method. Even though they are known as "flower waters", a hydrosol is simply a distillation of any part of the plant that contains essential oils, like the leaves or inner bark. You can buy them commercially or, with a little effort, make your own. Small commercial stills are available so you can make your own essential oils and hydrosols. If you don't want to buy a still, you can get almost the same effect on your stove. You'll want a large (20 quart or so) pot that has a domed lid. Put about three quarts of water and ten ounces of *fresh* herb in the pot and let it sit for a few hours before proceeding. Then put a vegetable steamer basket upside down in the center of the pot and a cereal-sized bowl right-side up on top of the basket to catch the hydrosol. Cover and bring to just under a boil. As soon as the water begins to simmer, reduce the heat, turn the lid upside down on the pot and put a large bag of ice in the lid. The ice will help condense the steam faster. The hydrosol is the condensed steam that will drip from the lid into your cereal bowl. Be sure to keep an eye on your preparation – make sure the water doesn't boil away and burn your herb. Once you've obtained a goodly amount of hydrosol in your cereal bowl, remove everything from the heat and allow to cool. Pour the water from the bowl through a coffee filter into a sterile bottle, then refrigerate. If you're lucky, you'll also have a few drops of essential oil in the bottom of the filter. Draw this off with a pipette and put into a separate bottle.

If you don't want to go to the trouble of distilling, you can pour two cups of boiling water over one cup of tightly-packed, fresh herb. Allow your mixture to cool completely, strain and pour into a sterilized bottle. This will not be as strong-smelling as a distilled hydrosol but is a simpler method.

An even quicker method of making a flower water involves essential oils. To one-quarter cup of distilled water, add six to eight drops of your chosen essential oil and bottle. Shake before use. This will have a much lighter fragrance than a regular hydrosol and is known as a "voile", which is French for "veil".

Hydrosols are generally used for skin issues, most often as an ingredient in a cream. However, Rose water on its own is an ages-old natural skin cleanser and astringent. My grandmother used to sprinkle her bedsheets with Lavender water. This not only kept bugs out of the bed but they smelled wonderful. Magically you can use them for asperging, sprinkling or virtually anywhere you would use a tea or brew.

The use of **Ointments** is pretty much limited to the skin. (I'm not sure why you would want to eat an ointment!) Medicinally, rub them into the area you want to affect, like a sore muscle or on a rash. Magically, massage it into pulse points to get the energies into your body. The old method of making an ointment was to use lard but nowadays, vegetable shortening is available and smells *much* better. Melt one cup shortening over low heat (do not allow it to get so hot the shortening smokes). Add three tablespoons of dried herb(s) and allow to "cook" for about ten minutes. Strain and cool the mixture before use. Or, melt the shortening and add up to ten drops of essential oils before cooling. If you like something firmer than shortening, add a couple of tablespoons of melted beeswax to the mixture. You can also use anhydrous lanolin (available in health food stores) with a little beeswax to thicken the mixture. A caution: if you're allergic to wool, don't use lanolin. It's the oil collected from the skin of sheep, which is where wool comes from, too. Ointments should be stored in an airtight container in a cool, dark place.

**Infused Oils** can be used the same as an ointment, as an all-over massage oil or as a salad dressing. There are a variety of good base oils on the market today but the easiest is plain ol' cold-pressed, extra virgin olive oil, which is available on virtually every grocer's shelf. My personal feeling is that olive oil is a bit too heavy to use for most skin preparations and it does have a distinct smell so other, lighter options include apricot, avocado, cocoanut, grapeseed, and sweet almond. (If ordering cocoanut oil over the Internet, be sure to get the "fractionated" kind. Cocoanut oil is solid in its normal state.) Jojoba oil is also available but it's actually a liquid wax and is somewhat heavy. It is also more expensive compared to other alternatives. Put one part herb in ten parts oil (the equivalent of one ounce by weight of herb in ten fluid ounces oil) into a jar that has a tight-fitting lid. Place in a cool, dark place. Shake ten times once a day for ten days. Strain, bottle and store in a cool, dark place. If you want a stronger infused oil, simply strain out the herb and repeat the process. Use your original oil and add another batch of herbs in the same proportion as the first time.

**Incense** of the "raw" or "granular" type is just plant material smoldered on a charcoal tablet. The use of incense has been documented for over 4,000 years – the residue of burnt Copal has been found on Mayan altars. Although today "fumigation" generally means "pest control", it really means "to apply smoke". Even after World War I, French hospitals not only strewed herbs on the floor, they wafted the smoke of burning herbs in the sick wards to purify the air. Today's Catholic Church still uses incense during their Masses. Incense smoke can be used to purify the air in a room; its vibrations are great as background when you're meditating; or you can pass ritual items through the smoke to purify them. Pick an herb or combination thereof and grind it down to about the size of peppercorns or coarsely-ground salt. Light the edge of a charcoal tablet held in a heat-proof container and once the tablet is fully lit, sprinkle a small amount of your herb onto the tablet every few minutes. Easy does it! You don't want to set off your smoke alarm. Also remember that a lot of herbs don't smell as good while burning as you might think.

If you've a mind, you can make your own cone or stick incense: choose your herbs, add a little gum arabic or gum traganth (to make it sticky), and either charcoal or saltpeter (for combustion). Powder your ingredients very, very fine. Mix your powder with a little distilled water to make a dough and then form into cones or roll around bamboo sticks. Place on a sheet of waxed paper and allow to dry at least two or three weeks, turning every couple of days to expose all surfaces to air. I haven't included any proportions because the recipe varies depending on the herbs used and your climate. You'll need to experiment on your own and be sure to keep a record!

**Baths**, believe it or not, do have a medicinal application. They are great to loosen tense muscles, for some skin issues, and for problems in the genital area. They are a luxurious method of herbal magic – especially if you add some soap to make a bubble bath. This spreads the herb's energies all over your body. You can use a tea, essential oils or bath salts in your bath.

To make bath salts, add up to fifteen drops of essential oil(s) into one cup Epsom salts or a combination of sea and Epsom salts – add until your nose tells you its right. Use your hands to mix the oils thoroughly into the salts. (You'll find your hands will get dried out from the salt so rinse with water and rub some oil or lotion into them afterwards.) Put two to four tablespoons of your salt mixture into a warm bath and swish around a bit. Only soak for about ten minutes if you're using salts. You'll re-absorb all the toxins your body has released into the bath if you soak longer.

If you don't like to take baths (or don't have a bathtub) you can get the same effect in the shower by using finer-ground salts as a body scrub or putting herbs in a sachet bag and hanging it from the showerhead so the water flows through the bag and then onto you.

I wouldn't recommend that you use loose herbs in either the bath or shower. They have a tendency to clog up the pipes and that sort of problem generates negative thoughts and energy, as well as high plumber's bills. Instead, either brew a tea and put that into your bathwater or as noted before, put the loose herbs in a sachet bag and allow the water to run through the bag. If you're in a romantic mood, by all means float a few rose petals on the surface of your bath but be sure to scoop them out before pulling the plug.

**Soaps** are another way to use herbs in the bath or shower, either medicinally or magically. They have become popular as a craft in recent years and glycerin soap-making kits are readily available at craft stores. You can powder dried herbs and add these to your mixture (ground oatmeal is great as a skin softener) or add a few drops of essential oil.

**Sachets** or herbal **Amulets** are an easy way to carry an herb (or a combination of herbs) with you all day long. I've seen sachets used as decongestants: they contain strong-smelling herbs such as Eucalyptus. One inhales the aroma to clear up congestion. For magical purposes you can carry a piece of dried herb in your pocket (like carrying a "lucky" Buckeye) or follow the example of the residents of the Isle of Man: on Tynwald Day (St. John's Feast Day), everyone wears a sprig of Mugwort in their lapel. Although Mugwort is the Manx official flower, this is a holdover from the Middle Ages when wearing a crown or carrying a posy of Mugwort was thought to ward off witchcraft. (Little did they know that most witches consider Mugwort one of their favorite herbs!)

A small muslin bag that has a drawstring or a small piece of cotton cloth that has been sewn up works great to carry a combination of herbs (or you can simply place the herb in the middle of a square of cloth, pull the corners together and use a ribbon to tie it up). Select the herb(s) you want to use, put a small amount in the bag and close it. Carry it in your pocket or somewhere on your person so the herbs can add their energies to yours during the day. Sachets can also be hung over doors or beds, in cars or placed wherever they can do the most good. Remember to replace your sachet every three months and recycle (compost) the herbs back to the Earth.

**Pillows** are usually used for dream magic or nightly protection but can be made for any type of magic. They should be fairly small (no more than 6" x 6"). Use those small squares of fabric you bought to make your sachets. Take two pieces, stitch up three sides and fill before closing the fourth side. You can fill them with dried herbs and add other things germane to your work like gems or other objects (you don't actually have to sleep *on* them, just have them near you at night). Aromatherapy has heightened the interest in dream pillows. A dream pillow made of sedative herbs can be used for insomnia. You can make your pillow stronger-smelling by putting a few drops of essential oils onto the dried herbs. Again, recycle the herbs every three months or so.

**Powders** are simply finely ground herbs. Sprinkle powders around your house or area where you're performing your magic or use them as incense. Yarrow (*Achillea millefolium*) powder is a good styptic (to staunch bleeding).

**Candles** can also be used with herbs! If you make your own candles, you can powder herbs and add them to the hot wax or add a few drops of essential oil(s) prior to pouring into your chosen mold or container. If you use store-bought candles, rub a little vegetable oil on the candle and then roll it lightly in powdered herbs. Don't use too much of your herbal powder as it tends to burn quickly and can cause a flash fire similar to sawdust.

**Pomanders** are what I made as a kid at Christmas. Mom hung them up in the house; they looked pretty and made the house smell good.

However, they do have a magical application. Depending on what you're trying to accomplish, you'll stud a citrus fruit with cloves, roll it in other powdered herbs, tie it with a ribbon and hang it up in your house. Not only will the house smell good but you'll be infusing the area with magical intentions. These will need to be recycled every few weeks as the fruit won't last as long as the herbs.

**Poppets** are generally associated with negative magic but they do have a positive use, especially for healing, love, and fertility spells. You can make one out of wax or clay, or simply use a child's doll that you have altered to look as much like the person in question as possible. If you make one out of wax or clay, be sure to leave a hollow area – usually in the torso but sometimes in the head. You can stuff the poppet with herbs appropriate to the situation or if you need to do a health working for a specific part of the body, the poppet makes a good substitute for the sore leg or broken arm you need to heal that is 100 miles away. Apply a poultice or fomentation to the area on the poppet corresponding to the body part that needs healing.

**Magical Inks** are used when a spell requires something written. Many practitioners use magical inks when writing in their Workbook. They are sometimes made with resins (most often Dragon's Blood which is red, unlike most other resins which are clear to whitish), lampblack (very tedious), or you can simply crush fresh fruit (like elderberries) and use the juice as an "ink". You'll want a pen you can use with your ink – a fountain, feather or wood pen that can either draw the ink into its own well or be used dipping-style. If you've never used a dipping pen, be sure to practice with it before writing in your Workbook or using it for a written working. Practice until you're proficient enough to write without smears and blotches.

If you want to go all the way and make your own ink, here's how you make ink with lampblack. Light a candle of a color appropriate to your intention. (This was once done with oil lamps instead of candles, hence the name "lampblack".) Once the flame takes hold, hold a spoon over the flame. You'll soon see soot starting to collect on the spoon. As you get a good coating, use a knife to scrape the soot into a bowl.

Repeat. And repeat. It's not only very time-consuming, it's also very messy as the flakes won't always cooperate and float directly into your bowl. Once you've collected enough soot flakes, add distilled water until your mixture is thin enough to use. You can use the same method but instead of using a candle, use the soot of burning resin(s) like Frankincense or Myrrh.

To make an ink with Dragon's Blood, soak a tablespoon of crushed resin in five tablespoons of alcohol (grain alcohol is best but 90 proof vodka will work). It will take an hour or so, but when the two substances have combined well, you'll have a very red liquid substance in your bowl. Strain out any remaining resin. Add some powdered gum arabic or gum traganth to thicken enough for use.

You can also use charcoal as an ink. Simply take a dried twig of an appropriate tree, light the end, gently blow the flame out and allow it to smolder until the end is blackened enough to write with. Be sure to wait until it stops smoldering before actually writing on paper or you may have a conflagration on your hands. You'll have to pause and relight often to keep the end black.

However, there is an easier method to make (and use) magical ink. You can magically charge a bottle of regular ink by adding essential oils and your own energies to one you've purchased. I generally add fifteen drops to a one ounce bottle of ink. Any more and the ink gets too oily to adhere to paper.

**Paper** can be magically charged for written work … either your Workbook or a written spell. I have read that parchment paper should be used because "its organic properties are compatible with nature". Parchment is traditionally made from calfskin, goatskin or sheepskin; there are still sources out there for this type and I'm sure that it's all ethically made. However, it's *expensive*, so I use plant-based parchment – writing paper! If you choose to use magical ink with a dipping-style pen, I believe you'll find that using a heavier grade of paper than simply notebook or copier paper will work better – the ink won't bleed through to the other side as easily. There are plenty of heavier-weight papers available at office supply stores that will suffice. To charge paper, soak it in a tincture or put a few drops of essential oil(s) onto the page (use herbs associated with your project) and let it air dry.

If you're really into crafts and the "do-it-all-yourself" mentality, you can make your own paper. I haven't tried but there are quite a few books and web sites that give good instructions for doing so. Again, use herbs appropriate to your project.

# In Conclusion

This book is meant as a starting point for those interested in herbs. There is an abundance of other books around and I truly hope you will read as many as you can get your hands on to see what others have discovered.

You will probably find as you walk your herbal path that you feel more connected to Nature. This isn't an accident. The more you work with plants and the rest of the natural world, the more connected you *are*. Enjoy your awakening senses and what the Universe is telling you about the properties and energies of herbs.

Use herbs wisely, for the good of all and enjoy the adventure! I'll close with the Celtic Blessing of the Nine Elements:

May you go forth under the strength of heaven, under the light of sun, under the radiance of moon;

May you go forth with the splendor of fire, with the speed of lightning, with the swiftness of wind;

May you go forth surrounded by the depth of sea, by the stability of earth, by the firmness of rock;

May you be surrounded and encircled, with the protection of the nine elements.

DJ

# Suggested Reading

Many of the books listed below have excellent (and extensive) bibliographies. I would recommend you read many of those books, as well.

**Books**

Agrippa, Henry Cornelius. *The Philosophy of Natural Magic.* Antwerp, 1531. Secaucus, NJ: University Books, 1974.

Beith, Mary. *Healing Threads.* Edinburgh: Polygon, 1995.

Beyerl, Paul. *A Compendium of Herbal Magick.* Custer, WA: Phoenix Publishing, Inc., 1998.

Bolton, Brett L. *The Secret Powers of Plants.* New York: Berkeley, 1974.

Carmichael, A. *Carmina Gaedelica.* Edinburgh: Floris Books, 1992.

Culpeper, Nicholas. *The Complete Herbal.* London: 1649. Berkshire, England: W. Foulsham & Co., Ltd. (no date).

Cunningham, Scott. *Encyclopedia of Magical Herbs 2$^{nd}$ Edition.* Woodbury, MN: Llewellyn Publications, 2000.

Cunningham, Scott. *Magical Herbalism.* St. Paul, MN: Llewellyn Publications, 1982, 1983.

Dugan, Ellen. *Herb Magic for Beginners.* Woodbury, MN: Llewellyn Publications, 2006.

Garrett, J.T. *The Cherokee Herbal.* Rochester, VT: Bear & Company, 2003.

Green, James. *The Herbal Medicine-Maker's Handbook.* Berkeley, CA: The Crossing Press, 2000.

Grieve, M. *A Modern Herbal.* New York, 1931; New York: Dover, 1971.

Griggs, Barbara. *Green Pharmacy: The History and Evolution of Western Herbal Medicine.* Rochester, VT: Healing Arts Press, 1997.

Hoffman, David. *The Herbal Handbook: A User's Guide to Medical Herbalism.* Rochester, VT: Inner Traditions, Ltd., 1998.

Hoffman, David. *Medical Herbalism: The Science and Practice of Herbal Medicine.* Rochester, VT: Healing Arts Press, 2003.

Illes, Judika. *The Element Encyclopedia of 5000 Spells.* London: HarperElement, 2004.

Illes, Judika. *The Element Encyclopedia of Witchcraft.* London: HarperElement, 2005.

Kieckhefer, Richard. *Magic in the Middle Ages.* London: Cambridge University Press, 2000.

Lust, John. *The Herb Book.* New York: Bantam, 1974.

Lyon, William S. *Encyclopedia of Native American Healing.* New York, NY: W. W. Norton & Co., Inc., 1996

Morrison, Dorothy. *Everyday Magic.* St. Paul, MN: Llewellyn Publications, 1998.

Pollington, Stephen. *Leechcraft, Early English Charms, Plantlore & Healing.* Norfolk, UK: Anglo-Saxon Books, 2001.

Thompkins, Peter and Christopher Bird. *The Secret Life of Plants.* New York: Avon Books, 1974.

Thompson, R. Campbell. *Devils and Evile Spirits of Babylonia* (translated from the original Cuneiform). Whitefish, MT: Kessinger Publishing, 2003 (reprinted from a 1903 book).

Wood, Matthew. *The Practice of Traditional Western Herbalism.* Berkeley, CA: North Atlantic Books, 2004.

Worwood, Valerie Ann. *Aromatherapy for the Soul.* Novato, CA: New World Library, 1999.

## Internet

American Herbalists Guild http://www.americanherbalistsguild.com The AHG has a very handy (and free) daily email that is a digest of the latest scientific research on herbs from PubMed – a service of the National Institutes of Health. You can also use this site to find a Registered Herbalist in the United States.

National Institute of Medical Herbalists http://www.nimh.org.uk. Use this site to find a Medical Herbalist in the United Kingdom.

American Association of Naturopathic Physicians http://www.naturopathic.org This site explains the difference between a Medical Doctor (MD) and a Naturopathic Physician (ND). You can also use this site to find a Naturopathic Physician in the United States.

Sacred Texts http://www.sacred-texts.com. This is a wonderful resource site for old books that are now in the public domain. Their collection is varied and extensive.

Google Books. http://books.google.com. Another resource for old books.

# My Herbal Medicine Diary

Today's Date: _____

Problem: _____

Herb(s) Used:_____
_____
_____
_____

Preparation: _____
_____
_____
_____

Dosage Notes: _____
_____
_____
_____

What I did (list dates as well as actions, note outcomes): _____
_____
_____
_____

Reference Books (list author, title, page & other notes): _____
_____
_____
_____
_____

# My Herbal Magic Diary

Today's Date: _____

Intention: _____

Herbs Used: _____
_____
_____

Method Employed: _____
_____
_____

Reference Books (list author, title, page & other notes): _____
_____
_____
_____
_____
_____
_____
_____
_____
_____

What I did (list dates as well as actions, note outcomes): _____
_____
_____
_____
_____

# The Herbs

The following appendices are not by any means complete! As I stated earlier, there are more than 50,000 plants used in a medicinal sense and probably considerably more used in a magical sense. However, they are the most widely known as far as my current research has taken me.

Two abbreviations you may not be familiar with are

spp.    This means "Species" so any plant in that Genus will work the same way.

var.    This means "varietal". It's usually used to describe wine but in this case means a hybridized plant. The majority of varietals will work the same as any of the specific Species but where there is a difference, I've included it.

Should you come across a Latin binomial for a commonly-named plant that you don't see here, it may be that the two binomials are synonyms for each other. For example, *Chrysopogon zizinoides* and *Vetiveria zizanioides* are both Vetivert and refer to the *identical plant*. Despite the age of the Linnaeus system for naming plants, researchers are still refining it. A quick Internet search of the Latin binomial will tell you if you're looking at a synonym or an entirely different plant.

# Appendix A

## Herbal Cheat Sheet

| Common Name | Latin Binomial |
|---|---|
| Adam & Eve | *Orchis spp.* |
| Agrimony | *Agrimonia eupatoria* |
| Alfalfa | *Medicago Sativa* |
| Alkanet | *Alkanna tinctoria* |
| Allspice | *Pimenta dioica* |
| Almond (Sweet) | *Prunus amygdalus var. dulcis* |
| Aloe Vera | *Aloe barbadensis* |
| Amaranth | *Amaranthus hypochondriacus* |
| Angelica | *Angelica archangelica* |
| Angelica, Chinese | *Angelica sinensis* |
| Anise | *Pimpinella anisum* |
| Anise, Star | *Illicium verum* |
| Apple | *Pyrus malus* |
| Apricot | *Prunus armeniaca* |
| Arbutus | *Arbutus unedo* |
| Arnica | *Arnica montana* |
| Asafoetida | *Ferula assa-foetida* |
| Ash | *Fraxinus exelsior* |
| Avens | *Geum urbanum* |
| Avocado | *Persea americana* |
| Balm of Gilead | *Populus candicans* |
| Balm of Gilead | *Abies balsamea* |
| Balsam Fir | *Abies balsamea* |
| Banana | *Musa sapientum* |
| Barberry | *Berberis vulgaris* |
| Barley | *Hordeum distichon* |
| Basil (Sweet) | *Ocimum basilicum* |
| Bay | *Laurus nobilis* |

| | |
|---|---|
| Bayberry | *Myrica cerifera* |
| Bearberry | *Arctostaphylos uva-ursi* |
| Bee Balm | *Monarda fistulosa* |
| Beech | *Fagus sylvatica* |
| Beet (White or Red) | *Beta vulgaris* |
| Belladonna | *Atropa belladonna* |
| Benzoin | *Styrax benzoin* |
| Bergamot | *Citrus bergamia* |
| Bilberry | *Vaccinium myrtillus* |
| Birch | *Betula alba* |
| Bishop's Wort | *Stachys officinalis* |
| Bistort | *Polygonum bistorta* |
| Bittersweet (American) | *Celastrus scandens* |
| Black Cohosh | *Cimicifuga racemosa* |
| Blackberry | *Rubus villosus* |
| Bladderwrack | *Fucus vesiculosus* |
| Blessed Thistle | *Cnicus benedictus* |
| Bloodroot | *Sanguinaria canadensis* |
| Blue Flag | *Iris versicolor* |
| Blueberry | *Vaccinium myrtillus* |
| Boneset | *Eupatorium perfoliatum* |
| Borage | *Borago officinalis* |
| Bromeliad | *Cryptanthus spp.* |
| Broom | *Cytisus scoparius* |
| Buchu | *Agathosma betulina* |
| Buckthorn | *Rhamnus frangula* |
| Buckwheat | *Fagopyrum esculentum* |
| Burdock | *Arctium lappa* |
| Cabbage | *Brassica oleracea* |
| Calendula | *Calendula officinalis* |
| Camphor | *Cinnamomum camphora* |
| Caper | *Capparis spinosa* |
| Caraway | *Carum carvi* |
| Cardamom | *Eletteria cardamomum* |

| | |
|---|---|
| Carnation | *Dianthus caryophyllus* |
| Carrot, Wild | *Daucus carota* |
| Cascara Sagrada | *Rhamnus purshiana* |
| Cashew | *Anacardium occidentale* |
| Catnip | *Nepeta cataria* |
| Cayenne | *Capsicum minimum* |
| Cedar | *Cedrus spp.* |
| Celandine | *Chelidonium majus* |
| Celery | *Apium graveolens* |
| Centaury | *Erythraea centarium* |
| Chamomile, German | *Matricaria recutita* |
| Chamomile, Roman | *Chamamelum nobile* |
| Chasteberry | *Vitex agnus-castus* |
| Cherry, Black | *Prunus serotina* |
| Cherry, Sweet | *Prunus avium* |
| Cherry, Wild | *Prunus serotina* |
| Chestnut | *Castanea sativa* |
| Chickweed | *Stellaria media* |
| Chicory | *Cichorium intybus* |
| Chinese Angelica | *Angelica sinensis* |
| Chinese Rhubarb | *Rheum palmatum* |
| Chrysanthemum | *Chrysanthemum x morifolium* |
| Cilantro | *Coriandrum sativum* |
| Cinchona | *Cinchona spp.* |
| Cinnamon | *Cinnamomum cassia* |
| Cinquefoil | *Potentilla erecta* |
| Citron | *Citrus medica* |
| Cleavers | *Galium aparine* |
| Clover (Red) | *Trifolium pratense* |
| Cloves | *Syzgium aromaticum* |
| Club Moss | *Lycopodium clavatum* |
| Coconut | *Cocos nucifera* |
| Coltsfoot | *Tussilago farfara* |
| Columbine | *Aquilegia vulgaris* |

| | |
|---|---|
| Comfrey | *Symphytum officinale* |
| Copal | *Bursera fagaroides* |
| Coriander | *Coriandrum sativum* |
| Corn | *Zea mays* |
| Cotton | *Gossypium herbaceum* |
| Couch Grass | *Elymus repens* |
| Cowslip | *Primula veris* |
| Cranesbill | *Geranium maculatum* |
| Cubeb | *Piper cubeba* |
| Cucumber | *Cucumis sativus* |
| Cumin | *Cuminum cyminum* |
| Cypress | *Cupressus sempervirens* |
| Daffodil | *Narcissus spp.* |
| Damiana | *Turnera diffusa* |
| Dandelion | *Taraxacum officinale* |
| Date Palm | *Phoenix dactylifera* |
| Datura | *Datura stramonium* |
| Deer's Tongue | *Trilisa odoratissima* |
| Devil's Bit | *Succisa pratensis* |
| Dill | *Anethum graveolens* |
| Dittany of Crete | *Origanum dictamnus* |
| Dock, Yellow | *Rumex crispus* |
| Dong Quai | *Angelica sinensis* |
| Dragon's Blood | *Daemonorops draco* |
| Dulse | *Rhodymenia palmata* |
| Echinacea | *Echinacea spp.* |
| Elder (Black) | *Sambucus nigra* |
| Elecampane | *Inula helenium* |
| Elm | *Ulmus campestris* |
| Elm, Slippery | *Ulmus fulva* |
| Ephedra | *Ephedra sinica* |
| Eryngo | *Eryngium spp.* |
| Eucalyptus | *Eucalyptus globulus* |
| Eyebright | *Euphrasia officinalis* |

| | |
|---|---|
| Fennel | *Foeniculum vulgare* |
| Fenugreek | *Trigonella foenum-graecum* |
| Feverfew | *Tanacetum parthenium* |
| Fig | *Ficus carica* |
| Figwort | *Scrophularia nodosa* |
| Flax | *Linim usitatissimum* |
| Foxglove | *Digitalis purpurea* |
| Frankincense | *Boswellia carterii* |
| Fumitory | *Fumaria officinalis* |
| Galangal | *Alpinia officinarum* |
| Gardenia | *Gardenia jasminoides* |
| Garlic | *Allium sativum* |
| Gentian | *Gentiana lutea* |
| Geranium | *Pelargonium spp.* |
| Gillyflower | *Dianthus caryophyllus* |
| Ginger | *Zingiber officinale* |
| Gingko | *Gingko biloba* |
| Ginseng, American | *Panax quinquefolius* |
| Ginseng, Siberian | *Eleutherococcus senticosus* |
| Goat's Rue | *Galega officinalis* |
| Goldenrod | *Solidago virgaurea* |
| Goldenseal | *Hydrastis canadensis* |
| Grains of Paradise | *Aframomum melegueta* |
| Grape | *Vitis vinifera* |
| Gravel Root | *Eupatorium purpureum* |
| Greater Celandine | *Chelidonium majus* |
| Grounsel | *Senecio vulgaris* |
| Gum Arabic | *Acacia senegal* |
| Hawthorn | *Crataegus laevigata* |
| Heartsease | *Viola tricolor* |
| Heather | *Erica vulgaris* |
| Hibiscus | *Hibiscus sabdariffa* |
| High John the Conqueror | *Ipomoea purga* |
| Holly | *Ilex aquifolium* |

| | |
|---|---|
| Hollyhock | *Althea rosea* |
| Holy Thistle | *Cnicus benedictus* |
| Honeysuckle | *Lonicera caprifolium* |
| Hops | *Humulus lupulus* |
| Horehound (White) | *Marrubium vulgare* |
| Horsemint | *Monarda fistulosa* |
| Horseradish | *Armoracia rusticana* |
| Horsetail | *Equisetum arvense* |
| Huckleberry | *Vaccinium myrtillus* |
| Hyacinth | *Hyacinthus orientalis* |
| Hyssop | *Hyssopus officinalis* |
| Iceland Moss | *Centraria islandica* |
| Irish Moss | *Chondrus crispus* |
| Ivy | *Hedera helix* |
| Jalap | *Ipomoea purga* |
| Jasmine | *Jasminum officinale* |
| Job's Tears | *Coix lachryma-jobi* |
| Joe Pye Weed | *Eupatorium purpureum* |
| Ju Hua | *Chrysanthemum x morifolium* |
| Juniper | *Juniperus communis* |
| Kale | *Brassica oleracea* |
| Kava Kava | *Piper methysticum* |
| Kelp | *Fucus vesiculosus* |
| Knotgrass | *Polygonum aviculare* |
| Knotweed | *Polygonum aviculare* |
| Lady's Mantle | *Alchemilla vulgaris* |
| Lady's Slipper (Yellow) | *Cypripedium pubescens* |
| Lavender | *Lavandula angustifolia* |
| Lemon | *Citrus limon* |
| Lemon Balm | *Melissa officinalis* |
| Lemon Verbena | *Lippia citriodora* |
| Lemongrass | *Cymbopogon citratus* |
| Lettuce, Wild | *Lactuca virosa* |
| Licorice | *Glycyrrhiza glabra* |

| | |
|---|---|
| Lilac | *Syringa vulgaris* |
| Lily of the Valley | *Convallaria majalis* |
| Lime (fruit) | *Citrus aurantifolia* |
| Lime (tree) | *Tilia platyphyllos* |
| Linden | *Tilia platyphyllos* |
| Liquidamber | *Liquidamber styraciflua* |
| Lobelia | *Lobelia inflata* |
| Loosestrife | *Lythrum salicaria* |
| Lovage | *Levisticum officinale* |
| Ma Huang | *Ephedra sinica* |
| Mace | *Myristica fragrans* |
| Maidenhair Fern | *Adiantum capillus-veneris* |
| Mallow | *Malva sylvestris* |
| Mandrake | *Mandragora officinarum* |
| Maple | *Acer spp.* |
| Marjoram | *Origanum vulgare* |
| Marshmallow | *Althaea officinalis* |
| Masterwort | *Imperatoria ostruthium* |
| Mastic | *Pistacia lentiscus* |
| Meadow Rue | *Thalictrum spp.* |
| Meadowsweet | *Filipendula ulmaria* |
| Milk Thistle | *Silybum marianum* |
| Mistletoe | *Viscum album* |
| Motherwort | *Leonurus cardiaca* |
| Mugwort | *Artemisia vulgaris* |
| Mulberry | *Morus spp.* |
| Mullein | *Verbascum thapsus* |
| Mustard (Black) | *Brassica nigra* |
| Myrrh | *Commiphora molmol* |
| Myrtle | *Myrtus communis* |
| Narcissus | *Narcissus spp.* |
| Nettle | *Urtica dioica* |
| Nightshade, Deadly | *Atropa belladonna* |
| Nutmeg | *Myristica fragrans* |

| | |
|---|---|
| Oak | *Quercus alba* |
| Oat | *Avena sativa* |
| Oatstraw | *Avena sativa* |
| Olive | *Olea europaea* |
| Onion | *Allium cepa* |
| Orange | *Citrus sinensis* |
| Oregon Grape | *Mahonia aquifolium* |
| Orris | *Iris germanica var. florentina* |
| Oswego Tea | *Monarda fistulosa* |
| Palm, Date | *Phoenix dactylifera* |
| Pansy | *Viola tricolor* |
| Papaya | *Carica papaya* |
| Parsley | *Petroselinum crispum* |
| Pasqueflower | *Pulsatilla vulgaris* |
| Passionflower | *Passiflora incarnata* |
| Patchouli | *Pogostemon cablin* |
| Peach | *Prunus persica* |
| Pecan | *Carya illinoinensis* |
| Pennyroyal | *Mentha pulegium* |
| Peony | *Paeonia officinalis* |
| Pepper | *Piper nigrum* |
| Peppermint | *Mentha x piperita* |
| Periwinkle | *Vinca minor* |
| Persimmon | *Diospyros virginiana* |
| Peruvian Bark | *Cinchona spp.* |
| Pimento | *Pimenta dioica* |
| Pine | *Pinus spp.* |
| Pineapple | *Ananas comosus* |
| Pipsissewa | *Chimaphila umbellata* |
| Pistachio | *Pistacia vera* |
| Plantain (Broad-leafed) | *Plantago major* |
| Plum | *Prunus domestica* |
| Poke | *Phytolacca americana* |
| Pomegranate | *Punica granatum* |

| | |
|---|---|
| Poppy | *Papaver spp.* |
| Pot Marigold | *Calendula officinalis* |
| Potato | *Solanum tuberosum* |
| Prickly Ash | *Zanthoxylum americanum* |
| Pumpkin | *Cucurbita pepo* |
| Purslane | *Portulaca oleracea* |
| Qing Hao | *Artemisia annua* |
| Queen Anne's Lace | *Daucus carota* |
| Radish | *Raphanus sativus* |
| Raspberry (Red) | *Rubus idaeus* |
| Red Clover | *Trifolium pratense* |
| Red Sage | *Salvia officinalis var. rubia* |
| Rhubarb, Chinese | *Rheum palmatum* |
| Rhubarb, Turkey | *Rheum officinale* |
| Rice | *Oryza sativa* |
| Rose | *Rosa spp.* |
| Rose Geranium | *Pelargonium spp.* |
| Rosemary | *Rosmarinus officinalis* |
| Rue | *Ruta graveolens* |
| Saffron | *Crocus sativus* |
| Sage | *Salvia officinalis* |
| Sage, Red | *Salvia officinalis var. rubia* |
| Sandalwood (Red) | *Pterocarpus santalinus* |
| Sandalwood (White) | *Santalum album* |
| Sanderswood | *Pterocarpus santalinus* |
| Sarsaparilla | *Smilax spp.* |
| Savory | *Satureja hortensis* |
| Scullcap | *Scutellaria lateriflora* |
| Sea Holly | *Eryngium spp.* |
| Seneca Snakeroot | *Polygala senega* |
| Senna | *Senna alexandrina* |
| Shepherd's Purse | *Capsella bursa-pastoris* |
| Skunk Cabbage | *Symplocarpus foetidus* |
| Slippery Elm | *Ulmus fulva* |

| | |
|---|---|
| Snapdragon | *Antirrhinum majus* |
| Solomon's Seal | *Polygonatum multiflorum* |
| Spearmint | *Mentha spicata* |
| Spikenard | *Inula conyza* |
| Squill | *Urginea scilla* |
| St. John's Wort | *Hypericum perforatum* |
| Star Anise | *Illicium verum* |
| Stinging Nettle | *Urtica dioica* |
| Strawberry | *Fragaria vesca* |
| Styrax | *Styrax benzoin* |
| Sugar Cane | *Saccharum officinarum* |
| Sunflower | *Helianthus annuus* |
| Sweet Annie | *Artemisia annua* |
| Sweet Flag | *Acorus calamus* |
| Sweet Violet | *Viola odorata* |
| Sweetgum | *Liquidamber styraciflua* |
| Tamarind | *Tamarindus indicus* |
| Tansy | *Tanacetum vulgare* |
| Tea | *Camellia sinensis* |
| Tea Tree | *Melaleuca alternifolia* |
| Thornapple | *Datura stramonium* |
| Thyme | *Thymus vulgaris* |
| Ti Plant | *Cordyline spp.* |
| Tobacco | *Nicotiana tabacum* |
| Tomato | *Solanum lycopersicum* |
| Tonka | *Dipteryx odorata* |
| Tormentil | *Potentilla erecta* |
| Traganth | *Astragalus gummifer* |
| Turkey Rhubarb | *Rheum officinale* |
| Turmeric | *Curcuma longa* |
| Turnip | *Brassica rapa* |
| Uva Ursi | *Arctostaphylos uva-ursi* |
| Valerian | *Valeriana officinalis* |
| Vanilla | *Vanilla spp.* |

| | |
|---|---|
| Vervain | *Verbena officinalis* |
| Vetivert | *Chrysopogon zizinoides* |
| Violet, Sweet | *Viola odorata* |
| Vitex | *Vitex agnus-castus* |
| Wahoo | *Euonymus atropurpureus* |
| Walnut (Black) | *Juglans nigra* |
| Wax Myrtle | *Myrica cerifera* |
| Wheat | *Triticum spp.* |
| Willow (White) | *Salix alba* |
| Wintergreen | *Gaultheria procumbens* |
| Witch Hazel | *Hamamelis virginiana* |
| Wolf's Bane | *Arnica montana* |
| Wood Betony | *Stachys officinalis* |
| Woodruff | *Galium odoratum* |
| Wormwood | *Artemisia absinthium* |
| Yarrow | *Achillea millefolium* |
| Yellow Dock | *Rumex crispus* |
| Yerba Mate | *Ilex paraguariensis* |
| Yerba Santa | *Eriodictyon californicum* |
| Yucca | *Yucca spp.* |

# Appendix B

## Medicinal Uses

| Medicinal Use | Latin Binomial |
| --- | --- |
| Abrasions | *Aloe barbadensis* |
| | *Commiphora molmol* |
| Abscess | *Aloe barbadensis* |
| | *Althaea officinalis (root)* |
| | *Arctium lappa* |
| | *Chamamelum nobile* |
| | *Coix lachryma-jobi* |
| | *Matricaria recutita* |
| Acne | *Aloe barbadensis* |
| | *Arctium lappa* |
| | *Chrysanthemum x morifolium* |
| | *Fragaria vesca* |
| | *Fumaria officinalis* |
| | *Juglans nigra* |
| | *Ocimum basilicum* |
| | *Rumex crispus* |
| | *Trifolium pratense* |
| | *Viola tricolor* |
| ADHD | *Gingko biloba* |
| Alopecia | *Aloe barbadensis* |
| | *Rosmarinus officinalis* |
| Alzheimers | *Gingko biloba* |
| Amenorrhea (missing periods) | *Ananas comosus* |
| | *Angelica sinensis* |
| | *Artemisia vulgaris* |
| | *Commiphora molmol* |
| | *Crocus sativus* |
| | *Gentiana lutea* |

44

*Levisticum officinale*
*Marrubium vulgare*
*Petroselinum crispum*
*Salvia officinalis*
*Tanacetum vulgare*
*Thymus vulgaris*
*Zingiber officinale*

Anemia
*Erythraea centarium*
*Petroselinum crispum*
*Rumex crispus*
*Trifolium pratense*

Angina
*Allium cepa*
*Eleutherococcus senticosus*

Anorexia
*Angelica archangelica*
*Arctium lappa*
*Artemisia absinthium*
*Cnicus benedictus*
*Eletteria cardamomum*
*Erythraea centarium*
*Gentiana lutea*
*Trigonella foenum-graecum*

Anxiety
*Humulus lupulus*
*Hypericum perforatum*
*Jasminum officinale*
*Leonurus cardiaca*
*Matricaria recutita*
*Piper methysticum*
*Valeriana officinalis*

Appendicitis
*Agrimonia eupatoria*
*Portulaca oleracea*

Appetite Loss
*Acorus calamus*
*Ananas comosus*
*Angelica archangelica*
*Armoracia rusticana*

*Berberis vulgaris*

*Carum carvi*

*Chamamelum nobile*

*Cinnamomum cassia*

*Erythraea centarium*

*Gentiana lutea*

*Hordeum distichon*

*Hydrastis canadensis*

*Marrubium vulgare*

*Matricaria recutita*

*Medicago sativa*

*Mentha x piperita*

*Myristica fragrans*

*Petroselinum crispum*

*Piper nigrum*

*Prunus armeniaca*

*Rheum officinale*

*Trigonella foenum-graecum*

*Zingiber officinale*

Arrhythmia        *Crataegus laevigata*

Arteriosclerosis    *Oryza sativa*

Arthritis            *Aloe barbadensis*

*Apium graveolens*

*Arctium lappa*

*Armoracia rusticana*

*Capsicum minimum*

*Cimicifuga racemosa*

*Coix lachryma-jobi*

*Curcuma longa*

*Fraxinus exelsior*

*Gaultheria procumbens*

*Juniperus communis*

*Mandragora officinarum*

*Matricaria recutita*

|                        | *Myristica fragrans* |
|                        | *Petroselinum crispum* |
|                        | *Pinus spp.* |
|                        | *Prunus avium* |
|                        | *Saccharum officinarum* |
| Arthritis, rheumatoid  | *Alpinia officinarum* |
|                        | *Arctium lappa* |
|                        | *Arnica montana* |
|                        | *Betula alba* |
|                        | *Capparis spinosa* |
|                        | *Celastrus scandens* |
|                        | *Cichorium intybus* |
|                        | *Cimicifuga racemosa* |
|                        | *Gaultheria procumbens* |
|                        | *Gentiana lutea* |
|                        | *Glycyrrhiza glabra* |
|                        | *Ilex aquifolium* |
|                        | *Illicium verum* |
|                        | *Laurus nobilis* |
|                        | *Mandragora officinarum* |
|                        | *Myristica fragrans* |
|                        | *Petroselinum crispum* |
|                        | *Pinus spp.* |
|                        | *Rumex crispus* |
|                        | *Salix alba* |
|                        | *Stellaria media* |
|                        | *Taraxacum officinale* |
|                        | *Thymus vulgaris* |
|                        | *Urtica dioica* |
|                        | *Viola odorata* |
|                        | *Zanthoxylum americanum* |
| Asthma                 | *Arctium lappa* |
|                        | *Armoracia rusticana* |
|                        | *Capsicum minimum* |

*Commiphora molmol*
*Cordyline spp.*
*Curcuma longa*
*Datura stramonium*
*Eletteria cardamomum*
*Ephedra sinica*
*Eriodictyon californicum*
*Eucalyptus globulus*
*Hyssopus officinalis*
*Inula helenium*
*Lobelia inflata*
*Marrubium vulgare*
*Petroselinum crispum*
*Pulsatilla vulgaris*
*Sanguinaria canadensis*
*Symplocarpus foetidus*
*Syzgium aromaticum*
*Thymus vulgaris*
*Tussilago farfara*
*Ulmus fulva*
*Verbascum thapsus*

Athletes Foot     *Anacardium occidentale*
*Curcuma longa*
*Juglans nigra*
*Melaleuca alternifolia*

Bedwetting     *Equisetum arvense*
*Thymus vulgaris*

Bee stings     *Aloe barbadensis*
*Althaea officinalis (leaf)*

Bladder inflammation     *Agathosma betulina*
*Althea rosea*
*Armoracia rusticana*
*Juniperus communis*
*Zea mays*

| | |
|---|---|
| Bleeding | *Achillea millefolium* |
| | *Capsicum minimum* |
| | *Citrus limon* |
| | *Juglans nigra* |
| | *Plantago major* |
| | *Polygonum aviculare* |
| | *Primula veris* |
| | *Salvia officinalis* |
| Bloating | *Ananas comosus* |
| | *Coriandrum sativum* |
| | *Piper nigrum* |
| Blood pressure, high | *Allium sativum* |
| | *Chrysanthemum x morifolium* |
| | *Eleutherococcus senticosus* |
| | *Fagopyrum esculentum* |
| | *Ferula assa-foetida* |
| | *Galium aparine* |
| | *Hibiscus sabdariffa* |
| | *Passiflora incarnata* |
| | *Petroselinum crispum* |
| | *Rubus idaeus* |
| | *Ruta graveolens* |
| | *Scutellaria lateriflora* |
| | *Tilia platyphyllos* |
| | *Valeriana officinalis* |
| | *Viscum album* |
| | *Yucca spp.* |
| Blood Pressure, low | *Eleutherococcus senticosus* |
| | *Rosmarinus officinalis* |
| Boils | *Althaea officinalis (root)* |
| | *Arctium lappa* |
| | *Commiphora molmol* |
| | *Juglans nigra* |
| | *Melaleuca alternifolia* |

*Myrica cerifera*

*Plantago major*

*Portulaca oleracea*

*Pulsatilla vulgaris*

*Saccharum officinarum*

Broken bones    *Symphytum officinale*

Bronchial asthma    *Carum carvi*

*Chelidonium majus*

*Eryngium spp.*

*Lobelia inflata*

*Polygala senega*

*Syzgium aromaticum*

Bronchial spasm    *Althaea officinalis (leaf)*

Bronchitis    *Abies balsamea*

*Achillea millefolium*

*Adiantum capillus-veneris*

*Agathosma betulina*

*Althaea officinalis (leaf)*

*Angelica archangelica*

*Arctium lappa*

*Armoracia rusticana*

*Boswellia carterii*

*Brassica nigra*

*Centraria islandica*

*Chelidonium majus*

*Chondrus crispus*

*Citrus sinensis*

*Commiphora molmol*

*Eletteria cardamomum*

*Eleutherococcus senticosus*

*Ephedra sinica*

*Eriodictyon californicum*

*Eryngium spp.*

*Eucalyptus globulus*

*Fagus sylvatica*
*Ferula assa-foetida*
*Foeniculum vulgare*
*Glycyrrhiza glabra*
*Hedera helix*
*Hyssopus officinalis*
*Inula helenium*
*Iris germanica var. florentina*
*Levisticum officinale*
*Lobelia inflata*
*Marrubium vulgare*
*Musa sapientum*
*Nepeta cataria*
*Pimpinella anisum*
*Piper cubeba*
*Populus candicans*
*Primula veris*
*Prunus persica*
*Prunus serotina*
*Sanguinaria canadensis*
*Santalum album*
*Styrax benzoin*
*Symplocarpus foetidus*
*Syzgium aromaticum*
*Thymus vulgaris*
*Trifolium pratense*
*Tussilago farfara*
*Ulmus fulva*
*Urginea scilla*
*Verbascum thapsus*
*Viola odorata*
*Viola tricolor*

Bruises        *Arnica montana*
*Artemisia absinthium*

|  | *Capsicum minimum* |
|--|--|
|  | *Fagopyrum esculentum* |
|  | *Hamamelis virginiana* |
|  | *Hyssopus officinalis* |
|  | *Inula conyza* |
|  | *Olea europaea* |
|  | *Polygonatum multiflorum* |
|  | *Sambucus nigra* |
| Burns | *Aloe barbadensis* |
|  | *Althaea officinalis (root)* |
|  | *Althea rosea* |
|  | *Carica papaya* |
|  | *Galium aparine* |
|  | *Hamamelis virginiana* |
|  | *Olea europaea* |
|  | *Plantago major* |
|  | *Polygonum bistorta* |
|  | *Potentilla erecta* |
|  | *Rubus villosus* |
|  | *Solanum tuberosum* |
|  | *Thymus vulgaris* |
|  | *Trifolium pratense* |
|  | *Ulmus fulva* |
| Calculus | *Althaea officinalis (leaf)* |
|  | *Arctium lappa* |
| Cancer | *Artemisia absinthium* |
|  | *Beta vulgaris* |
|  | *Brassica oleracea* |
|  | *Camellia sinensis* |
|  | *Coix lachryma-jobi* |
|  | *Cuminum cyminum* |
|  | *Eleutherococcus senticosus* |
|  | *Ilex paraguariensis* |
|  | *Monarda fistulosa* |

*Saccharum officinarum*

*Salvia officinalis*

*Solanum lycopersicum*

*Trifolium pratense*

*Triticum spp*

*Viscum album*

Candida            *Achillea millefolium*

*Alpinia officinarum*

*Cymbopogon citratus*

*Medicago sativa*

*Thymus vulgaris*

Cardiac disease    *Carya illinoinensis*

*Digitalis purpurea*

Catarrh            *Allium sativum*

*Althaea officinalis (leaf)*

*Cnicus benedictus*

*Coix lachryma-jobi*

*Cucumis sativus*

*Geranium maculatum*

*Hedera helix*

*Hyssopus officinalis*

*Marrubium vulgare*

*Phoenix dactylifera*

*Phytolacca americana*

*Rubus idaeus*

*Rumex crispus*

*Salvia officinalis*

Chapped Skin       *Althaea officinalis (root)*

*Cocos nucifera*

*Pelargonium spp.*

*Stellaria media*

Chickenpox         *Achillea millefolium*

*Hyssopus officinalis*

Childbirth         *Rubus idaeus*

|                    | *Ulmus fulva* |
|--------------------|---------------|
| Chillblains        | *Armoracia rusticana* |
|                    | *Brassica nigra* |
|                    | *Capsicum minimum* |
|                    | *Sambucus nigra* |
|                    | *Thymus vulgaris* |
|                    | *Zanthoxylum americanum* |
|                    | *Zingiber officinale* |
| Chills             | *Capsicum minimum* |
|                    | *Myrica cerifera* |
| Cholesterol, High  | *Beta vulgaris* |
|                    | *Curcuma longa* |
|                    | *Olea europaea* |
|                    | *Oryza sativa* |
|                    | *Persea americana* |
|                    | *Pistacia vera* |
|                    | *Prunus amygdalus var dulcis* |
|                    | *Trigonella foenum-graecum* |
|                    | *Yucca spp.* |
|                    | *Zingiber officinale* |
| Circulation, poor  | *Crataegus laevigata* |
|                    | *Rosmarinus officinalis* |
| Cirrhosis, liver   | *Silybum marianum* |
| Cold extremities   | *Capsicum minimum* |
| Cold sores         | *Cinnamomum camphora* |
|                    | *Juglans nigra* |
|                    | *Styrax benzoin* |
| Colds              | *Acacia senegal* |
|                    | *Achillea millefolium* |
|                    | *Allium cepa* |
|                    | *Castanea sativa* |
|                    | *Cedrus spp.* |
|                    | *Chimaphila umbellata* |
|                    | *Cinnamomum cassia* |

*Citrus aurantifolia*

*Citrus limon*

*Echinacea spp.*

*Erica vulgaris*

*Galium aparine*

*Helianthus annuus*

*Marrubium vulgare*

*Matricaria recutita*

*Melaleuca alternifolia*

*Mentha x piperita*

*Myrica cerifera*

*Nepeta cataria*

*Origanum vulgare*

*Phoenix dactylifera*

*Pinus spp.*

*Saccharum officinarum*

*Sambucus nigra*

*Styrax benzoin*

*Symphytum officinale*

*Tilia platyphyllos*

*Verbena officinalis*

Colic

*Acorus calamus*

*Anethum graveolens*

*Atropa belladonna*

*Capsicum minimum*

*Chamamelum nobile*

*Crocus sativus*

*Daucus carota*

*Erica vulgaris*

*Foeniculum vulgare*

*Illicium verum*

*Iris germanica var. florentina*

*Juglans nigra*

*Levisticum officinale*

|  |  |
|---|---|
|  | *Matricaria recutita* |
|  | *Mentha spicata* |
|  | *Mentha x piperita* |
|  | *Nepeta cataria* |
|  | *Petroselinum crispum* |
|  | *Pimpinella anisum* |
|  | *Thymus vulgaris* |
| Colitis | *Althaea officinalis (leaf)* |
|  | *Althaea officinalis (root)* |
|  | *Hamamelis virginiana* |
|  | *Hydrastis canadensis* |
|  | *Myrica cerifera* |
|  | *Potentilla erecta* |
|  | *Vinca minor* |
| Congestive heart failure | *Convallaria majalis* |
|  | *Crataegus laevigata* |
| Conjunctivitis | *Chamamelum nobile* |
|  | *Foeniculum vulgare* |
|  | *Fumaria officinalis* |
|  | *Hydrastis canadensis* |
|  | *Matricaria recutita* |
|  | *Petroselinum crispum* |
|  | *Stellaria media* |
|  | *Thymus vulgaris* |
| Constipation | *Aloe barbadensis* |
|  | *Ananas comosus* |
|  | *Armoracia rusticana* |
|  | *Artemisia absinthium* |
|  | *Astragalus gummifer* |
|  | *Ferula assa-foetida* |
|  | *Ficus carica* |
|  | *Fraxinus exelsior* |
|  | *Glycyrrhiza glabra* |
|  | *Juglans nigra* |

*Linum usitatissimum*
*Mahonia aquifolium*
*Marrubium vulgare*
*Olea europaea*
*Olea europaea*
*Piper nigrum*
*Prunus domestica*
*Pyrus malus*
*Rhamnus frangula*
*Rhamnus purshiana*
*Rheum officinale*
*Rheum palmatum*
*Rubus idaeus*
*Rumex crispus*
*Scrophularia nodosa*
*Senna alexandrina*
*Triticum spp*
*Ulmus fulva*

Cough
*Acacia senegal*
*Achillea millefolium*
*Adiantum capillus-veneris*
*Althaea officinalis (leaf)*
*Angelica archangelica*
*Berberis vulgaris*
*Castanea sativa*
*Chondrus crispus*
*Citrus aurantifolia*
*Citrus limon*
*Erica vulgaris*
*Ficus carica*
*Glycyrrhiza glabra*
*Helianthus annuus*
*Hyssopus officinalis*
*Inula helenium*

|  | *Iris germanica var. florentina* |
|  | *Juniperus communis* |
|  | *Malva sylvestris* |
|  | *Melaleuca alternifolia* |
|  | *Morus spp.* |
|  | *Musa sapientum* |
|  | *Origanum vulgare* |
|  | *Persea americana* |
|  | *Petroselinum crispum* |
|  | *Pinus spp.* |
|  | *Populus candicans* |
|  | *Primula veris* |
|  | *Prunus persica* |
|  | *Prunus serotina* |
|  | *Rumex crispus* |
|  | *Saccharum officinarum* |
|  | *Styrax benzoin* |
|  | *Succisa pratensis* |
|  | *Symphytum officinale* |
|  | *Thymus vulgaris* |
|  | *Trifolium pratense* |
|  | *Triticum spp* |
|  | *Ulmus fulva* |
|  | *Verbascum thapsus* |
|  | *Verbena officinalis* |
|  | *Vitis vinifera* |
| Cracked skin | *Calendula officinalis* |
|  | *Stellaria media* |
| Cradle cap | *Arctium lappa* |
|  | *Rumex crispus* |
|  | *Viola tricolor* |
| Cramp | *Chamamelum nobile* |
|  | *Cinchona spp.* |
|  | *Datura stramonium* |

*Eletteria cardamomum*
*Rosa spp.*
*Thymus vulgaris*
*Verbascum thapsus*
*Zingiber officinale*

Cystitis  *Abies balsamea*
*Althaea officinalis (leaf)*
*Althaea officinalis (root)*
*Althea rosea*
*Arctostaphylos uva-ursi*
*Betula alba*
*Cedrus spp.*
*Chimaphila umbellata*
*Commiphora molmol*
*Daucus carota*
*Elymus repens*
*Eupatorium purpureum*
*Galium aparine*
*Petroselinum crispum*
*Plantago major*
*Prunus avium*
*Santalum album*
*Solidago virgaurea*
*Tussilago farfara*
*Viola tricolor*
*Zea mays*

Dandruff  *Arctium lappa*
*Beta vulgaris*
*Laurus nobilis*
*Olea europaea*
*Petroselinum crispum*

Debility  *Eletteria cardamomum*
*Panax quinquefolius*

Depression  *Artemisia vulgaris*

*Avena sativa*

*Capsicum minimum*

*Ilex paraguariensis*

*Lavandula angustifolia*

*Matricaria recutita*

*Piper methysticum*

*Turnera diffusa*

Dermatitis     *Aloe barbadensis*

*Althaea officinalis (root)*

*Rumex crispus*

*Stellaria media*

*Stellaria media*

*Ulmus fulva*

Diabetes     *Achillea millefolium*

*Arctium lappa*

*Berberis vulgaris*

*Carum carvi*

*Cuminum cyminum*

*Galega officinalis*

*Juglans nigra*

*Persea americana*

*Plantago major*

*Prunus amygdalus var dulcis*

*Pterocarpus santalinus*

*Salvia officinalis*

*Vaccinium myrtillus*

*Vitis vinifera*

*Yucca spp.*

Diarrhea     *Acacia senegal*

*Agrimonia eupatoria*

*Alchemilla vulgaris*

*Artemisia absinthium*

*Camellia sinensis*

*Capsella bursa-pastoris*

*Capsicum minimum*

*Castanea sativa*

*Chamamelum nobile*

*Fragaria vesca*

*Galium aparine*

*Geranium maculatum*

*Geum urbanum*

*Hamamelis virginiana*

*Hordeum distichon*

*Liquidambar styraciflua*

*Lythrum salicaria*

*Matricaria recutita*

*Musa sapientum*

*Myrica cerifera*

*Myristica fragrans*

*Nepeta cataria*

*Oryza sativa*

*Pimenta dioica*

*Polygonum aviculare*

*Polygonum bistorta*

*Portulaca oleracea*

*Quercus alba*

*Rheum palmatum*

*Rubus idaeus*

*Rubus villosus*

*Rumex crispus*

*Saccharum officinarum*

*Syzgium aromaticum*

*Thymus vulgaris*

*Ulmus fulva*

*Vaccinium myrtillus*

*Vinca minor*

Digestion, sluggish      *Achillea millefolium*

*Acorus calamus*

*Artemisia vulgaris*
*Cinchona spp.*
*Foeniculum vulgare*
*Gentiana lutea*
*Linum usitatissimum*
*Myristica fragrans*
*Origanum vulgare*
*Prunus serotina*
*Rheum officinale*
*Rosmarinus officinalis*
*Scutellaria lateriflora*
*Thymus vulgaris*
*Verbascum thapsus*

Dizziness
*Artemisia annua*
*Chrysanthemum x morifolium*
*Gingko biloba*
*Morus spp.*
*Rosa spp.*
*Salvia officinalis*
*Tanacetum parthenium*

Drug Withdrawal
*Scutellaria lateriflora*

Dysentery
*Acacia senegal*
*Althaea officinalis (root)*
*Camellia sinensis*
*Coix lachryma-jobi*
*Fragaria vesca*
*Geum urbanum*
*Lythrum salicaria*
*Polygonum bistorta*
*Portulaca oleracea*
*Potentilla erecta*
*Quercus alba*
*Rheum palmatum*
*Rubus villosus*

|  | *Saccharum officinarum* |
|---|---|
|  | *Verbascum thapsus* |
| Dysmenorrhea (painful periods) | *Ananas comosus* |
|  | *Angelica sinensis* |
|  | *Capsicum minimum* |
|  | *Carum carvi* |
|  | *Chamamelum nobile* |
|  | *Cimicifuga racemosa* |
|  | *Crocus sativus* |
|  | *Gossypium herbaceum* |
|  | *Hibiscus sabdariffa* |
|  | *Hydrastis canadensis* |
|  | *Lactuca virosa* |
|  | *Levisticum officinale* |
|  | *Petroselinum crispum* |
|  | *Pulsatilla vulgaris* |
|  | *Salvia officinalis* |
|  | *Thymus vulgaris* |
|  | *Vitex agnus-castus* |
|  | *Zingiber officinale* |
| Dyspepsia | *Agathosma betulina* |
|  | *Alpinia officinarum* |
|  | *Artemisia absinthium* |
|  | *Capsicum minimum* |
|  | *Centraria islandica* |
|  | *Chamamelum nobile* |
|  | *Citrus sinensis* |
|  | *Cnicus benedictus* |
|  | *Erythraea centarium* |
|  | *Eucalyptus globulus* |
|  | *Eupatorium perfoliatum* |
|  | *Gentiana lutea* |
|  | *Humulus lupulus* |
|  | *Lippia citriodora* |

*Matricaria recutita*
*Melissa officinalis*
*Mentha x piperita*
*Nepeta cataria*
*Pimenta dioica*
*Rheum palmatum*
*Rosmarinus officinalis*
*Salvia officinalis var rubia*
*Solidago virgaurea*
*Turnera diffusa*
*Zingiber officinale*

Earache
*Allium cepa*
*Hydrastis canadensis*
*Pulsatilla vulgaris*
*Rosa spp.*
*Verbascum thapsus*

Eczema
*Aloe barbadensis*
*Arctium lappa*
*Chelidonium majus*
*Curcuma longa*
*Fragaria vesca*
*Fumaria officinalis*
*Hydrastis canadensis*
*Iris versicolor*
*Juglans nigra*
*Mahonia aquifolium*
*Myristica fragrans*
*Plantago major*
*Populus candicans*
*Rumex crispus*
*Scrophularia nodosa*
*Stellaria media*
*Thymus vulgaris*
*Trifolium pratense*

|                   | *Ulmus fulva* |
|-------------------|----------------|
|                   | *Urtica dioica* |
|                   | *Viola odorata* |
| Edema             | *Armoracia rusticana* |
|                   | *Viola tricolor* |
| Emphysema         | *Sanguinaria canadensis* |
|                   | *Tussilago farfara* |
| Epilepsy          | *Lobelia inflata* |
|                   | *Scutellaria lateriflora* |
| Eye inflammation  | *Althaea officinalis (leaf)* |
|                   | *Euphrasia officinalis* |
|                   | *Hydrastis canadensis* |
|                   | *Morus spp.* |
|                   | *Prunus serotina* |
|                   | *Pyrus malus* |
| Eye Strain        | *Acer spp.* |
|                   | *Chrysanthemum x morifolium* |
|                   | *Morus spp.* |
| Fever             | *Achillea millefolium* |
|                   | *Acorus calamus* |
|                   | *Arctium lappa* |
|                   | *Artemisia absinthium* |
|                   | *Artemisia annua* |
|                   | *Borago officinalis* |
|                   | *Brassica nigra* |
|                   | *Chamamelum nobile* |
|                   | *Chimaphila umbellata* |
|                   | *Cinchona spp.* |
|                   | *Coix lachryma-jobi* |
|                   | *Eucalyptus globulus* |
|                   | *Hyssopus officinalis* |
|                   | *Ilex aquifolium* |
|                   | *Juglans nigra* |
|                   | *Liquidambar styraciflua* |

*Mentha spicata*
*Mentha x piperita*
*Morus spp.*
*Nepeta cataria*
*Olea europaea*
*Phoenix dactylifera*
*Piper nigrum*
*Portulaca oleracea*
*Pyrus malus*
*Rubus idaeus*
*Rumex crispus*
*Saccharum officinarum*
*Salix alba*
*Salvia officinalis*
*Succisa pratensis*
*Symplocarpus foetidus*
*Syringa vulgaris*
*Thymus vulgaris*
*Trigonella foenum-graecum*

Flatulence

*Acorus calamus*
*Agathosma betulina*
*Alpinia officinarum*
*Ananas comosus*
*Anethum graveolens*
*Angelica archangelica*
*Artemisia absinthium*
*Cinnamomum cassia*
*Citrus sinensis*
*Cnicus benedictus*
*Coriandrum sativum*
*Daucus carota*
*Foeniculum vulgare*
*Gentiana lutea*
*Illicium verum*

*Juniperus communis*
*Levisticum officinale*
*Lippia citriodora*
*Melissa officinalis*
*Mentha pulegium*
*Mentha spicata*
*Mentha x piperita*
*Nepeta cataria*
*Pimenta dioica*
*Pimpinella anisum*
*Piper cubeba*
*Piper nigrum*
*Punica granatum*
*Salvia officinalis*
*Syzgium aromaticum*
*Thymus vulgaris*
*Zingiber officinale*

Flu

*Cinnamomum cassia*
*Eupatorium perfoliatum*
*Matricaria recutita*
*Mentha x piperita*
*Myrica cerifera*
*Nepeta cataria*
*Origanum vulgare*
*Sambucus nigra*
*Solidago virgaurea*
*Tilia platyphyllos*

Fluid Retention

*Agathosma betulina*
*Chamamelum nobile*
*Cucurbita pepo*
*Galium aparine*
*Juniperus communis*
*Mentha spicata*
*Morus spp.*

|  | *Vaccinium myrtillus* |
| Fungal infection | *Aloe barbadensis* |
| Gall stones | *Berberis vulgaris* |
|  | *Chelidonium majus* |
|  | *Galium aparine* |
|  | *Urtica dioica* |
| Gallbladder problems | *Berberis vulgaris* |
|  | *Calendula officinalis* |
|  | *Erythraea centarium* |
|  | *Euonymus atropurpureus* |
|  | *Hydrastis canadensis* |
|  | *Nepeta cataria* |
|  | *Rumex crispus* |
| Gastritis | *Acorus calamus* |
|  | *Althaea officinalis (leaf)* |
|  | *Althaea officinalis (root)* |
|  | *Centraria islandica* |
|  | *Chondrus crispus* |
|  | *Curcuma longa* |
|  | *Eletteria cardamomum* |
|  | *Filipendula ulmaria* |
|  | *Glycyrrhiza glabra* |
|  | *Lycopodium clavatum* |
|  | *Myristica fragrans* |
|  | *Trigonella foenum-graecum* |
|  | *Ulmus fulva* |
| Gingivitis | *Commiphora molmol* |
|  | *Echinacea spp.* |
|  | *Salvia officinalis var rubia* |
| Glaucoma | *Juniperus communis* |
| Goiter | *Fucus vesiculosus* |
| Gout | *Apium graveolens* |
|  | *Arctium lappa* |
|  | *Artemisia absinthium* |

|  | *Betula alba* |
|---|---|
|  | *Cichorium intybus* |
|  | *Juniperus communis* |
|  | *Persea americana* |
|  | *Prunus avium* |
|  | *Salix alba* |
| Gum inflammation | *Alpinia officinarum* |
| Halitosis | *Anethum graveolens* |
|  | *Commiphora molmol* |
|  | *Coriandrum sativum* |
|  | *Petroselinum crispum* |
|  | *Senna alexandrina* |
|  | *Thymus vulgaris* |
|  | *Trigonella foenum-graecum* |
| Hayfever | *Arctium lappa* |
|  | *Verbascum thapsus* |
| Headache, Tension | *Artemisia annua* |
|  | *Chamamelum nobile* |
|  | *Chrysanthemum x morifolium* |
|  | *Citrus aurantifolia* |
|  | *Citrus limon* |
|  | *Humulus lupulus* |
|  | *Lavandula angustifolia* |
|  | *Mentha x piperita* |
|  | *Morus spp.* |
|  | *Nepeta cataria* |
|  | *Origanum vulgare* |
|  | *Piper methysticum* |
|  | *Pulsatilla vulgaris* |
|  | *Rosa spp.* |
|  | *Rosmarinus officinalis* |
|  | *Ruta graveolens* |
|  | *Scutellaria lateriflora* |
|  | *Solanum tuberosum* |

*Stachys officinalis*
*Thymus vulgaris*

Heartburn
*Aloe barbadensis*
*Chamamelum nobile*
*Filipendula ulmaria*

Hemorrhoids
*Achillea millefolium*
*Geum urbanum*
*Hamamelis virginiana*
*Juglans nigra*
*Mentha spicata*
*Polygonum aviculare*
*Polygonum bistorta*
*Potentilla erecta*
*Quercus alba*
*Rhamnus purshiana*
*Rheum officinale*
*Solanum tuberosum*
*Vaccinium myrtillus*
*Verbascum thapsus*

Hepatitis
*Erythraea centarium*
*Glycyrrhiza glabra*
*Iris versicolor*
*Petroselinum crispum*
*Silybum marianum*

Herpes simplex
*Hypericum perforatum*
*Iris versicolor*
*Melaleuca alternifolia*
*Melissa officinalis*
*Myrtus communis*
*Passiflora incarnata*
*Persea americana*

Herpes zoster
*Capsicum minimum*
*Hypericum perforatum*
*Passiflora incarnata*

|  |  |
|---|---|
|  | *Trifolium pratense* |
| Hiatal hernia | *Althaea officinalis (root)* |
|  | *Ulmus fulva* |
| Hiccoughs | *Alpinia officinarum* |
|  | *Mentha spicata* |
|  | *Nepeta cataria* |
|  | *Saccharum officinarum* |
|  | *Scutellaria lateriflora* |
| Hoarseness | *Althaea officinalis (leaf)* |
| Hyperglycemia | *Chamamelum nobile* |
|  | *Rubus idaeus* |
| Hypoglycemia | *Arctium lappa* |
| Hysteria | *Scutellaria lateriflora* |
| Immune System | *Plantago major* |
| Impotence | *Turnera diffusa* |
| Incontinence | *Equisetum arvense* |
| Indigestion | *Acorus calamus* |
|  | *Aframomum melegueta* |
|  | *Agathosma betulina* |
|  | *Agrimonia eupatoria* |
|  | *Alpinia officinarum* |
|  | *Armoracia rusticana* |
|  | *Capsicum minimum* |
|  | *Chamamelum nobile* |
|  | *Commiphora molmol* |
|  | *Crocus sativus* |
|  | *Eletteria cardamomum* |
|  | *Erythraea centarium* |
|  | *Ferula assa-foetida* |
|  | *Gentiana lutea* |
|  | *Humulus lupulus* |
|  | *Hyssopus officinalis* |
|  | *Illicium verum* |
|  | *Juniperus communis* |

|                |                              |
| -------------- | ---------------------------- |
|                | *Levisticum officinale*      |
|                | *Lippia citriodora*          |
|                | *Lycopodium clavatum*        |
|                | *Mentha spicata*             |
|                | *Punica granatum*            |
|                | *Salvia officinalis*         |
|                | *Valeriana officinalis*      |
| Infection      | *Allium sativum*             |
|                | *Aloe barbadensis*           |
|                | *Arctium lappa*              |
|                | *Boswellia carterii*         |
|                | *Cinchona spp.*              |
|                | *Juglans nigra*              |
|                | *Plantago major*             |
|                | *Trifolium pratense*         |
| Inflammation   | *Althaea officinalis (leaf)* |
|                | *Chamamelum nobile*          |
|                | *Ficus carica*               |
|                | *Inula helenium*             |
|                | *Plantago major*             |
|                | *Prunus armeniaca*           |
|                | *Saccharum officinarum*      |
|                | *Zingiber officinale*        |
| Insect bites   | *Althaea officinalis (root)* |
|                | *Hamamelis virginiana*       |
|                | *Melaleuca alternifolia*     |
|                | *Olea europaea*              |
|                | *Petroselinum crispum*       |
|                | *Plantago major*             |
|                | *Salvia officinalis*         |
| Insomnia       | *Chrysanthemum x morifolium* |
|                | *Galium aparine*             |
|                | *Humulus lupulus*            |
|                | *Lactuca virosa*             |

*Matricaria recutita*
*Mentha x piperita*
*Nepeta cataria*
*Pulsatilla vulgaris*
*Scutellaria lateriflora*
*Ulmus fulva*
*Valeriana officinalis*
*Verbascum thapsus*

Intestinal cramps    *Carum carvi*
Irritability    *Jasminum officinale*
Irritable bowel disease    *Althaea officinalis (leaf)*
*Cinnamomum cassia*

Irritable bowel syndrome    *Geum urbanum*
*Polygonum bistorta*
*Potentilla erecta*
Itching    *Olea europaea*
Jaundice    *Artemisia absinthium*
*Berberis vulgaris*
*Chelidonium majus*
*Curcuma longa*
*Eryngium spp.*
*Erythraea centarium*
*Euonymus atropurpureus*
*Gentiana lutea*
*Ilex aquifolium*
*Petroselinum crispum*
*Rumex crispus*
*Taraxacum officinale*
*Verbena officinalis*
Kidney stones    *Agathosma betulina*
*Althea rosea*
*Arctostaphylos uva-ursi*
*Chimaphila umbellata*
*Eletteria cardamomum*

|  | *Elymus repens* |
|---|---|
|  | *Erica vulgaris* |
|  | *Eupatorium purpureum* |
|  | *Galium aparine* |
|  | *Hyssopus officinalis* |
|  | *Lycopodium clavatum* |
|  | *Ocimum basilicum* |
|  | *Petroselinum crispum* |
|  | *Raphanus sativus* |
|  | *Senecio vulgaris* |
|  | *Zea mays* |
| Lactation, promote milk | *Trifolium pratense* |
| Laryngitis | *Agrimonia eupatoria* |
|  | *Alchemilla vulgaris* |
|  | *Althaea officinalis (leaf)* |
|  | *Capsicum minimum* |
|  | *Echinacea spp.* |
|  | *Melaleuca alternifolia* |
|  | *Phytolacca americana* |
|  | *Polygala senega* |
|  | *Populus candicans* |
|  | *Quercus alba* |
|  | *Saccharum officinarum* |
|  | *Salvia officinalis* |
|  | *Salvia officinalis var rubia* |
|  | *Sanguinaria canadensis* |
|  | *Solidago virgaurea* |
|  | *Thymus vulgaris* |
| Leukorrhea | *Arctostaphylos uva-ursi* |
|  | *Celastrus scandens* |
|  | *Eucalyptus globulus* |
|  | *Geum urbanum* |
|  | *Juniperus communis* |
|  | *Lythrum salicaria* |

|  |  |
|---|---|
|  | *Myrica cerifera* |
|  | *Plantago major* |
|  | *Polygonum bistorta* |
|  | *Quercus alba* |
|  | *Rubus villosus* |
|  | *Trigonella foenum-graecum* |
|  | *Vitis vinifera* |
| Lice | *Rhamnus purshiana* |
| Liver congestion | *Arctium lappa* |
|  | *Berberis vulgaris* |
|  | *Gentiana lutea* |
|  | *Iris germanica var. florentina* |
|  | *Juglans nigra* |
| Lumbago | *Arctium lappa* |
|  | *Plantago major* |
| Lymphatic inflammation | *Phytolacca americana* |
|  | *Rumex crispus* |
| Malaria | *Syringa vulgaris* |
| Mastitis | *Phytolacca americana* |
|  | *Plantago major* |
|  | *Verbascum thapsus* |
| Measles | *Achillea millefolium* |
|  | *Mentha x piperita* |
| Memory Loss | *Gingko biloba* |
| Menopause | *Hamamelis virginiana* |
|  | *Vitex agnus-castus* |
| Menorrhagia (scant periods) | *Alchemilla vulgaris* |
|  | *Amaranthus hypochondriacus* |
|  | *Capsella bursa-pastoris* |
|  | *Myrica cerifera* |
|  | *Rubus idaeus* |
|  | *Vinca minor* |
| Metrorrhagia (heavy periods) | *Calendula officinalis* |
|  | *Cimicifuga racemosa* |

|  | *Erythraea centarium* |
|---|---|
|  | *Inula helenium* |
|  | *Leonurus cardiaca* |
|  | *Liquidambar styraciflua* |
|  | *Lythrum salicaria* |
|  | *Mentha pulegium* |
|  | *Polygonum aviculare* |
|  | *Ruta graveolens* |
|  | *Tanacetum parthenium* |
|  | *Vinca minor* |
|  | *Vitis vinifera* |
| Migraine | *Chamamelum nobile* |
|  | *Matricaria recutita* |
|  | *Rosmarinus officinalis* |
|  | *Scutellaria lateriflora* |
|  | *Tanacetum parthenium* |
|  | *Tilia platyphyllos* |
| Miscarriage, threatened | *Hamamelis virginiana* |
| Morning sickness | *Mentha spicata* |
|  | *Mentha x piperita* |
|  | *Tamarindus indicus* |
| Motion sickness | *Alpinia officinarum* |
|  | *Matricaria recutita* |
|  | *Zingiber officinale* |
| Mumps | *Phytolacca americana* |
| Muscle strain | *Capsicum minimum* |
|  | *Cinnamomum camphora* |
|  | *Matricaria recutita* |
|  | *Pinus spp.* |
|  | *Salix alba* |
|  | *Symphytum officinale* |
| Myalgia | *Hypericum perforatum* |
|  | *Urtica dioica* |
| Nausea | *Berberis vulgaris* |

|  | *Chamamelum nobile* |
|---|---|
|  | *Curcuma longa* |
|  | *Erythraea centarium* |
|  | *Filipendula ulmaria* |
|  | *Mentha spicata* |
|  | *Mentha x piperita* |
|  | *Myristica fragrans* |
|  | *Piper nigrum* |
|  | *Rubus idaeus* |
|  | *Tanacetum vulgare* |
|  | *Zingiber officinale* |
| Nephritis | *Arctostaphylos uva-ursi* |
|  | *Petroselinum crispum* |
| Nervous tension | *Arctium lappa* |
|  | *Chamamelum nobile* |
|  | *Cordyline spp.* |
|  | *Cypripedium pubescens* |
|  | *Dianthus caryophyllus* |
|  | *Humulus lupulus* |
|  | *Jasminum officinale* |
|  | *Olea europaea* |
|  | *Paeonia officinalis* |
|  | *Papaver spp.* |
|  | *Salvia officinalis* |
|  | *Scutellaria lateriflora* |
|  | *Stachys officinalis* |
|  | *Trifolium pratense* |
| Neuralgia | *Armoracia rusticana* |
|  | *Artemisia absinthium* |
|  | *Cypripedium pubescens* |
|  | *Gaultheria procumbens* |
|  | *Humulus lupulus* |
|  | *Hypericum perforatum* |
|  | *Inula helenium* |

| | |
|---|---|
| | *Matricaria recutita* |
| | *Melissa officinalis* |
| | *Rosmarinus officinalis* |
| Nosebleed | *Achillea millefolium* |
| | *Artemisia annua* |
| | *Capsella bursa-pastoris* |
| | *Hamamelis virginiana* |
| | *Stachys officinalis* |
| | *Vinca minor* |
| Pertussis | *Althaea officinalis (leaf)* |
| | *Castanea sativa* |
| | *Chelidonium majus* |
| | *Datura stramonium* |
| | *Ferula assa-foetida* |
| | *Inula helenium* |
| | *Lactuca virosa* |
| | *Lobelia inflata* |
| | *Marrubium vulgare* |
| | *Nepeta cataria* |
| | *Pimpinella anisum* |
| | *Prunus persica* |
| | *Prunus serotina* |
| | *Saccharum officinarum* |
| | *Symplocarpus foetidus* |
| | *Thymus vulgaris* |
| | *Trifolium pratense* |
| | *Tussilago farfara* |
| | *Urginea scilla* |
| | *Verbascum thapsus* |
| | *Viola tricolor* |
| Pharyngitis | *Althaea officinalis (leaf)* |
| | *Commiphora molmol* |
| | *Polygala senega* |
| | *Quercus alba* |

|  |  |
|---|---|
|  | *Salvia officinalis var rubia* |
|  | *Solidago virgaurea* |
| Phlebitis | *Arnica montana* |
| Pleurisy | *Angelica archangelica* |
| PMS | *Angelica sinensis* |
|  | *Leonurus cardiaca* |
|  | *Stachys officinalis* |
|  | *Vitex agnus-castus* |
| Pneumonia | *Ulmus fulva* |
| Psoriasis | *Aloe barbadensis* |
|  | *Arctium lappa* |
|  | *Curcuma longa* |
|  | *Galium aparine* |
|  | *Iris versicolor* |
|  | *Juglans nigra* |
|  | *Mahonia aquifolium* |
|  | *Melaleuca alternifolia* |
|  | *Populus candicans* |
|  | *Rumex crispus* |
|  | *Scrophularia nodosa* |
|  | *Smilax spp.* |
|  | *Stellaria media* |
|  | *Thymus vulgaris* |
|  | *Trifolium pratense* |
|  | *Ulmus fulva* |
|  | *Viola tricolor* |
| Pyorrhea | *Anacardium occidentale* |
|  | *Commiphora molmol* |
|  | *Echinacea spp.* |
|  | *Potentilla erecta* |
| Respiratory infection | *Abies balsamea* |
|  | *Althea rosea* |
|  | *Citrus bergamia* |
|  | *Echinacea spp.* |

|                          | *Glycyrrhiza glabra* |
|                          | *Pulsatilla vulgaris* |
|                          | *Salvia officinalis* |
| Respiratory inflammation | *Althaea officinalis (leaf)* |
| Ringworm                 | *Chimaphila umbellata* |
|                          | *Hydrastis canadensis* |
|                          | *Juglans nigra* |
|                          | *Plantago major* |
|                          | *Rumex crispus* |
|                          | *Thymus vulgaris* |
| Scabies                  | *Tanacetum vulgare* |
| Scalds                   | *Plantago major* |
| Sciatica                 | *Armoracia rusticana* |
|                          | *Cimicifuga racemosa* |
|                          | *Gaultheria procumbens* |
|                          | *Hypericum perforatum* |
|                          | *Inula helenium* |
|                          | *Juniperus communis* |
|                          | *Rosmarinus officinalis* |
| Seizures                 | *Scutellaria lateriflora* |
| Shock                    | *Capsicum minimum* |
| Sinusitis                | *Armoracia rusticana* |
|                          | *Commiphora molmol* |
|                          | *Ephedra sinica* |
|                          | *Euphrasia officinalis* |
|                          | *Gentiana lutea* |
|                          | *Hydrastis canadensis* |
|                          | *Matricaria recutita* |
|                          | *Melaleuca alternifolia* |
|                          | *Phytolacca americana* |
|                          | *Sambucus nigra* |
| Sore throat              | *Adiantum capillus-veneris* |
|                          | *Agrimonia eupatoria* |
|                          | *Althea rosea* |

*Berberis vulgaris*
*Capsicum minimum*
*Cinchona spp.*
*Citrus aurantifolia*
*Citrus limon*
*Glycyrrhiza glabra*
*Hordeum distichon*
*Hyssopus officinalis*
*Iris germanica var. florentina*
*Juglans nigra*
*Marrubium vulgare*
*Morus spp.*
*Myrica cerifera*
*Phoenix dactylifera*
*Polygonum bistorta*
*Populus candicans*
*Rubus idaeus*
*Saccharum officinarum*
*Salvia officinalis*
*Thymus vulgaris*
*Triticum spp*
*Ulmus fulva*
*Zingiber officinale*

Sores      *Galium aparine*
*Hordeum distichon*
*Rumex crispus*
*Trifolium pratense*
*Verbascum thapsus*

Spasm      *Scutellaria lateriflora*
*Thymus vulgaris*

Sprain      *Arnica montana*
*Artemisia absinthium*
*Capsicum minimum*
*Gaultheria procumbens*

|                    |                              |
|--------------------|------------------------------|
|                    | *Olea europaea*              |
|                    | *Sambucus nigra*             |
|                    | *Symphytum officinale*       |
|                    | *Verbascum thapsus*          |
| Stress             | *Avena sativa*               |
|                    | *Eleutherococcus senticosus* |
|                    | *Ulmus fulva*                |
| Stretch marks      | *Aloe barbadensis*           |
| Sunburn            | *Aloe barbadensis*           |
|                    | *Citrus limon*               |
|                    | *Cucumis sativus*            |
|                    | *Galium aparine*             |
|                    | *Hypericum perforatum*       |
|                    | *Ulmus fulva*                |
| Suppressed urine   | *Mentha spicata*             |
| Swelling           | *Artemisia absinthium*       |
|                    | *Chamamelum nobile*          |
|                    | *Malva sylvestris*           |
|                    | *Rumex crispus*              |
| Tachycardia        | *Leonurus cardiaca*          |
| Teething, babies   | *Chamamelum nobile*          |
|                    | *Matricaria recutita*        |
|                    | *Mentha x piperita*          |
| Tension            | *Artemisia vulgaris*         |
|                    | *Humulus lupulus*            |
|                    | *Hypericum perforatum*       |
|                    | *Leonurus cardiaca*          |
|                    | *Valeriana officinalis*      |
| Throat infection   | *Althaea officinalis (leaf)* |
|                    | *Geum urbanum*               |
|                    | *Potentilla erecta*          |
|                    | *Salvia officinalis var rubia* |
| Thrush             | *Achillea millefolium*       |
|                    | *Agathosma betulina*         |

*Commiphora molmol*
*Geranium maculatum*
*Hydrastis canadensis*
*Juniperus communis*
*Melaleuca alternifolia*
*Myrica cerifera*
*Ulmus fulva*

Tinnitus
*Gingko biloba*
*Tanacetum parthenium*

Tonsillitis
*Echinacea spp.*
*Juglans nigra*
*Phytolacca americana*
*Quercus alba*
*Salvia officinalis*
*Salvia officinalis var rubia*

Tooth extraction
*Geranium maculatum*

Toothache
*Acorus calamus*
*Anacardium occidentale*
*Mentha x piperita*
*Morus spp.*
*Piper nigrum*
*Plantago major*
*Rosa spp.*
*Thymus vulgaris*
*Verbascum thapsus*

Tremors
*Atropa belladonna*
*Scutellaria lateriflora*

Tuberculosis
*Inula helenium*

Tumors
*Rumex crispus*

Ulcer, duodenal
*Calendula officinalis*
*Geranium maculatum*
*Glycyrrhiza glabra*
*Hypericum perforatum*
*Juglans nigra*

| | |
|---|---|
| Ulcer, gastric | *Calendula officinalis* |
| | *Carica papaya* |
| | *Chamamelum nobile* |
| | *Chimaphila umbellata* |
| | *Glycyrrhiza glabra* |
| | *Hypericum perforatum* |
| | *Juglans nigra* |
| | *Matricaria recutita* |
| | *Musa sapientum* |
| | *Trigonella foenum-graecum* |
| Ulcer, mouth | *Alchemilla vulgaris* |
| | *Althaea officinalis (root)* |
| | *Arctium lappa* |
| | *Commiphora molmol* |
| | *Geranium maculatum* |
| | *Juglans nigra* |
| | *Myrica cerifera* |
| | *Polygonum bistorta* |
| Ulcer, peptic | *Aloe barbadensis* |
| | *Anacardium occidentale* |
| | *Atropa belladonna* |
| | *Filipendula ulmaria* |
| | *Geum urbanum* |
| | *Hydrastis canadensis* |
| | *Juglans nigra* |
| | *Medicago sativa* |
| | *Polygonum bistorta* |
| | *Solanum tuberosum* |
| | *Thymus vulgaris* |
| Ulcer, skin | *Aloe barbadensis* |
| | *Calendula officinalis* |
| | *Cedrus spp.* |
| | *Chimaphila umbellata* |
| | *Cnicus benedictus* |

|  | *Geranium maculatum* |
|---|---|
|  | *Humulus lupulus* |
|  | *Juglans nigra* |
|  | *Liquidambar styraciflua* |
|  | *Lythrum salicaria* |
|  | *Mandragora officinarum* |
| Urethritis | *Arctostaphylos uva-ursi* |
|  | *Elymus repens* |
|  | *Eupatorium purpureum* |
|  | *Portulaca oleracea* |
|  | *Solidago virgaurea* |
|  | *Zea mays* |
| Urinary gravel | *Althaea officinalis (leaf)* |
|  | *Arctostaphylos uva-ursi* |
|  | *Erica vulgaris* |
| Urinary incontinence | *Agrimonia eupatoria* |
| Urinary tract infection | *Abies balsamea* |
|  | *Achillea millefolium* |
|  | *Agathosma betulina* |
|  | *Apium graveolens* |
|  | *Arctostaphylos uva-ursi* |
|  | *Armoracia rusticana* |
|  | *Chimaphila umbellata* |
|  | *Chondrus crispus* |
|  | *Cichorium intybus* |
|  | *Daucus carota* |
|  | *Elymus repens* |
|  | *Erica vulgaris* |
|  | *Hordeum distichon* |
|  | *Levisticum officinale* |
|  | *Myrtus communis* |
|  | *Piper cubeba* |
|  | *Santalum album* |
|  | *Solidago virgaurea* |

|  |  |
|---|---|
|  | *Viola odorata* |
| Uterine fibroids | *Iris versicolor* |
| Uterus, prolapsed | *Arctium lappa* |
| Vaginal infection | *Achillea millefolium* |
|  | *Hydrastis canadensis* |
|  | *Ulmus fulva* |
| Varicose ulcers | *Althaea officinalis (root)* |
|  | *Hamamelis virginiana* |
|  | *Zanthoxylum americanum* |
| Varicose veins | *Althaea officinalis (root)* |
|  | *Fagopyrum esculentum* |
|  | *Hamamelis virginiana* |
|  | *Juglans nigra* |
|  | *Zanthoxylum americanum* |
| Vertigo | *Gingko biloba* |
|  | *Matricaria recutita* |
|  | *Morus spp.* |
| Vomiting | *Alpinia officinarum* |
|  | *Centraria islandica* |
|  | *Chamamelum nobile* |
|  | *Cinnamomum cassia* |
|  | *Gentiana lutea* |
|  | *Mentha spicata* |
|  | *Myristica fragrans* |
| Warts | *Echinacea spp.* |
| Water retention | *Capsella bursa-pastoris* |
|  | *Inula helenium* |
|  | *Iris germanica var. florentina* |
|  | *Medicago sativa* |
|  | *Plantago major* |
|  | *Taraxacum officinale* |
| Worms | *Alkanna tinctoria* |
|  | *Allium sativum* |
|  | *Armoracia rusticana* |

*Artemisia absinthium*
*Cucurbita pepo*
*Erythraea centarium*
*Gentiana lutea*
*Hyssopus officinalis*
*Inula helenium*
*Juglans nigra*
*Marrubium vulgare*
*Persea americana*
*Plantago major*
*Polygonum aviculare*
*Portulaca oleracea*
*Punica granatum*
*Senna alexandrina*
*Syzgium aromaticum*
*Tanacetum vulgare*
*Thymus vulgaris*
*Zingiber officinale*

Wounds

*Agrimonia eupatoria*
*Alkanna tinctoria*
*Althaea officinalis (root)*
*Althea rosea*
*Arctium lappa*
*Calendula officinalis*
*Capsella bursa-pastoris*
*Carica papaya*
*Cedrus spp.*
*Chamamelum nobile*
*Cnicus benedictus*
*Commiphora molmol*
*Equisetum arvense*
*Galium aparine*
*Hypericum perforatum*
*Hyssopus officinalis*

*Inula conyza*
*Inula helenium*
*Juniperus communis*
*Lythrum salicaria*
*Marrubium vulgare*
*Myrica cerifera*
*Persea americana*
*Plantago major*
*Polygonum bistorta*
*Saccharum officinarum*
*Salvia officinalis*
*Salvia officinalis var rubia*
*Sambucus nigra*
*Solidago virgaurea*
*Symphytum officinale*
*Thymus vulgaris*
*Trifolium pratense*
*Verbascum thapsus*

# Appendix C

# Magical Intentions

| Magical Intention | Latin Binomial |
|---|---|
| Anger Management | *Inula helenium* |
| | *Lavandula angustifolia* |
| | *Matricaria recutita* |
| | *Melissa officinalis* |
| | *Mentha spicata* |
| | *Mentha x piperita* |
| | *Nepeta cataria* |
| | *Passiflora incarnata* |
| | *Prunus amygdalus var dulcis* |
| | *Rosa spp.* |
| | *Verbena officinalis* |
| Anti-Hunger | *Medicago sativa* |
| Astral Projection, To Aid | *Artemisia vulgaris* |
| | *Atropa belladonna* |
| | *Origanum dictamnus* |
| | *Styrax benzoin* |
| Beauty, To Attain | *Eriodictyon californicum* |
| | *Linum usitatissimum* |
| | *Nepeta cataria* |
| | *Persea americana* |
| | *Syringa vulgaris* |
| Chastity, To Maintain | *Ananas comosus* |
| | *Cinnamomum camphora* |
| | *Cocos nucifera* |
| | *Crataegus laevigata* |
| | *Cucumis sativus* |
| | *Hamamelis virginiana* |

| | |
|---|---|
| | *Lactuca virosa* |
| | *Lavandula angustifolia* |
| | *Verbena officinalis* |
| Courage, To Attain | *Achillea millefolium* |
| | *Aquilegia vulgaris* |
| | *Borago officinalis* |
| | *Camellia sinensis* |
| | *Cedrus spp.* |
| | *Cimicifuga racemosa* |
| | *Dipteryx odorata* |
| | *Euonymus atropurpureus* |
| | *Imperatoria ostruthium* |
| | *Phytolacca americana* |
| | *Thymus vulgaris* |
| | *Verbascum thapsus* |
| Depression Management | *Capsella bursa-pastoris* |
| | *Chelidonium majus* |
| | *Convallaria majalis* |
| | *Crataegus laevigata* |
| | *Crocus sativus* |
| | *Hyacinthus orientalis* |
| | *Lonicera caprifolium* |
| | *Melissa officinalis* |
| | *Nepeta cataria* |
| | *Origanum vulgare* |
| Divination | *Artemisia absinthium* |
| | *Boswellia carterii* |
| | *Cichorium intybus* |
| | *Cinnamomum camphora* |
| | *Citrus sinensis* |
| | *Cytisus scoparius* |
| | *Eletteria cardamomum* |
| | *Ficus carica* |
| | *Filipendula ulmaria* |

*Foeniculum vulgare*
*Hibiscus sabdariffa*
*Hypericum perforatum*
*Iris germanica var. florentina*
*Juniperus communis*
*Lactuca virosa*
*Petroselinum crispum*
*Pimpinella anisum*
*Potentilla erecta*
*Prunus avium*
*Pterocarpus santalinus*
*Punica granatum*
*Rosa spp.*
*Salix alba*
*Solidago virgaurea*
*Syzgium aromaticum*
*Taraxacum officinale*
*Thalictrum spp.*
*Valeriana officinalis*
*Verbascum thapsus*
*Viola odorata*
*Viola tricolor*
*Zea mays*

Employment, To Attain/Maintain   *Anethum graveolens*
*Carya illinoinensis*
*Citrus bergamia*
*Laurus nobilis*
*Myrica cerifera*
*Pinus spp.*

Exorcism   *Achillea millefolium*
*Adiantum capillus-veneris*
*Allium cepa*
*Allium sativum*
*Angelica archangelica*

*Arbutus unedo*
*Armoracia rusticana*
*Betula alba*
*Boswellia carterii*
*Commiphora molmol*
*Cuminum cyminum*
*Daemonorops draco*
*Eupatorium perfoliatum*
*Ferula assa-foetida*
*Fumaria officinalis*
*Geum urbanum*
*Juniperus communis*
*Malva sylvestris*
*Marrubium vulgare*
*Ocimum basilicum*
*Paeonia officinalis*
*Pinus spp.*
*Piper nigrum*
*Polygonatum multiflorum*
*Prunus persica*
*Pterocarpus santalinus*
*Rhamnus frangula*
*Rosmarinus officinalis*
*Ruta graveolens*
*Sambucus nigra*
*Santalum album*
*Succisa pratensis*
*Syringa vulgaris*
*Syzgium aromaticum*
*Trifolium pratense*
*Urtica dioica*
*Verbascum thapsus*
*Viscum album*

Fertility, To Increase    *Brassica nigra*

*Crataegus laevigata*
*Cucumis sativus*
*Daucus carota*
*Equisetum arvense*
*Ficus carica*
*Helianthus annuus*
*Hypericum perforatum*
*Mandragora officinarum*
*Musa sapientum*
*Myrtus communis*
*Narcissus spp.*
*Nepeta cataria*
*Olea europaea*
*Oryza sativa*
*Papaver spp.*
*Pelargonium spp.*
*Phoenix dactylifera*
*Pinus spp.*
*Pogostemon cablin*
*Polygonum bistorta*
*Punica granatum*
*Quercus alba*
*Rumex crispus*
*Stellaria media*
*Triticum spp*
*Viscum album*
*Vitis vinifera*

Fidelity, to Ensure     *Cuminum cyminum*
*Glycyrrhiza glabra*
*Ilex paraguariensis*
*Scutellaria lateriflora*
*Trifolium pratense*

Friendship, To Promote     *Citrus limon*
*Citrus sinensis*

|  |  |
|---|---|
|  | *Dipteryx odorata* |
|  | *Galium aparine* |
|  | *Helianthus annuus* |
|  | *Passiflora incarnata* |
|  | *Vanilla spp* |
| Gossip, To Halt | *Antirrhinum majus* |
|  | *Ruta graveolens* |
|  | *Syzgium aromaticum* |
|  | *Trilisa odoratissima* |
|  | *Ulmus fulva* |
|  | *Urtica dioica* |
| Happiness, To Promote | *Chelidonium majus* |
|  | *Convallaria majalis* |
|  | *Crataegus laevigata* |
|  | *Crocus sativus* |
|  | *Filipendula ulmaria* |
|  | *Hyacinthus orientalis* |
|  | *Hypericum perforatum* |
|  | *Ipomoea purga* |
|  | *Lavandula angustifolia* |
|  | *Nepeta cataria* |
|  | *Orchis spp.* |
|  | *Origanum vulgare* |
|  | *Portulaca oleracea* |
| Healing, To Promote | *Abies balsamea* |
|  | *Acorus calamus* |
|  | *Allium cepa* |
|  | *Allium sativum* |
|  | *Angelica archangelica* |
|  | *Angelica sinensis* |
|  | *Arctium lappa* |
|  | *Artemisia vulgaris* |
|  | *Cedrus spp.* |
|  | *Celastrus scandens* |

*Cinnamomum cassia*
*Citrus aurantifolia*
*Citrus medica*
*Coix lachryma-jobi*
*Commiphora molmol*
*Cordyline spp.*
*Coriandrum sativum*
*Crocus sativus*
*Cucumis sativus*
*Cupressus sempervirens*
*Dianthus caryophyllus*
*Diospyros virginiana*
*Eriodictyon californicum*
*Eucalyptus globulus*
*Foeniculum vulgare*
*Galega officinalis*
*Gardenia jasminoides*
*Gaultheria procumbens*
*Gossypium herbaceum*
*Hedera helix*
*Helianthus annuus*
*Hordeum distichon*
*Humulus lupulus*
*Hydrastis canadensis*
*Juniperus communis*
*Laurus nobilis*
*Linum usitatissimum*
*Marrubium vulgare*
*Melissa officinalis*
*Mentha spicata*
*Mentha x piperita*
*Nicotiana tabacum*
*Olea europaea*
*Origanum vulgare*

*Panax quinquefolius*
*Pimenta dioica*
*Pinus spp.*
*Plantago major*
*Primula veris*
*Prunus domestica*
*Pterocarpus santalinus*
*Pulsatilla vulgaris*
*Pyrus malus*
*Quercus alba*
*Rosa spp.*
*Rosmarinus officinalis*
*Rubus villosus*
*Rumex crispus*
*Ruta graveolens*
*Salix alba*
*Sambucus nigra*
*Santalum album*
*Senecio vulgaris*
*Solanum tuberosum*
*Thymus vulgaris*
*Urtica dioica*
*Verbena officinalis*
*Viola odorata*
*Viscum album*

Health, To Maintain

*Adiantum capillus-veneris*
*Allium sativum*
*Alpinia officinarum*
*Carum carvi*
*Cinnamomum camphora*
*Coriandrum sativum*
*Fraxinus exelsior*
*Galega officinalis*
*Hypericum perforatum*

*Juglans nigra*
*Juniperus communis*
*Mandragora officinarum*
*Myristica fragrans*
*Origanum vulgare*
*Pelargonium spp.*
*Polygonum aviculare*
*Pulsatilla vulgaris*
*Quercus alba*
*Ruta graveolens*
*Scrophularia nodosa*
*Senecio vulgaris*
*Tanacetum vulgare*
*Thymus vulgaris*
*Verbascum thapsus*
*Viscum album*

Hexes, To Break     *Alpinia officinarum*
*Capsicum minimum*
*Chrysopogon zizinoides*
*Cnicus benedictus*
*Datura stramonium*
*Erythraea centarium*
*Euonymus atropurpureus*
*Gaultheria procumbens*
*Leonurus cardiaca*
*Phytolacca americana*
*Urginea scilla*
*Urtica dioica*
*Vaccinium myrtillus*

Hunting, To Aid     *Viscum album*
Immortality, To Attain     *Prunus amygdalus var dulcis*
*Pyrus malus*
*Salvia officinalis*
*Salvia officinalis var rubia*

|                               | *Tilia platyphyllos*            |
| Infertility, To Create        | *Juglans nigra*                 |
| Invisibility, To Attain       | *Amaranthus hypochondriacus*    |
|                               | *Arnica montana*                |
|                               | *Cichorium intybus*             |
|                               | *Papaver spp.*                  |
| Legal Matters, To Assist In   | *Alpinia officinarum*           |
|                               | *Calendula officinalis*         |
|                               | *Chelidonium majus*             |
|                               | *Ipomoea purga*                 |
|                               | *Matricaria recutita*           |
|                               | *Rhamnus frangula*              |
|                               | *Rhamnus purshiana*             |
|                               | *Symplocarpus foetidus*         |
| Longevity, To Attain          | *Acer spp.*                     |
|                               | *Citrus limon*                  |
|                               | *Cupressus sempervirens*        |
|                               | *Lavandula angustifolia*        |
|                               | *Salvia officinalis*            |
|                               | *Salvia officinalis var rubia*  |
|                               | *Tanacetum vulgare*             |
| Love Spells, To Break         | *Pistacia vera*                 |
| Love, Divination Of           | *Hypericum perforatum*          |
|                               | *Lactuca virosa*                |
|                               | *Narcissus spp.*                |
|                               | *Pyrus malus*                   |
|                               | *Rosa spp.*                     |
|                               | *Salix alba*                    |
|                               | *Viola tricolor*                |
| Love, To Attract              | *Abies balsamea*                |
|                               | *Acer spp.*                     |
|                               | *Achillea millefolium*          |
|                               | *Aframomum melegueta*           |
|                               | *Alchemilla vulgaris*           |

*Anethum graveolens*

*Aquilegia vulgaris*

*Artemisia absinthium*

*Beta vulgaris*

*Bursera fagaroides*

*Capsicum minimum*

*Carica papaya*

*Castanea sativa*

*Chamamelum nobile*

*Chrysopogon zizinoides*

*Cimicifuga racemosa*

*Cinnamomum cassia*

*Citrus aurantifolia*

*Citrus limon*

*Citrus sinensis*

*Coriandrum sativum*

*Crocus sativus*

*Daemonorops draco*

*Dipteryx odorata*

*Eletteria cardamomum*

*Eryngium spp.*

*Eupatorium purpureum*

*Ficus carica*

*Filipendula ulmaria*

*Fragaria vesca*

*Galium aparine*

*Gardenia jasminoides*

*Gentiana lutea*

*Geum urbanum*

*Glycyrrhiza glabra*

*Hibiscus sabdariffa*

*Hordeum distichon*

*Hyacinthus orientalis*

*Ilex paraguariensis*

*Inula conyza*

*Inula helenium*

*Ipomoea purga*

*Iris germanica var. florentina*

*Jasminum officinale*

*Juniperus communis*

*Lavandula angustifolia*

*Leonurus cardiaca*

*Levisticum officinale*

*Lippia citriodora*

*Lobelia inflata*

*Malva sylvestris*

*Matricaria recutita*

*Melissa officinalis*

*Mentha spicata*

*Mentha x piperita*

*Myrtus communis*

*Nepeta cataria*

*Ocimum basilicum*

*Orchis spp.*

*Origanum vulgare*

*Panax quinquefolius*

*Papaver spp.*

*Pelargonium spp.*

*Persea americana*

*Pimenta dioica*

*Pimpinella anisum*

*Piper cubeba*

*Portulaca oleracea*

*Potentilla erecta*

*Prunus armeniaca*

*Prunus avium*

*Pterocarpus santalinus*

*Rosa spp.*

*Rosmarinus officinalis*
*Rubus idaeus*
*Ruta graveolens*
*Saccharum officinarum*
*Salix alba*
*Sanguinaria canadensis*
*Scutellaria lateriflora*
*Senna alexandrina*
*Smilax spp.*
*Solanum lycopersicum*
*Stachys officinalis*
*Stellaria media*
*Syzgium aromaticum*
*Tamarindus indicus*
*Thymus vulgaris*
*Tilia platyphyllos*
*Trifolium pratense*
*Turnera diffusa*
*Tussilago farfara*
*Ulmus campestris*
*Valeriana officinalis*
*Vanilla spp*
*Verbascum thapsus*
*Verbena officinalis*
*Vinca minor*
*Viola odorata*
*Viola tricolor*
*Viscum album*
*Zanthoxylum americanum*
*Zingiber officinale*

**Luck, To Obtain**

*Acorus calamus*
*Adiantum capillus-veneris*
*Aframomum melegueta*
*Aloe barbadensis*

*Ananas comosus*
*Anethum graveolens*
*Brassica oleracea*
*Capparis spinosa*
*Centraria islandica*
*Chondrus crispus*
*Chrysopogon zizinoides*
*Cinchona spp.*
*Citrus sinensis*
*Coix lachryma-jobi*
*Diospyros virginiana*
*Erica vulgaris*
*Fragaria vesca*
*Gossypium herbaceum*
*Ilex aquifolium*
*Illicium verum*
*Myristica fragrans*
*Narcissus spp.*
*Papaver spp.*
*Pimenta dioica*
*Piper methysticum*
*Polygala senega*
*Portulaca oleracea*
*Punica granatum*
*Quercus alba*
*Rosa spp.*
*Succisa pratensis*
*Tilia platyphyllos*
*Trifolium pratense*
*Vaccinium myrtillus*
*Verbena officinalis*
*Viola odorata*
*Zea mays*

Lust, To Increase/Create     *Aframomum melegueta*

*Allium cepa*
*Allium sativum*
*Alpinia officinarum*
*Anethum graveolens*
*Apium graveolens*
*Capparis spinosa*
*Carum carvi*
*Cinnamomum cassia*
*Crocus sativus*
*Cymbopogon citratus*
*Daucus carota*
*Eletteria cardamomum*
*Eryngium spp.*
*Glycyrrhiza glabra*
*Hibiscus sabdariffa*
*Ilex paraguariensis*
*Olea europaea*
*Panax quinquefolius*
*Pelargonium spp.*
*Persea americana*
*Petroselinum crispum*
*Pistacia lentiscus*
*Pogostemon cablin*
*Raphanus sativus*
*Rhodymenia palmata*
*Rosmarinus officinalis*
*Saccharum officinarum*
*Succisa pratensis*
*Trilisa odoratissima*
*Turnera diffusa*
*Urtica dioica*
*Vanilla spp*
*Vinca minor*
*Viola odorata*

| | |
|---|---|
| Manifestations, To Aid | *Abies balsamea* |
| | *Origanum dictamnus* |
| | *Pistacia lentiscus* |
| Meditation, To Aid | *Erythraea centarium* |
| | *Pterocarpus santalinus* |
| | *Styrax benzoin* |
| Mental Powers, To Strengthen | *Apium graveolens* |
| | *Brassica nigra* |
| | *Carum carvi* |
| | *Convallaria majalis* |
| | *Euphrasia officinalis* |
| | *Jasminum officinale* |
| | *Juglans nigra* |
| | *Marrubium vulgare* |
| | *Mentha spicata* |
| | *Monarda fistulosa* |
| | *Myristica fragrans* |
| | *Rosmarinus officinalis* |
| | *Ruta graveolens* |
| | *Salvia officinalis* |
| | *Salvia officinalis var rubia* |
| | *Satureja hortensis* |
| | *Styrax benzoin* |
| | *Vanilla spp* |
| | *Vinca minor* |
| | *Vitis vinifera* |
| Money, Riches, Treasures, Wealth | *Acacia senegal* |
| | *Acer spp.* |
| | *Acorus calamus* |
| | *Adiantum capillus-veneris* |
| | *Aframomum melegueta* |
| | *Allium cepa* |
| | *Alpinia officinarum* |
| | *Althea rosea* |

*Anacardium occidentale*

*Ananas comosus*

*Anethum graveolens*

*Avena sativa*

*Camellia sinensis*

*Carya illinoinensis*

*Cedrus spp.*

*Centraria islandica*

*Chamamelum nobile*

*Chimaphila umbellata*

*Chondrus crispus*

*Chrysopogon zizinoides*

*Citrus bergamia*

*Citrus sinensis*

*Cryptanthus spp.*

*Dipteryx odorata*

*Fagopyrum esculentum*

*Fucus vesiculosus*

*Fumaria officinalis*

*Galium odoratum*

*Hydrastis canadensis*

*Ipomoea purga*

*Iris versicolor*

*Jasminum officinale*

*Linum usitatissimum*

*Lonicera caprifolium*

*Mahonia aquifolium*

*Mandragora officinarum*

*Matricaria recutita*

*Medicago sativa*

*Myristica fragrans*

*Myrtus communis*

*Ocimum basilicum*

*Origanum vulgare*

*Oryza sativa*
*Papaver spp.*
*Pimenta dioica*
*Pinus spp.*
*Pogostemon cablin*
*Polygala senega*
*Potentilla erecta*
*Primula veris*
*Prunus amygdalus var dulcis*
*Punica granatum*
*Quercus alba*
*Rhamnus purshiana*
*Rubus villosus*
*Rumex crispus*
*Smilax spp.*
*Solidago virgaurea*
*Symphytum officinale*
*Syzgium aromaticum*
*Trifolium pratense*
*Trigonella foenum-graecum*
*Triticum spp*
*Urginea scilla*
*Verbena officinalis*
*Vinca minor*
*Vitis vinifera*
*Zingiber officinale*

Obstacles, to Remove      *Cichorium intybus*
Peace/Harmony, To Instill      *Eryngium spp.*
*Filipendula ulmaria*
*Gardenia jasminoides*
*Lavandula angustifolia*
*Lythrum salicaria*
*Mentha pulegium*
*Myrtus communis*

|  | *Olea europaea* |
|  | *Passiflora incarnata* |
|  | *Scutellaria lateriflora* |
|  | *Tussilago farfara* |
|  | *Verbena officinalis* |
|  | *Viola odorata* |
| Power, To Obtain | *Cinnamomum cassia* |
|  | *Gentiana lutea* |
|  | *Hypericum perforatum* |
|  | *Lycopodium clavatum* |
|  | *Zingiber officinale* |
| Prophetic Dreams, To Cause | *Agathosma betulina* |
|  | *Allium cepa* |
|  | *Artemisia vulgaris* |
|  | *Calendula officinalis* |
|  | *Jasminum officinale* |
|  | *Ocimum basilicum* |
|  | *Potentilla erecta* |
| Prosperity, To Obtain | *Alkanna tinctoria* |
|  | *Fraxinus exelsior* |
|  | *Mahonia aquifolium* |
|  | *Medicago sativa* |
|  | *Musa sapientum* |
|  | *Prunus amygdalus var dulcis* |
|  | *Sambucus nigra* |
|  | *Solanum lycopersicum* |
|  | *Styrax benzoin* |
| Protection | *Abies balsamea* |
|  | *Acorus calamus* |
|  | *Adiantum capillus-veneris* |
|  | *Agrimonia eupatoria* |
|  | *Allium cepa* |
|  | *Allium sativum* |
|  | *Aloe barbadensis* |

*Alpinia officinarum*
*Althaea officinalis*
*Amaranthus hypochondriacus*
*Anethum graveolens*
*Angelica archangelica*
*Angelica sinensis*
*Antirrhinum majus*
*Arbutus unedo*
*Arctium lappa*
*Arnica montana*
*Artemisia absinthium*
*Artemisia vulgaris*
*Betula alba*
*Borago officinalis*
*Boswellia carterii*
*Brassica nigra*
*Brassica rapa*
*Calendula officinalis*
*Carica papaya*
*Carum carvi*
*Cedrus spp.*
*Celastrus scandens*
*Chelidonium majus*
*Chondrus crispus*
*Chrysanthemum x morifolium*
*Cimicifuga racemosa*
*Cinchona spp.*
*Cinnamomum cassia*
*Citrus aurantifolia*
*Cnicus benedictus*
*Cocos nucifera*
*Commiphora molmol*
*Cordyline spp.*
*Cryptanthus spp.*

*Cucurbita pepo*

*Cuminum cyminum*

*Cupressus sempervirens*

*Cypripedium pubescens*

*Cytisus scoparius*

*Daemonorops draco*

*Datura stramonium*

*Dianthus caryophyllus*

*Digitalis purpurea*

*Erica vulgaris*

*Eriodictyon californicum*

*Eucalyptus globulus*

*Eupatorium perfoliatum*

*Fagopyrum esculentum*

*Ferula assa-foetida*

*Foeniculum vulgare*

*Fraxinus exelsior*

*Fucus vesiculosus*

*Galium aparine*

*Galium odoratum*

*Gaultheria procumbens*

*Gossypium herbaceum*

*Hamamelis virginiana*

*Hedera helix*

*Hordeum distichon*

*Hyacinthus orientalis*

*Hypericum perforatum*

*Hyssopus officinalis*

*Ilex aquifolium*

*Imperatoria ostruthium*

*Inula helenium*

*Iris germanica var. florentina*

*Juniperus communis*

*Lactuca virosa*

*Laurus nobilis*
*Lavandula angustifolia*
*Leonurus cardiaca*
*Linum usitatissimum*
*Liquidambar styraciflua*
*Lonicera caprifolium*
*Lycopodium clavatum*
*Lythrum salicaria*
*Malva sylvestris*
*Mandragora officinarum*
*Marrubium vulgare*
*Mentha pulegium*
*Mentha spicata*
*Morus spp.*
*Ocimum basilicum*
*Olea europaea*
*Origanum vulgare*
*Oryza sativa*
*Paeonia officinalis*
*Panax quinquefolius*
*Pelargonium spp.*
*Petroselinum crispum*
*Pimpinella anisum*
*Pinus spp.*
*Piper methysticum*
*Piper nigrum*
*Plantago major*
*Pogostemon cablin*
*Polygala senega*
*Polygonatum multiflorum*
*Portulaca oleracea*
*Potentilla erecta*
*Prunus persica*
*Pterocarpus santalinus*

*Pulsatilla vulgaris*
*Quercus alba*
*Raphanus sativus*
*Rhamnus frangula*
*Rhamnus purshiana*
*Rheum officinale*
*Rheum palmatum*
*Rosa spp.*
*Rosmarinus officinalis*
*Rubus idaeus*
*Rubus villosus*
*Ruta graveolens*
*Salix alba*
*Salvia officinalis*
*Salvia officinalis var rubia*
*Sambucus nigra*
*Sanguinaria canadensis*
*Santalum album*
*Scrophularia nodosa*
*Solanum lycopersicum*
*Stachys officinalis*
*Succisa pratensis*
*Syringa vulgaris*
*Syzgium aromaticum*
*Tanacetum parthenium*
*Tilia platyphyllos*
*Trifolium pratense*
*Urginea scilla*
*Urtica dioica*
*Vaccinium myrtillus*
*Valeriana officinalis*
*Verbascum thapsus*
*Verbena officinalis*
*Vinca minor*

*Viola odorata*

*Viscum album*

*Yucca spp.*

*Zea mays*

Psychic Powers, To Strengthen   *Acacia senegal*

*Achillea millefolium*

*Agathosma betulina*

*Alpinia officinarum*

*Althaea officinalis*

*Apium graveolens*

*Arctostaphylos uva-ursi*

*Artemisia absinthium*

*Artemisia vulgaris*

*Borago officinalis*

*Calendula officinalis*

*Cinnamomum cassia*

*Citrus medica*

*Crocus sativus*

*Cymbopogon citratus*

*Eriodictyon californicum*

*Euphrasia officinalis*

*Fucus vesiculosus*

*Illicium verum*

*Inula helenium*

*Laurus nobilis*

*Linum usitatissimum*

*Lonicera caprifolium*

*Mentha x piperita*

*Myristica fragrans*

*Pistacia lentiscus*

*Polygonum bistorta*

*Rosa spp.*

*Thymus vulgaris*

*Trilisa odoratissima*

Purification

*Acacia senegal*
*Alkanna tinctoria*
*Angelica archangelica*
*Armoracia rusticana*
*Betula alba*
*Bursera fagaroides*
*Cedrus spp.*
*Chamamelum nobile*
*Citrus limon*
*Cnicus benedictus*
*Cocos nucifera*
*Curcuma longa*
*Cytisus scoparius*
*Ferula assa-foetida*
*Foeniculum vulgare*
*Geum urbanum*
*Hyssopus officinalis*
*Laurus nobilis*
*Lavandula angustifolia*
*Lippia citriodora*
*Matricaria recutita*
*Mentha x piperita*
*Nicotiana tabacum*
*Petroselinum crispum*
*Pimpinella anisum*
*Rosmarinus officinalis*
*Sanguinaria canadensis*
*Stachys officinalis*
*Styrax benzoin*
*Thymus vulgaris*
*Valeriana officinalis*
*Verbena officinalis*
*Yucca spp.*

Rain, To Cause To Fall          *Erica vulgaris*

|  |  |
|---|---|
|  | *Gossypium herbaceum* |
|  | *Oryza sativa* |
|  | *Viola tricolor* |
| Relationships, to End | *Brassica rapa* |
| Sexual Potency, To Regain | *Cnicus benedictus* |
| or Maintain | *Satureja hortensis* |
| Sleep | *Agrimonia eupatoria* |
|  | *Chamamelum nobile* |
|  | *Datura stramonium* |
|  | *Humulus lupulus* |
|  | *Lactuca virosa* |
|  | *Lavandula angustifolia* |
|  | *Matricaria recutita* |
|  | *Mentha x piperita* |
|  | *Papaver spp.* |
|  | *Passiflora incarnata* |
|  | *Portulaca oleracea* |
|  | *Potentilla erecta* |
|  | *Rosmarinus officinalis* |
|  | *Sambucus nigra* |
|  | *Thymus vulgaris* |
|  | *Tilia platyphyllos* |
|  | *Valeriana officinalis* |
|  | *Verbena officinalis* |
| Snakes, To Call | *Equisetum arvense* |
| Snakes, To Enrage | *Silybum marianum* |
| Snakes, To Repel | *Cymbopogon citratus* |
|  | *Erythraea centarium* |
|  | *Pelargonium spp.* |
|  | *Plantago major* |
| Spirits, To Call | *Artemisia absinthium* |
|  | *Chimaphila umbellata* |
|  | *Taraxacum officinale* |
| Spirituality, To Strengthen | *Acacia senegal* |

*Boswellia carterii*
*Cinnamomum cassia*
*Commiphora molmol*
*Gardenia jasminoides*
*Pterocarpus santalinus*
*Santalum album*

Strength, To Instill
*Artemisia vulgaris*
*Camellia sinensis*
*Crocus sativus*
*Dianthus caryophyllus*
*Echinacea spp.*
*Hypericum perforatum*
*Imperatoria ostruthium*
*Laurus nobilis*
*Mentha pulegium*
*Morus spp.*
*Plantago major*

Stress Management
*Avena sativa*
*Calendula officinalis*
*Humulus lupulus*
*Hypericum perforatum*
*Lavandula angustifolia*
*Matricaria recutita*
*Passiflora incarnata*
*Scutellaria lateriflora*
*Symphytum officinale*
*Urtica dioica*

Success, To Attain
*Cinnamomum cassia*
*Citrus bergamia*
*Euonymus atropurpureus*
*Galium odoratum*
*Ipomoea purga*
*Melissa officinalis*
*Trifolium pratense*

|  |  |
|---|---|
|  | *Zingiber officinale* |
| Theft, To Prevent | *Allium sativum* |
|  | *Carum carvi* |
|  | *Chrysopogon zizinoides* |
|  | *Gentiana lutea* |
|  | *Juniperus communis* |
|  | *Rosmarinus officinalis* |
|  | *Sambucus nigra* |
| Travelling, to Protect While | *Eryngium spp.* |
|  | *Lavandula angustifolia* |
|  | *Symphytum officinale* |
| Visions, To Induce | *Angelica archangelica* |
|  | *Atropa belladonna* |
|  | *Piper methysticum* |
|  | *Turnera diffusa* |
|  | *Tussilago farfara* |
| Wisdom, To Promote | *Helianthus annuus* |
|  | *Prunus amygdalus var dulcis* |
|  | *Salvia officinalis* |
|  | *Salvia officinalis var rubia* |
| Wishes, To Manifest | *Aframomum melegueta* |
|  | *Coix lachryma-jobi* |
|  | *Dipteryx odorata* |
|  | *Fagus sylvatica* |
|  | *Helianthus annuus* |
|  | *Juglans nigra* |
|  | *Panax quinquefolius* |
|  | *Punica granatum* |
|  | *Rhamnus frangula* |
|  | *Salvia officinalis* |
|  | *Salvia officinalis var rubia* |
|  | *Taraxacum officinale* |
|  | *Viola odorata* |
| Youth, To Maintain or Regain | *Adiantum capillus-veneris* |

*Myrtus communis*
*Pimpinella anisum*
*Primula veris*
*Rosmarinus officinalis*
*Verbena officinalis*

# Appendix D

# Herbs by Element

| Element | Latin Binomial |
| --- | --- |
| Air | *Acacia senegal* |
| | *Acer spp.* |
| | *Adiantum capillus-veneris* |
| | *Agrimonia eupatoria* |
| | *Borago officinalis* |
| | *Carum carvi* |
| | *Carya illinoinensis* |
| | *Celastrus scandens* |
| | *Cichorium intybus* |
| | *Citrus bergamia* |
| | *Citrus medica* |
| | *Convallaria majalis* |
| | *Cryptanthus spp.* |
| | *Cymbopogon citratus* |
| | *Cytisus scoparius* |
| | *Euphrasia officinalis* |
| | *Filipendula ulmaria* |
| | *Galega officinalis* |
| | *Humulus lupulus* |
| | *Illicium verum* |
| | *Inula helenium* |
| | *Lavandula angustifolia* |
| | *Lippia citriodora* |
| | *Marrubium vulgare* |
| | *Monarda fistulosa* |
| | *Morus spp.* |
| | *Origanum vulgare* |
| | *Oryza sativa* |

*Petroselinum crispum*

*Phoenix dactylifera*

*Pimpinella anisum*

*Pinus spp.*

*Pistacia lentiscus*

*Pistacia vera*

*Rumex crispus*

*Salvia officinalis*

*Satureja hortensis*

*Senna alexandrina*

*Solidago virgaurea*

*Styrax benzoin*

*Taraxacum officinale*

*Tilia platyphyllos*

*Trifolium pratense*

*Trigonella foenum-graecum*

*Ulmus fulva*

*Viscum album*

Earth

*Artemisia annua*

*Artemisia vulgaris*

*Avena sativa*

*Beta vulgaris*

*Brassica rapa*

*Chrysopogon zizinoides*

*Cupressus sempervirens*

*Echinacea spp.*

*Equisetum arvense*

*Fagopyrum esculentum*

*Fumaria officinalis*

*Gossypium herbaceum*

*Hordeum distichon*

*Lonicera caprifolium*

*Lythrum salicaria*

*Mahonia aquifolium*

*Medicago sativa*
*Plantago major*
*Pogostemon cablin*
*Polygonum aviculare*
*Polygonum bistorta*
*Rheum officinale*
*Rheum palmatum*
*Solanum tuberosum*
*Triticum spp*
*Verbena officinalis*
*Zea mays*

Fire

*Aframomum melegueta*
*Allium cepa*
*Allium sativum*
*Alpinia officinarum*
*Amaranthus hypochondriacus*
*Anacardium occidentale*
*Ananas comosus*
*Anethum graveolens*
*Angelica archangelica*
*Angelica sinensis*
*Antirrhinum majus*
*Apium graveolens*
*Arbutus unedo*
*Armoracia rusticana*
*Artemisia absinthium*
*Astragalus gummifer*
*Boswellia carterii*
*Brassica nigra*
*Bursera fagaroides*
*Calendula officinalis*
*Camellia sinensis*
*Capsicum minimum*
*Castanea sativa*

*Cedrus spp.*
*Chelidonium majus*
*Chrysanthemum x morifolium*
*Cinnamomum cassia*
*Citrus aurantifolia*
*Citrus sinensis*
*Cnicus benedictus*
*Cordyline spp.*
*Coriandrum sativum*
*Crataegus laevigata*
*Crocus sativus*
*Cuminum cyminum*
*Daemonorops draco*
*Daucus carota*
*Dianthus caryophyllus*
*Erythraea centarium*
*Ferula assa-foetida*
*Ficus carica*
*Foeniculum vulgare*
*Fraxinus exelsior*
*Galium aparine*
*Galium odoratum*
*Gentiana lutea*
*Geum urbanum*
*Hamamelis virginiana*
*Helianthus annuus*
*Hydrastis canadensis*
*Hypericum perforatum*
*Hyssopus officinalis*
*Ilex aquifolium*
*Imperatoria ostruthium*
*Ipomoea purga*
*Juglans nigra*
*Juniperus communis*

*Laurus nobilis*
*Levisticum officinale*
*Linum usitatissimum*
*Liquidambar styraciflua*
*Mandragora officinarum*
*Mentha pulegium*
*Mentha x piperita*
*Myristica fragrans*
*Nicotiana tabacum*
*Ocimum basilicum*
*Olea europaea*
*Paeonia officinalis*
*Panax quinquefolius*
*Phytolacca americana*
*Pimenta dioica*
*Piper cubeba*
*Piper nigrum*
*Potentilla erecta*
*Prunus persica*
*Pulsatilla vulgaris*
*Punica granatum*
*Quercus alba*
*Raphanus sativus*
*Rosmarinus officinalis*
*Ruta graveolens*
*Sanguinaria canadensis*
*Silybum marianum*
*Smilax spp.*
*Stachys officinalis*
*Stachys officinalis*
*Syzgium aromaticum*
*Trilisa odoratissima*
*Turnera diffusa*
*Urginea scilla*

Water

*Urtica dioica*

*Verbascum thapsus*

*Yucca spp.*

*Zanthoxylum americanum*

*Zingiber officinale*

*Abies balsamea*

*Achillea millefolium*

*Acorus calamus*

*Agathosma betulina*

*Alchemilla vulgaris*

*Alkanna tinctoria*

*Aloe barbadensis*

*Althaea officinalis*

*Aquilegia vulgaris*

*Arctium lappa*

*Arnica montana*

*Atropa belladonna*

*Betula alba*

*Brassica oleracea*

*Capparis spinosa*

*Carica papaya*

*Chamamelum nobile*

*Chondrus crispus*

*Cimicifuga racemosa*

*Cinnamomum camphora*

*Citrus limon*

*Cocos nucifera*

*Commiphora molmol*

*Cucumis sativus*

*Cucurbita pepo*

*Cypripedium pubescens*

*Datura stramonium*

*Digitalis purpurea*

*Diospyros virginiana*

*Dipteryx odorata*
*Eletteria cardamomum*
*Erica vulgaris*
*Eryngium spp.*
*Eucalyptus globulus*
*Eupatorium perfoliatum*
*Eupatorium purpureum*
*Fragaria vesca*
*Fucus vesiculosus*
*Gardenia jasminoides*
*Gaultheria procumbens*
*Glycyrrhiza glabra*
*Hedera helix*
*Hibiscus sabdariffa*
*Hyacinthus orientalis*
*Inula conyza*
*Iris germanica var. florentina*
*Iris versicolor*
*Jasminum officinale*
*Lactuca virosa*
*Lobelia inflata*
*Lycopodium clavatum*
*Malva sylvestris*
*Matricaria recutita*
*Melissa officinalis*
*Mentha spicata*
*Musa sapientum*
*Myrtus communis*
*Narcissus spp.*
*Nepeta cataria*
*Orchis spp.*
*Origanum dictamnus*
*Papaver spp.*
*Passiflora incarnata*

*Pelargonium spp.*

*Persea americana*

*Piper methysticum*

*Polygonatum multiflorum*

*Populus candicans*

*Portulaca oleracea*

*Primula veris*

*Prunus amygdalus var dulcis*

*Prunus armeniaca*

*Prunus avium*

*Prunus domestica*

*Prunus serotina*

*Pterocarpus santalinus*

*Pyrus malus*

*Rhamnus frangula*

*Rhodymenia palmata*

*Rosa spp.*

*Rubus idaeus*

*Rubus villosus*

*Saccharum officinarum*

*Salix alba*

*Sambucus nigra*

*Santalum album*

*Scrophularia nodosa*

*Scutellaria lateriflora*

*Senecio vulgaris*

*Solanum lycopersicum*

*Stellaria media*

*Symphytum officinale*

*Symplocarpus foetidus*

*Syringa vulgaris*

*Tamarindus indicus*

*Tanacetum parthenium*

*Tanacetum vulgare*

*Thymus vulgaris*
*Tussilago farfara*
*Ulmus campestris*
*Vaccinium myrtillus*
*Valeriana officinalis*
*Vanilla spp*
*Vinca minor*
*Viola odorata*
*Viola tricolor*
*Vitis vinifera*

# Appendix E

# Herbs by Planet

| Planet | Latin Binomial |
|--------|----------------|
| Jupiter | *Acer spp.* |
| | *Agrimonia eupatoria* |
| | *Borago officinalis* |
| | *Castanea sativa* |
| | *Cordyline spp.* |
| | *Echinacea spp.* |
| | *Ficus carica* |
| | *Filipendula ulmaria* |
| | *Geum urbanum* |
| | *Hyssopus officinalis* |
| | *Illicium verum* |
| | *Lonicera caprifolium* |
| | *Myristica fragrans* |
| | *Pimpinella anisum* |
| | *Potentilla erecta* |
| | *Rumex crispus* |
| | *Salvia officinalis* |
| | *Smilax spp.* |
| | *Stachys officinalis* |
| | *Syzgium aromaticum* |
| | *Taraxacum officinale* |
| | *Tilia platyphyllos* |
| Mars | *Aframomum melegueta* |
| | *Allium cepa* |
| | *Allium sativum* |
| | *Alpinia officinarum* |
| | *Antirrhinum majus* |
| | *Arbutus unedo* |

*Arctostaphylos uva-ursi*
*Armoracia rusticana*
*Artemisia absinthium*
*Berberis vulgaris*
*Brassica nigra*
*Capsicum minimum*
*Cnicus benedictus*
*Coriandrum sativum*
*Crataegus laevigata*
*Cuminum cyminum*
*Cytisus scoparius*
*Daemonorops draco*
*Daucus carota*
*Ferula assa-foetida*
*Galium odoratum*
*Gentiana lutea*
*Humulus lupulus*
*Ilex aquifolium*
*Imperatoria ostruthium*
*Ipomoea purga*
*Mentha pulegium*
*Nicotiana tabacum*
*Ocimum basilicum*
*Phytolacca americana*
*Pimenta dioica*
*Pinus spp.*
*Piper cubeba*
*Piper nigrum*
*Pulsatilla vulgaris*
*Raphanus sativus*
*Ruta graveolens*
*Sanguinaria canadensis*
*Silybum marianum*
*Styrax benzoin*

*Trilisa odoratissima*
*Turnera diffusa*
*Urginea scilla*
*Urtica dioica*
*Yucca spp.*
*Zanthoxylum americanum*
*Zingiber officinale*

**Mercury**     *Adiantum capillus-veneris*
*Anethum graveolens*
*Carum carvi*
*Carya illinoinensis*
*Celastrus scandens*
*Citrus bergamia*
*Convallaria majalis*
*Cymbopogon citratus*
*Foeniculum vulgare*
*Galega officinalis*
*Inula helenium*
*Lavandula angustifolia*
*Linum usitatissimum*
*Lippia citriodora*
*Mandragora officinarum*
*Marrubium vulgare*
*Mentha x piperita*
*Morus spp.*
*Origanum vulgare*
*Petroselinum crispum*
*Pistacia vera*
*Punica granatum*
*Satureja hortensis*
*Senna alexandrina*
*Trifolium pratense*
*Trigonella foenum-graecum*

**Moon**     *Acorus calamus*

*Agathosma betulina*
*Aloe barbadensis*
*Brassica oleracea*
*Brassica rapa*
*Carica papaya*
*Chondrus crispus*
*Cinnamomum camphora*
*Citrus limon*
*Cocos nucifera*
*Commiphora molmol*
*Cucumis sativus*
*Cucurbita pepo*
*Eucalyptus globulus*
*Fucus vesiculosus*
*Gardenia jasminoides*
*Gaultheria procumbens*
*Gossypium herbaceum*
*Jasminum officinale*
*Lactuca virosa*
*Lycopodium clavatum*
*Lythrum salicaria*
*Malva sylvestris*
*Melissa officinalis*
*Papaver spp.*
*Portulaca oleracea*
*Rhodymenia palmata*
*Salix alba*
*Santalum album*
*Solanum tuberosum*
*Stellaria media*
*Vitex agnus-castus*
*Vitis vinifera*

Saturn      *Amaranthus hypochondriacus*
*Arnica montana*

*Atropa belladonna*
*Beta vulgaris*
*Cupressus sempervirens*
*Cypripedium pubescens*
*Datura stramonium*
*Equisetum arvense*
*Eupatorium perfoliatum*
*Eupatorium purpureum*
*Fagus sylvatica*
*Fumaria officinalis*
*Galium aparine*
*Hedera helix*
*Lobelia inflata*
*Piper methysticum*
*Pogostemon cablin*
*Polygonatum multiflorum*
*Polygonum aviculare*
*Polygonum bistorta*
*Populus candicans*
*Rhamnus frangula*
*Scutellaria lateriflora*
*Symphytum officinale*
*Symplocarpus foetidus*
*Tamarindus indicus*
*Ulmus campestris*
*Ulmus fulva*
*Verbascum thapsus*
*Viola tricolor*

Sun
*Acacia senegal*
*Anacardium occidentale*
*Ananas comosus*
*Angelica archangelica*
*Angelica sinensis*
*Apium graveolens*

*Boswellia carterii*
*Bursera fagaroides*
*Calendula officinalis*
*Camellia sinensis*
*Cedrus spp.*
*Chamamelum nobile*
*Chelidonium majus*
*Chrysanthemum x morifolium*
*Cichorium intybus*
*Cinnamomum cassia*
*Citrus aurantifolia*
*Citrus medica*
*Citrus sinensis*
*Crocus sativus*
*Cryptanthus spp.*
*Dianthus caryophyllus*
*Erythraea centarium*
*Euphrasia officinalis*
*Fraxinus exelsior*
*Hamamelis virginiana*
*Helianthus annuus*
*Hydrastis canadensis*
*Hypericum perforatum*
*Juglans nigra*
*Juniperus communis*
*Laurus nobilis*
*Levisticum officinale*
*Liquidambar styraciflua*
*Matricaria recutita*
*Olea europaea*
*Oryza sativa*
*Paeonia officinalis*
*Panax quinquefolius*
*Phoenix dactylifera*

*Pistacia lentiscus*

*Prunus amygdalus var dulcis*

*Prunus persica*

*Quercus alba*

*Rosmarinus officinalis*

*Viscum album*

Venus

*Abies balsamea*

*Achillea millefolium*

*Alchemilla vulgaris*

*Althaea officinalis*

*Althea rosea*

*Aquilegia vulgaris*

*Arctium lappa*

*Artemisia annua*

*Artemisia vulgaris*

*Avena sativa*

*Betula alba*

*Capparis spinosa*

*Chrysopogon zizinoides*

*Cimicifuga racemosa*

*Digitalis purpurea*

*Diospyros virginiana*

*Dipteryx odorata*

*Eletteria cardamomum*

*Erica vulgaris*

*Eryngium spp.*

*Fagopyrum esculentum*

*Fragaria vesca*

*Glycyrrhiza glabra*

*Hibiscus sabdariffa*

*Hordeum distichon*

*Hyacinthus orientalis*

*Inula conyza*

*Iris germanica var. florentina*

*Iris versicolor*
*Leonurus cardiaca*
*Medicago sativa*
*Mentha spicata*
*Musa sapientum*
*Myrtus communis*
*Narcissus spp.*
*Nepeta cataria*
*Orchis spp.*
*Origanum dictamnus*
*Passiflora incarnata*
*Pelargonium spp.*
*Persea americana*
*Plantago major*
*Primula veris*
*Prunus armeniaca*
*Prunus avium*
*Prunus domestica*
*Prunus serotina*
*Pterocarpus santalinus*
*Pyrus malus*
*Rheum officinale*
*Rheum palmatum*
*Rosa spp.*
*Rubus idaeus*
*Rubus villosus*
*Saccharum officinarum*
*Sambucus nigra*
*Scrophularia nodosa*
*Senecio vulgaris*
*Solanum lycopersicum*
*Solidago virgaurea*
*Syringa vulgaris*
*Tanacetum parthenium*

*Tanacetum vulgare*
*Thymus vulgaris*
*Triticum spp*
*Tussilago farfara*
*Vaccinium myrtillus*
*Valeriana officinalis*
*Vanilla spp*
*Verbena officinalis*
*Vinca minor*
*Viola odorata*
*Zea mays*

# Appendix F

# Individual Herbs

## *Abies balsamea*

## Balsam Fir, Balm of Gilead

**Family** Pinaceae      □ **Low Therapeutic Margin**

| **Medicinal Uses** | **Magical Intentions** |
| --- | --- |
| Bronchitis | Healing, To Promote |
| Cystitis | Love, To Attract |
| Respiratory infection | Manifestations, To Aid |
| Urinary tract infection | Protection |

| **Parts Used** | **Element** | **Planet** |
| --- | --- | --- |
| Gum resin | Water | Venus |
| Leaves | | |

**Do Not Use**
Pregnancy □
Lactation □      **Male** □          **Female** ☑
Children □
Frail □

# *Acacia senegal*

## Gum Arabic

**Family** Fabaceae

☐ **Low Therapeutic Margin**

**Medicinal Uses**
Colds
Cough
Diarrhea
Dysentery

**Magical Intentions**
Money, Riches, Treasures, Wealth
Psychic Powers, To Strengthen
Purification
Spirituality, To Strengthen

**Parts Used**
Gum resin

**Element**
Air

**Planet**
Sun

**Do Not Use**
Pregnancy ☐
Lactation ☐
Children ☐
Frail ☐

**Male** ☑

**Female** ☐

# *Acer spp.*

## Maple

**Family** Sapindaceae                    ☐ **Low Therapeutic Margin**

**Medicinal Uses**          **Magical Intentions**
Eye Strain                 Longevity, To Attain
                           Love, To Attract
                           Money, Riches, Treasures, Wealth

**Parts Used**          **Element**          **Planet**
Bark                    Air                  Jupiter

**Do Not Use**
Pregnancy ☐
Lactation ☐          **Male** ☑          **Female** ☐
Children ☐
Frail ☐

**Cautions**
Leaves are toxic when taken internally.

# *Achillea millefolium*

## Yarrow

**Family** Asteraceae  □ **Low Therapeutic Margin**

**Medicinal Uses**
Bleeding
Bronchitis
Candida
Chickenpox
Colds
Cough
Diabetes
Digestion, sluggish
Fever
Hemorrhoids
Measles
Nosebleed
Thrush
Urinary tract infection
Vaginal infection

**Magical Intentions**
Courage, To Attain
Exorcism
Love, To Attract
Psychic Powers, To Strengthen

| **Parts Used** | **Element** | **Planet** |
| --- | --- | --- |
| Aerial | Water | Venus |

**Do Not Use**
Pregnancy  ☑
Lactation  ☑          **Male** □                    **Female** ☑
Children  □
Frail  □

**Cautions**

Avoid using with other herbs containing thujone, as may increase possibility of thujone toxicity.

Excessive doses may interfere with anticoagulant, hypo & hyper-tensive therapies & have sedative & diuretic effects.

# *Acorus calamus*

## Sweet Flag

**Family** Araceae       ☐ **Low Therapeutic Margin**

**Medicinal Uses**    **Magical Intentions**
Appetite Loss    Healing, To Promote
Colic    Luck, To Obtain
Digestion, sluggish    Money, Riches, Treasures, Wealth
Fever    Protection
Flatulence
Gastritis
Indigestion
Toothache

**Parts Used**    **Element**    **Planet**
Rhizome    Water    Moon

**Do Not Use**
Pregnancy  ☐
Lactation  ☐    **Male** ☐    **Female** ☑
Children  ☐
Frail  ☐

# *Adiantum capillus-veneris*

## Maidenhair Fern

**Family** Polypodiaceae          □ **Low Therapeutic Margin**

**Medicinal Uses**          **Magical Intentions**
Bronchitis          Exorcism
Cough          Health, To Maintain
Sore throat          Luck, To Obtain
          Money, Riches, Treasures, Wealth
          Protection
          Youth, To Maintain or Regain

**Parts Used**          **Element**          **Planet**
Aerial          Air          Mercury

**Do Not Use**
Pregnancy  ☑
Lactation  □          **Male** ☑          **Female** □
Children  □
Frail     □

# *Aframomum melegueta*

## Grains of Paradise

**Family** Zingiberaceae    ☐ **Low Therapeutic Margin**

**Medicinal Uses**
Indigestion

**Magical Intentions**
Love, To Attract
Luck, To Obtain
Lust, To Increase/Create
Money, Riches, Treasures, Wealth
Wishes, To Manifest

**Parts Used**
Oil
Seed

**Element**
Fire

**Planet**
Mars

**Do Not Use**
Pregnancy ☐
Lactation ☐
Children ☐
Frail ☐

**Male** ☑     **Female** ☐

# *Agathosma betulina*

## Buchu

**Family** Rutaceae     ☐ **Low Therapeutic Margin**

**Medicinal Uses**     **Magical Intentions**

Bladder inflammation     Prophetic Dreams, To Cause

Bronchitis     Psychic Powers, To Strengthen

Dyspepsia

Flatulence

Fluid Retention

Indigestion

Kidney stones

Thrush

Urinary tract infection

**Parts Used**     **Element**     **Planet**

Leaves     Water     Moon

**Do Not Use**

Pregnancy ☑

Lactation ☑     **Male** ☐     **Female** ☑

Children ☐

Frail ☐

**Cautions**

Do not use where there is kidney inflammation

# *Agrimonia eupatoria*

## Agrimony

**Family**                    ☐ **Low Therapeutic Margin**

**Medicinal Uses**            **Magical Intentions**
Appendicitis                  Protection
Diarrhea                      Sleep
Indigestion
Laryngitis
Sore throat
Urinary incontinence
Wounds

**Parts Used**        **Element**        **Planet**
Aerial                Air                Jupiter

**Do Not Use**
Pregnancy  ☐
Lactation  ☐        **Male** ☑        **Female** ☐
Children  ☐
Frail  ☐

# *Alchemilla vulgaris*

## Lady's Mantle

**Family** Rosaceae

☐**Low Therapeutic Margin**

**Medicinal Uses**
Diarrhea
Laryngitis
Menorrhagia
Ulcer, mouth

**Magical Intentions**
Love, To Attract

**Parts Used**
Flowering Tops
Leaves

**Element**
Water

**Planet**
Venus

**Do Not Use**
Pregnancy ☐
Lactation ☐
Children ☐
Frail ☐

**Male** ☐

**Female** ☑

# *Alkanna tinctoria*

## Alkanet

**Family** Boraginaceae          ☐ **Low Therapeutic Margin**

**Medicinal Uses**          **Magical Intentions**
Worms                         Prosperity, To Obtain
Wounds                        Purification

**Parts Used**          **Element**          **Planet**
Root                    Water

**Do Not Use**
Pregnancy   ☐
Lactation   ☐          **Male** ☐          **Female** ☑
Children    ☐
Frail       ☐

# *Allium cepa*

## Onion

**Family** Liliaceae          ☐ **Low Therapeutic Margin**

**Medicinal Uses**          **Magical Intentions**

Angina          Exorcism

Colds          Healing, To Promote

Earache          Lust, To Increase/Create

Money, Riches, Treasures, Wealth

Prophetic Dreams, To Cause

Protection

**Parts Used**          **Element**          **Planet**

Bulb          Fire          Mars

**Do Not Use**

Pregnancy  ☐

Lactation  ☐          **Male** ☑          **Female** ☐

Children  ☐

Frail  ☐

# *Allium sativum*

## Garlic

**Family** Liliaceae

☐ **Low Therapeutic Margin**

**Medicinal Uses**
Blood pressure, high
Catarrh
Infection
Worms

**Magical Intentions**
Exorcism
Healing, To Promote
Health, To Maintain
Lust, To Increase/Create
Protection
Theft, To Prevent

**Parts Used**
Bulb
Essential Oil
Leaves

**Element**
Fire

**Planet**
Mars

**Do Not Use**
Pregnancy ☐
Lactation ☐
Children ☐
Frail ☐

**Male** ☑

**Female** ☐

**Cautions**
May interfere with existing hypoglycemic and anticoagulant
therapies.

# *Aloe barbadensis*

## Aloe Vera

**Family** Liliaceae             □ **Low Therapeutic Margin**

**Medicinal Uses**            **Magical Intentions**
Abrasions                    Luck, To Obtain
Abscess                      Protection
Acne
Alopecia
Arthritis
Bee stings
Burns
Constipation
Dermatitis
Eczema
Fungal infection
Heartburn
Infection
Psoriasis
Stretch marks
Sunburn
Ulcer, peptic
Ulcer, skin

**Parts Used**          **Element**          **Planet**
Leaves                 Water                Moon

**Do Not Use**
Pregnancy  ☑
Lactation   ☑          **Male** □          **Female** ☑
Children    ☑
Frail       □

**Cautions**

Gel: when used topically, may delay wound healing following a laparoscopy or cesarean delivery.

Juice: do not use during pregnancy or lactation; with any intestinal obstruction, abdominal pain of unknown origin, or any inflammatory condition of the intestine; hemorrhoids; kidney dysfunction, menstruation; in children younger than 12 or for more than 8-10 days.

# *Alpinia officinarum*

## Galangal

**Family** Zingiberaceae    ☐ **Low Therapeutic Margin**

**Medicinal Uses**
Arthritis, rheumatoid
Candida
Dyspepsia
Flatulence
Gum inflammation
Hiccoughs
Indigestion
Motion sickness
Vomiting

**Magical Intentions**
Health, To Maintain
Hexes, To Break
Legal Matters, To Assist In
Lust, To Increase/Create
Money, Riches, Treasures, Wealth
Protection
Psychic Powers, To Strengthen

**Parts Used**
Root

**Element**
Fire

**Planet**
Mars

**Do Not Use**
Pregnancy ☐
Lactation ☐
Children ☐
Frail ☐

**Male** ☑    **Female** ☐

# *Althaea officinalis (leaf)*

## Marshmallow

**Family** Malvaceae            □ **Low Therapeutic Margin**

**Medicinal Uses**
Bee stings
Bronchial spasm
Bronchitis
Calculus
Catarrh
Colitis
Cough
Cystitis
Eye inflammation
Gastritis
Hoarseness
Inflammation
Irritable bowel disease
Laryngitis
Pertussis
Pharyngitis
Respiratory inflammation
Throat infection
Urinary gravel

**Magical Intentions**
Protection
Psychic Powers, To Strengthen

**Parts Used**
Flowers
Leaves
Root

**Element**
Water

**Planet**
Venus

**Do Not Use**

Pregnancy ☐

Lactation ☐        **Male** ☐        **Female** ☑

Children ☐

Frail ☐

**Cautions**

May slow absorption of other drugs.

# *Althaea officinalis (root)*

## Marshmallow

**Family** Malvaceae     ☐ **Low Therapeutic Margin**

**Medicinal Uses**
Abscess
Boils
Burns
Chapped Skin
Colitis
Cystitis
Dermatitis
Dysentery
Gastritis
Hiatal hernia
Insect bites
Ulcer, mouth
Varicose ulcers
Varicose veins
Wounds

**Magical Intentions**
Protection
Psychic Powers, To Strengthen

| **Parts Used** | **Element** | **Planet** |
|---|---|---|
| Root | Water | Venus |

**Do Not Use**
Pregnancy ☐
Lactation ☐     **Male** ☐      **Female** ☑
Children ☐
Frail ☐

**Cautions**
May slow absorption of other drugs

# *Althea rosea*

# Hollyhock

**Family** Malvaceae          ☐ **Low Therapeutic Margin**

**Medicinal Uses**               **Magical Intentions**
Bladder inflammation      Money, Riches, Treasures, Wealth
Burns
Cystitis
Kidney stones
Respiratory infection
Sore throat
Wounds

**Parts Used**          **Element**          **Planet**
Flowers                                        Venus
Leaves
Root

**Do Not Use**
Pregnancy  ☐
Lactation  ☐          **Male** ☐               **Female** ☑
Children  ☐
Frail      ☐

# *Amaranthus hypochondriacus*

## Amaranth

**Family** Amaranthaceae      □ **Low Therapeutic Margin**

**Medicinal Uses**      **Magical Intentions**
Menorrhagia      Invisibility, To Attain
Protection

**Parts Used**      **Element**      **Planet**
Root      Fire      Saturn

**Do Not Use**
Pregnancy  □
Lactation  □      **Male** □      **Female** ☑
Children  □
Frail      □

# *Anacardium occidentale*

## Cashew

**Family** Anacardiaceae       □ **Low Therapeutic Margin**

**Medicinal Uses**          **Magical Intentions**
Athletes Foot              Money, Riches, Treasures, Wealth
Pyorrhea
Toothache
Ulcer, peptic

**Parts Used**          **Element**          **Planet**
Bark                   Fire                 Sun
Fruit
Gum resin
Leaves
Root

**Do Not Use**
Pregnancy   □
Lactation   □          **Male** ☑          **Female** □
Children    □
Frail       □

**Cautions**
Shell oil & its vapor are highly irritant.

# *Ananas comosus*

# Pineapple

**Family** Bromeliaceae        ☐ **Low Therapeutic Margin**

**Medicinal Uses**        **Magical Intentions**
Amenorrhea        Chastity, To Maintain
Appetite Loss        Luck, To Obtain
Bloating        Money, Riches, Treasures, Wealth
Constipation
Dysmenorrhea
Flatulence

**Parts Used**        **Element**        **Planet**
Fruit        Fire        Sun
Juice
Leaves

**Do Not Use**
Pregnancy  ☐
Lactation  ☐        **Male** ☑        **Female** ☐
Children  ☐
Frail    ☐

# *Anethum graveolens*

## Dill

**Family** Apiaceae     ☐ **Low Therapeutic Margin**

**Medicinal Uses**

Colic

Flatulence

Halitosis

**Magical Intentions**

Employment, To Attain/Maintain

Love, To Attract

Luck, To Obtain

Lust, To Increase/Create

Money, Riches, Treasures, Wealth

Protection

| **Parts Used** | **Element** | **Planet** |
| --- | --- | --- |
| Seed | Fire | Mercury |

**Do Not Use**

Pregnancy ☐

Lactation ☐     **Male** ☑        **Female** ☐

Children ☐

Frail ☐

# *Angelica archangelica*

## Angelica

**Family** Apiaceae     ☐ **Low Therapeutic Margin**

| **Medicinal Uses** | **Magical Intentions** |
| --- | --- |
| Anorexia | Exorcism |
| Appetite Loss | Healing, To Promote |
| Bronchitis | Protection |
| Cough | Purification |
| Flatulence | Visions, To Induce |
| Pleurisy | |

| **Parts Used** | **Element** | **Planet** |
| --- | --- | --- |
| Leaves | Fire | Sun |
| Root | | |

**Do Not Use**

| | | | | |
| --- | --- | --- | --- | --- |
| Pregnancy | ☐ | | | |
| Lactation | ☐ | **Male** ☑ | **Female** ☐ |
| Children | ☐ | | | |
| Frail | ☐ | | | |

**Cautions**

May provoke photosensitivity reactions.

May interfere with anticoagulant therapy.

# *Angelica sinensis*

## Chinese Angelica, Dong Quai

**Family** Apiaceae          ☐ **Low Therapeutic Margin**

**Medicinal Uses**          **Magical Intentions**
Amenorrhea                Healing, To Promote
Dysmenorrhea              Protection
PMS

**Parts Used**          **Element**          **Planet**
Rhizome                Fire                Sun
Root

**Do Not Use**
Pregnancy  ☐
Lactation  ☐          **Male** ☑          **Female** ☐
Children  ☐
Frail  ☐

**Cautions**
Interactions with warfarin may occur.

# *Antirrhinum majus*

## Snapdragon

**Family** Plantaginaceae         □ **Low Therapeutic Margin**

**Medicinal Uses**              **Magical Intentions**
None known                       Gossip, To Halt
                                 Protection

**Parts Used**          **Element**              **Planet**
Flowers                  Fire                     Mars

**Do Not Use**
Pregnancy   □
Lactation   □            **Male** ☑              **Female** □
Children    □
Frail       □

# *Apium graveolens*

## Celery

**Family** Apiaceae          ☐   **Low Therapeutic Margin**

**Medicinal Uses**          **Magical Intentions**
Arthritis                   Lust, To Increase/Create
Gout                        Mental Powers, To Strengthen
Urinary tract infection     Psychic Powers, To Strengthen

**Parts Used**          **Element**          **Planet**
Seed                    Fire                 Sun

**Do Not Use**
Pregnancy   ☐
Lactation   ☐          **Male** ☑          **Female** ☐
Children    ☐
Frail       ☐

**Cautions**
May provoke photosensitivity reactions.

# *Aquilegia vulgaris*

## Columbine

**Family** Ranunculaceae          ☐ **Low Therapeutic Margin**

**Medicinal Uses**          **Magical Intentions**
None known          Courage, To Attain
          Love, To Attract

**Parts Used**          **Element**          **Planet**
Aerial          Water          Venus
Seed

**Do Not Use**
Pregnancy    ☑
Lactation    ☑          **Male** ☐          **Female** ☑
Children    ☑
Frail       ☑

**Cautions**
DO NOT TAKE INTERNALLY

# *Arbutus unedo*

## Arbutus

**Family** Ericaceae

☐ **Low Therapeutic Margin**

**Medicinal Uses**
None known

**Magical Intentions**
Exorcism
Protection

**Parts Used**
Aerial

**Element**
Fire

**Planet**
Mars

**Do Not Use**
Pregnancy ☐
Lactation ☐
Children ☐
Frail ☐

**Male** ☑

**Female** ☐

# *Arctium lappa*

## Burdock

**Family** Asteraceae ☐ **Low Therapeutic Margin**

**Medicinal Uses**

**Magical Intentions**
Healing, To Promote
Protection

Abscess
Acne
Anorexia
Arthritis
Arthritis, rheumatoid
Asthma
Boils
Bronchitis
Calculus
Cradle cap
Dandruff
Diabetes
Eczema
Fever
Gout
Hayfever
Hypoglycemia
Infection
Liver congestion
Lumbago
Nervous tension
Psoriasis
Ulcer, mouth
Uterus, prolapsed
Wounds

| **Parts Used** | **Element** | **Planet** |
|---|---|---|
| Leaves | Water | Venus |
| Root | | |
| Seed | | |

**Do Not Use**

Pregnancy ☑

Lactation ☐      **Male** ☐      **Female** ☑

Children ☐

Frail ☐

**Cautions**

Excessive doses may interfere with existing hypoglycemic therapy.

# *Arctostaphylos uva-ursi*

## Uva Ursi, Bearberry

**Family** Ericaceae  □ **Low Therapeutic Margin**

**Medicinal Uses**   **Magical Intentions**
Cystitis   Psychic Powers, To Strengthen
Kidney stones
Leukorrhea
Nephritis
Urethritis
Urinary gravel
Urinary tract infection

**Parts Used**   **Element**   **Planet**
Leaves    Mars

**Do Not Use**
Pregnancy  ☑
Lactation  ☑   **Male** ☑   **Female** □
Children  □
Frail   □

**Cautions**
High in tannin: may cause liver damage with prolonged use.
Contraindicated for kidney disorders, irritated digestive conditions,
acidic urine or in conjunction with therapies that cause acidic urine.
Do not use for more than 1 month in therapeutic quantities without
consulting a practitioner.

# *Armoracia rusticana*

# Horseradish

**Family** Brassicaceae    ☐ **Low Therapeutic Margin**

**Medicinal Uses**
Appetite Loss
Arthritis
Asthma
Bladder inflammation
Bronchitis
Chillblains
Constipation
Edema
Indigestion
Neuralgia
Sciatica
Sinusitis
Urinary tract infection
Worms

**Magical Intentions**
Exorcism
Purification

| **Parts Used** | **Element** | **Planet** |
|---|---|---|
| Root, fresh | Fire | Mars |

**Do Not Use**
Pregnancy ☑
Lactation ☑    **Male** ☑    **Female** ☐
Children ☑
Frail ☐

**Cautions**

Large doses can cause gastric & intestinal irritation, vomiting, excessive night sweats, diarrhea, mucous membrane irritation & irritation of the urinary tract. Contraindicated where there is inflammation of the gastric mucosa, gastrointestinal disorders, kidney disorders or for children under four.

# *Arnica montana*

# Arnica, Wolf's Bane

**Family** Asteraceae          ☑ **Low Therapeutic Margin**

**Medicinal Uses**          **Magical Intentions**
Arthritis, rheumatoid          Invisibility, To Attain
Bruises          Protection
Phlebitis
Sprain

**Parts Used**          **Element**          **Planet**
Flowering Tops          Water          Saturn

**Do Not Use**
Pregnancy   ☐
Lactation   ☐          **Male** ☐          **Female** ☑
Children   ☐
Frail      ☐

**Cautions**

Topical applications may cause an allergy in the form of painful, itchy, inflammatory changes to the skin in some people.

Due to the toxicity of the sesquiterpene lactones, oral use of arnica must be avoided altogether.

# *Artemisia absinthium*

## Wormwood

**Family** Asteraceae | ☑ **Low Therapeutic Margin**

**Medicinal Uses**
Anorexia
Bruises
Cancer
Constipation
Diarrhea
Dyspepsia
Fever
Flatulence
Gout
Jaundice
Neuralgia
Sprain
Swelling
Worms

**Magical Intentions**
Divination
Love, To Attract
Protection
Psychic Powers, To Strengthen
Spirits, To Call

**Parts Used**
Essential Oil
Flowering Herb
Leaves

**Element**
Fire

**Planet**
Mars

**Do Not Use**
Pregnancy ☑
Lactation ☑
Children ☑
Frail ☑

**Male** ☑     **Female** ☐

## Cautions

Volatile essential oil is extremely potent & dose as small as 3 teaspoons can cause coma & death.

# *Artemisia annua*

## Qing Hao, Sweet Annie

**Family** Asteraceae    ☐ **Low Therapeutic Margin**

**Medicinal Uses**
Dizziness
Fever
Headache, Tension
Nosebleed

**Magical Intentions**
None known

**Parts Used**
Leaves

**Element**
Earth

**Planet**
Venus

**Do Not Use**
Pregnancy ☑
Lactation ☐    **Male** ☐     **Female** ☑
Children ☐
Frail ☐

# *Artemisia vulgaris*

# Mugwort

**Family** Asteraceae

☐ **Low Therapeutic Margin**

| **Medicinal Uses** | **Magical Intentions** |
|---|---|
| Amenorrhea | Astral Projection, To Aid |
| Depression | Healing, To Promote |
| Digestion, sluggish | Prophetic Dreams, To Cause |
| Tension | Protection |
| | Psychic Powers, To Strengthen |
| | Strength, To Instill |

| **Parts Used** | **Element** | **Planet** |
|---|---|---|
| Leaves | Earth | Venus |
| Root | | |

**Do Not Use**

| | | |
|---|---|---|
| Pregnancy ☐ | | |
| Lactation ☐ | **Male** ☐ | **Female** ☑ |
| Children ☐ | | |
| Frail ☐ | | |

**Cautions**

Potentially allergenic to people sensitive to plants in Asteraceae Family.

# *Astragalus gummifer*

## Traganth

**Family** Fabaceae

☐ **Low Therapeutic Margin**

**Medicinal Uses**
Constipation

**Magical Intentions**
None known

**Parts Used**
Gum resin

**Element**
Fire

**Planet**

**Do Not Use**
Pregnancy ☐
Lactation ☐
Children ☐
Frail ☐

**Male** ☑

**Female** ☐

**Cautions**

**Notes**
Main use is as a thickening agent in pharmaceutical formulations.
Magically used to bring the ethereal into the subconcious.

# *Atropa belladonna*

# Deadly Nightshade

**Family** Solanaceae          ☑ **Low Therapeutic Margin**

**Medicinal Uses**          **Magical Intentions**

Colic                    Astral Projection, To Aid

Tremors                  Visions, To Induce

Ulcer, peptic

**Parts Used**          **Element**          **Planet**

Leaves                 Water              Saturn

**Do Not Use**

Pregnancy  ☑

Lactation   ☑          **Male** ☐          **Female** ☑

Children   ☑

Frail     ☑

**Cautions**

Excessive dosage can result in respiratory paralysis, coma and death.

# *Avena sativa*

# Oats, Oatstraw

**Family** Poaceae

☐ **Low Therapeutic Margin**

**Medicinal Uses**
Depression
Stress

**Magical Intentions**
Money, Riches, Treasures, Wealth
Stress Management

**Parts Used**
Seed
Whole Plant

**Element**
Earth

**Planet**
Venus

**Do Not Use**
Pregnancy ☐
Lactation ☐
Children ☐
Frail ☐

**Male** ☐

**Female** ☑

# *Berberis vulgaris*

## Barberry

**Family** Berberidaceae          ☐ **Low Therapeutic Margin**

**Medicinal Uses**          **Magical Intentions**
Appetite Loss          None known
Cough
Diabetes
Gall stones
Gallbladder problems
Jaundice
Liver congestion
Nausea
Sore throat

**Parts Used**          **Element**          **Planet**
Berries          Mars
Root Bark

**Do Not Use**
Pregnancy  ☑
Lactation  ☑          **Male** ☑          **Female** ☐
Children  ☑
Frail  ☐

**Cautions**
Do not use where diarrhea is present.

# *Beta vulgaris*

## Beet (White or Red)

**Family** Chenopodiaceae    ☐ **Low Therapeutic Margin**

**Medicinal Uses**
Cancer
Cholesterol, High
Dandruff

**Magical Intentions**
Love, To Attract

**Parts Used**
Root

**Element**
Earth

**Planet**
Saturn

**Do Not Use**
Pregnancy ☐
Lactation ☐
Children ☐
Frail ☐

**Male** ☐      **Female** ☑

# *Betula alba*

## Birch

**Family** Betulaceae          □ **Low Therapeutic Margin**

**Medicinal Uses**          **Magical Intentions**
Arthritis, rheumatoid          Exorcism
Cystitis          Protection
Gout          Purification

**Parts Used**          **Element**          **Planet**
Twigs          Water          Venus
Young Leaf

**Do Not Use**
Pregnancy   □
Lactation    □          **Male** □          **Female** ☑
Children   □
Frail        □

# *Borago officinalis*

## Borage

**Family** Boraginaceae ☐ **Low Therapeutic Margin**

**Medicinal Uses**
Fever

**Magical Intentions**
Courage, To Attain
Protection
Psychic Powers, To Strengthen

**Parts Used**
Leaves

**Element**
Air

**Planet**
Jupiter

**Do Not Use**
Pregnancy ☐
Lactation ☐    **Male** ☑    **Female** ☐
Children ☐
Frail ☐

**Cautions**
Contains pyrrolizidine alkaloids. Best used externally only.

# *Boswellia carterii*

## Frankincense

**Family** Burseraceae       □ **Low Therapeutic Margin**

**Medicinal Uses**          **Magical Intentions**
Bronchitis                 Divination
Infection                  Exorcism
                           Protection
                           Spirituality, To Strengthen

**Parts Used**        **Element**        **Planet**
Essential Oil         Fire               Sun
Gum resin

**Do Not Use**
Pregnancy  □
Lactation  □          **Male** □              **Female** ☑
Children   □
Frail      □

**Notes**
Modern use is chiefly external.

# *Brassica nigra*

## Mustard (Black)

**Family** Brassicaceae          ☐ **Low Therapeutic Margin**

**Medicinal Uses**          **Magical Intentions**
Bronchitis                Fertility, To Increase
Chillblains               Mental Powers, To Strengthen
Fever                     Protection

**Parts Used**          **Element**          **Planet**
Seed                    Fire                Mars

**Do Not Use**
Pregnancy   ☐
Lactation    ☐          **Male** ☑          **Female** ☐
Children    ☐
Frail      ☐

**Cautions**
May cause skin irritation when applied externally, especially to fair-skinned people.

**Notes**
Most commonly used as a poultice. Skin may be soothed by application of olive oil afterward.

# *Brassica oleracea*

## Cabbage, Kale, etc.

**Family** Brassicaceae          ☐ **Low Therapeutic Margin**

**Medicinal Uses**          **Magical Intentions**
Cancer                    Luck, To Obtain

**Parts Used**          **Element**          **Planet**
Leaves              Water              Moon

**Do Not Use**
Pregnancy  ☐
Lactation   ☐          **Male** ☐                    **Female** ☑
Children   ☐
Frail      ☐

**Notes**
Varietals determine which vegetable it is.

# *Brassica rapa*

## Turnip

**Family** Brassicaceae  □ **Low Therapeutic Margin**

**Medicinal Uses**  **Magical Intentions**
None known  Protection
Relationships, to End

**Parts Used**  **Element**  **Planet**
Root  Earth  Moon

**Do Not Use**
Pregnancy  □
Lactation  □  **Male** □  **Female** ☑
Children  □
Frail  □

# *Bursera fagaroides*

## Copal

**Family** Burseraceae       ☐ **Low Therapeutic Margin**

**Medicinal Uses**          **Magical Intentions**
None known                Love, To Attract
                          Purification

**Parts Used**            **Element**          **Planet**
Gum resin                 Fire                 Sun

**Do Not Use**
Pregnancy   ☐
Lactation   ☐            **Male** ☑           **Female** ☐
Children    ☐
Frail       ☐

# *Calendula officinalis*

## Calendula, Pot Marigold

**Family** Asteraceae          ☐ **Low Therapeutic Margin**

**Medicinal Uses**

Cracked skin

Gallbladder problems

Metrorrhagia

Ulcer, duodenal

Ulcer, gastric

Ulcer, skin

Wounds

**Magical Intentions**

Legal Matters, To Assist In

Prophetic Dreams, To Cause

Protection

Psychic Powers, To Strengthen

Stress Management

| **Parts Used** | **Element** | **Planet** |
|---|---|---|
| Flowering Tops | Fire | Sun |

**Do Not Use**

Pregnancy  ☐

Lactation  ☐          **Male** ☑          **Female** ☐

Children  ☐

Frail  ☐

**Cautions**

Possible allergen for those with known sensitivity to Asteraceae
Family.

# *Camellia sinensis*

## Tea

**Family** Theaceae  □ **Low Therapeutic Margin**

**Medicinal Uses**                **Magical Intentions**
Cancer                            Courage, To Attain
Diarrhea                          Money, Riches, Treasures, Wealth
Dysentery                         Strength, To Instill

**Parts Used**          **Element**          **Planet**
Leaves                  Fire                 Sun

**Do Not Use**
Pregnancy  □
Lactation  □          **Male** ☑          **Female** □
Children  □
Frail      □

**Cautions**

In excess can cause gastrointestinal upset & nervous irritability due to caffeine content.

# *Capparis spinosa*

## Caper

**Family** Capparaceae  ☐ **Low Therapeutic Margin**

**Medicinal Uses**

Arthritis, rheumatoid

**Magical Intentions**

Luck, To Obtain

Lust, To Increase/Create

**Parts Used**

Root

**Element**

Water

**Planet**

Venus

**Do Not Use**

Pregnancy ☐

Lactation ☐     **Male** ☐          **Female** ☑

Children ☐

Frail ☐

# *Capsella bursa-pastoris*

## Shepherd's Purse

**Family** Brassicaceae          □ **Low Therapeutic Margin**

**Medicinal Uses**          **Magical Intentions**
Diarrhea                    Depression Management
Menorrhagia
Nosebleed
Water retention
Wounds

**Parts Used**          **Element**          **Planet**
Aerial

**Do Not Use**
Pregnancy   □
Lactation   □          **Male** □          **Female** □
Children   □
Frail      □

# *Capsicum minimum*

## Cayenne

**Family** Solanaceae          □ **Low Therapeutic Margin**

**Medicinal Uses**          **Magical Intentions**
Arthritis                  Hexes, To Break
Asthma                     Love, To Attract
Bleeding
Bruises
Chillblains
Chills
Cold extremities
Colic
Depression
Diarrhea
Dysmenorrhea
Dyspepsia
Herpes zoster
Indigestion
Laryngitis
Muscle strain
Shock
Sore throat
Sprain

**Parts Used**          **Element**          **Planet**
Fruit                   Fire                 Mars

**Do Not Use**

Pregnancy ☐

Lactation ☐        **Male** ☑            **Female** ☐

Children ☐

Frail ☐

**Cautions**

Not used on mucous membranes; not used as a tincture.

Large doses may cause irritation of mucous membranes; can cause diarrhea or nausea.

# *Carica papaya*

## Papaya

**Family** Caricaceae     ☐ **Low Therapeutic Margin**

**Medicinal Uses**
Burns
Ulcer, gastric
Wounds

**Magical Intentions**
Love, To Attract
Protection

**Parts Used**
Fruit
Leaves
Seed

**Element**
Water

**Planet**
Moon

**Do Not Use**
Pregnancy ☐
Lactation ☐
Children ☐
Frail ☐

**Male** ☐       **Female** ☑

**Cautions**
Inhalation of enzyme powder has caused allergic reactions; care should be taken with high doses.

# *Carum carvi*

## Caraway

**Family** Apiaceae

☐ **Low Therapeutic Margin**

**Medicinal Uses**
Appetite Loss
Bronchial asthma
Diabetes
Dysmenorrhea
Intestinal cramps

**Magical Intentions**
Health, To Maintain
Lust, To Increase/Create
Mental Powers, To Strengthen
Protection
Theft, To Prevent

**Parts Used**
Seed

**Element**
Air

**Planet**
Mercury

**Do Not Use**
Pregnancy ☐
Lactation ☐
Children ☐
Frail ☐

**Male** ☑

**Female** ☐

# *Carya illinoinensis*

## Pecan

**Family** Juglandaceae      ☐ **Low Therapeutic Margin**

**Medicinal Uses**          **Magical Intentions**
Cardiac disease             Employment, To Attain/Maintain
                            Money, Riches, Treasures, Wealth

**Parts Used**       **Element**       **Planet**
Seed                 Air               Mercury

**Do Not Use**
Pregnancy  ☐
Lactation  ☐        **Male** ☑        **Female** ☐
Children   ☐
Frail      ☐

# *Castanea sativa*

# Chestnut

**Family** Fagaceae         □ **Low Therapeutic Margin**

**Medicinal Uses**      **Magical Intentions**
Colds                 Love, To Attract
Cough
Diarrhea
Pertussis

**Parts Used**        **Element**          **Planet**
Leaves                Fire                 Jupiter

**Do Not Use**
Pregnancy  □
Lactation   □      **Male** ☑         **Female** □
Children   □
Frail      □

# *Cedrus spp.*

## Cedar

**Family** Pinaceae          ☐ **Low Therapeutic Margin**

**Medicinal Uses** | **Magical Intentions**
--- | ---
Colds | Courage, To Attain
Cystitis | Healing, To Promote
Ulcer, skin | Money, Riches, Treasures, Wealth
Wounds | Protection
 | Purification

**Parts Used** | **Element** | **Planet**
--- | --- | ---
Leaves | Fire | Sun
Oil | |

**Do Not Use**
Pregnancy  ☐
Lactation  ☐          **Male** ☑          **Female** ☐
Children  ☐
Frail  ☐

**Cautions**

Do not take essential oil internally except under professional supervision.

# *Celastrus scandens*

## Bittersweet (American)

**Family** Celastraceae          ☐ **Low Therapeutic Margin**

**Medicinal Uses**          **Magical Intentions**
Arthritis, rheumatoid          Healing, To Promote
Leukorrhea          Protection

**Parts Used**          **Element**          **Planet**
Bark          Air          Mercury
Root

**Do Not Use**
Pregnancy  ☐
Lactation  ☐          **Male**  ☑          **Female**  ☐
Children  ☐
Frail  ☐

# *Centraria islandica*

## Iceland Moss

**Family** Parmeliaceae          ☐**Low Therapeutic Margin**

**Medicinal Uses**          **Magical Intentions**
Bronchitis          Luck, To Obtain
Dyspepsia          Money, Riches, Treasures, Wealth
Gastritis
Vomiting

**Parts Used**          **Element**          **Planet**
Whole Plant

**Do Not Use**
Pregnancy  ☐
Lactation  ☐          **Male**  ☐          **Female**  ☐
Children  ☐
Frail  ☐

# *Chamamelum nobile*

## Roman Chamomile

**Family** Asteraceae                    ☐ **Low Therapeutic Margin**

**Medicinal Uses**              **Magical Intentions**
Abscess                         Love, To Attract
Appetite Loss                   Money, Riches, Treasures, Wealth
Colic                           Purification
Conjunctivitis                  Sleep
Cramp
Diarrhea
Dysmenorrhea
Dyspepsia
Fever
Fluid Retention
Headache, Tension
Heartburn
Hyperglycemia
Indigestion
Inflammation
Migraine
Nausea
Nervous tension
Swelling
Teething, babies
Ulcer, gastric
Vomiting
Wounds

**Parts Used**          **Element**          **Planet**
Aerial                  Water                Sun
Essential Oil

**Do Not Use**
Pregnancy ☑
Lactation ☑             **Male** ☑                    **Female** ☐
Children ☐
Frail ☐

**Cautions**
Large doses have been reported to cause vomiting & stomach irritation. Excessive use during pregnancy & lactation should be avoided due to reputed abortifacient actions, its ability to affect the menstrual cycle & potential allergic effects. The coumarin constituent may interfere with anticoagulant therapy if used in excessive doses.

# *Chelidonium majus*

## Celandine, Greater Celandine

**Family** Papaveraceae        □ **Low Therapeutic Margin**

| **Medicinal Uses** | **Magical Intentions** |
| --- | --- |
| Bronchial asthma | Depression Management |
| Bronchitis | Happiness, To Promote |
| Eczema | Legal Matters, To Assist In |
| Gall stones | Protection |
| Jaundice | |
| Pertussis | |

| **Parts Used** | **Element** | **Planet** |
| --- | --- | --- |
| Aerial | Fire | Sun |

**Do Not Use**

Pregnancy  ☑
Lactation  ☑        **Male** ☑              **Female** □
Children  □
Frail  □

**Cautions**

Use only under professional supervision. Causes muscles of uterus to contract.

# *Chimaphila umbellata*

## Pipsissewa

**Family** Ericaceae          ☐ **Low Therapeutic Margin**

**Medicinal Uses**          **Magical Intentions**
Colds                      Money, Riches, Treasures, Wealth
Cystitis                   Spirits, To Call
Fever
Kidney stones
Ringworm
Ulcer, gastric
Ulcer, skin
Urinary tract infection

**Parts Used**          **Element**          **Planet**
Leaves
Root

**Do Not Use**
Pregnancy  ☐
Lactation  ☐          **Male** ☐          **Female** ☐
Children  ☐
Frail  ☐

**Notes**
Leaves recognized as most medicinally potent part of plant but the entire plant is used in folk medicine (root used to flavor root beer).

# *Chondrus crispus*

## Irish Moss

**Family** Gigartinaceae       □ **Low Therapeutic Margin**

**Medicinal Uses**          **Magical Intentions**
Bronchitis                  Luck, To Obtain
Cough                       Money, Riches, Treasures, Wealth
Gastritis                   Protection
Urinary tract infection

**Parts Used**          **Element**          **Planet**
Whole Plant             Water                Moon

**Do Not Use**
Pregnancy   □
Lactation   □          **Male** □                    **Female** ☑
Children   □
Frail      □

# *Chrysanthemum x morifolium*

## Chrysanthemum, Ju Hua

**Family** Asteraceae        □ **Low Therapeutic Margin**

**Medicinal Uses**                 **Magical Intentions**
Acne                               Protection
Blood pressure, high
Dizziness
Eye Strain
Headache, Tension
Insomnia

**Parts Used**          **Element**          **Planet**
Flowers                 Fire                 Sun

**Do Not Use**
Pregnancy   □
Lactation   □           **Male**  ☑          **Female**  □
Children    □
Frail       □

# *Chrysopogon zizinoides*

## Vetivert

**Family** Poaceae          □ **Low Therapeutic Margin**

**Medicinal Uses**          **Magical Intentions**

None known                 Hexes, To Break

Love, To Attract

Luck, To Obtain

Money, Riches, Treasures, Wealth

Theft, To Prevent

| **Parts Used** | **Element** | **Planet** |
|---|---|---|
| Root | Earth | Venus |

**Do Not Use**

Pregnancy    □

Lactation    □          **Male**  □                    **Female**  ☑

Children    □

Frail        □

**Cautions**

**Notes**

Recent research suggests antioxidant activity.

# *Cichorium intybus*

## Chicory

**Family** Asteraceae    ☐ **Low Therapeutic Margin**

**Medicinal Uses**
Arthritis, rheumatoid
Gout
Urinary tract infection

**Magical Intentions**
Divination
Invisibility, To Attain
Obstacles, to Remove

**Parts Used**
Flowers
Leaves
Root

**Element**
Air

**Planet**
Sun

**Do Not Use**
Pregnancy ☐
Lactation ☐
Children ☐
Frail ☐

**Male** ☑      **Female** ☐

**Notes**
An infusion is a mild-enough laxative to use on children. Also aids digestion.

# *Cimicifuga racemosa*

## Black Cohosh

**Family** Ranunculaceae    ☐ **Low Therapeutic Margin**

**Medicinal Uses**
Arthritis
Arthritis, rheumatoid
Dysmenorrhea
Metrorrhagia
Sciatica

**Magical Intentions**
Courage, To Attain
Love, To Attract
Protection

**Parts Used**
Rhizome
Root

**Element**
Water

**Planet**
Venus

**Do Not Use**
Pregnancy ☑
Lactation ☑    **Male** ☑    **Female** ☐
Children ☐
Frail ☐

# *Cinchona spp.*

## Cinchona, Peruvian Bark

**Family** Rubiaceae          ☑ **Low Therapeutic Margin**

**Medicinal Uses**          **Magical Intentions**
Cramp                      Luck, To Obtain
Digestion, sluggish        Protection
Fever
Infection
Sore throat

**Parts Used**          **Element**          **Planet**
Bark

**Do Not Use**
Pregnancy  ☑
Lactation  ☑          **Male** ☐          **Female** ☐
Children  ☑
Frail  ☐

**Cautions**
Excessive use can lead to death.

# *Cinnamomum camphora*

## Camphor

**Family** Lauraceae     ☑ **Low Therapeutic Margin**

**Medicinal Uses**     **Magical Intentions**

Cold sores     Chastity, To Maintain

Muscle strain     Divination

Health, To Maintain

**Parts Used**     **Element**     **Planet**

Oil     Water     Moon

**Do Not Use**

Pregnancy ☑

Lactation ☑     **Male** ☐     **Female** ☑

Children ☑

Frail ☑

**Cautions**

Should only be used in small amounts externally. May cause systemic toxicity.

# *Cinnamomum cassia*

## Cinnamon

**Family** Lauraceae      ☐ **Low Therapeutic Margin**

**Medicinal Uses**

Appetite Loss

Colds

Flatulence

Flu

Irritable bowel disease

Vomiting

**Magical Intentions**

Healing, To Promote

Love, To Attract

Lust, To Increase/Create

Power, To Obtain

Protection

Psychic Powers, To Strengthen

Spirituality, To Strengthen

Success, To Attain

**Parts Used**

Bark

**Element**

Fire

**Planet**

Sun

**Do Not Use**

Pregnancy ☐

Lactation ☐

Children ☐

Frail ☐

**Male** ☑      **Female** ☐

# *Citrus aurantifolia*

# Lime (fruit)

**Family** Rutaceae                    ☐ **Low Therapeutic Margin**

**Medicinal Uses**           **Magical Intentions**
Colds                         Healing, To Promote
Cough                         Love, To Attract
Headache, Tension             Protection
Sore throat

**Parts Used**           **Element**           **Planet**
Fruit                     Fire                  Sun
Juice

**Do Not Use**
Pregnancy   ☐
Lactation   ☐          **Male**  ☑          **Female**  ☐
Children   ☐
Frail      ☐

**Cautions**
May cause photosensitization; allergies.

# *Citrus bergamia*

## Bergamot

**Family** Rutaceae

☐ **Low Therapeutic Margin**

**Medicinal Uses**
Respiratory infection

**Magical Intentions**
Employment, To Attain/Maintain
Money, Riches, Treasures, Wealth
Success, To Attain

**Parts Used**
Fruit
Peel

**Element**
Air

**Planet**
Mercury

**Do Not Use**
Pregnancy ☐
Lactation ☐  **Male** ☑  **Female** ☐
Children ☐
Frail ☐

**Cautions**
May be photosensitizing.

**Notes**
Most widely known as a flavoring agent, especially in Earl Grey Tea.

# *Citrus limon*

## Lemon

**Family** Rutaceae           □ **Low Therapeutic Margin**

**Medicinal Uses**           **Magical Intentions**
Bleeding                     Friendship, To Promote
Colds                        Longevity, To Attain
Cough                        Love, To Attract
Headache, Tension            Purification
Sore throat
Sunburn

**Parts Used**          **Element**          **Planet**
Essential Oil           Water                Moon
Fruit
Juice
Peel

**Do Not Use**
Pregnancy   □
Lactation   □          **Male** □           **Female** ☑
Children    □
Frail       □

# *Citrus medica*

## Citron

**Family** Rutaceae

□ **Low Therapeutic Margin**

**Medicinal Uses**
None known

**Magical Intentions**
Healing, To Promote
Psychic Powers, To Strengthen

**Parts Used**
Peel
Seed

**Element**
Air

**Planet**
Sun

**Do Not Use**
Pregnancy □
Lactation □
Children □
Frail □

**Male** ☑

**Female** □

**Notes**
Not currently used in a medicinal sense but probably the same as
Lemon.

# *Citrus sinensis*

## Orange

**Family** Rutaceae    ☐ **Low Therapeutic Margin**

| **Medicinal Uses** | **Magical Intentions** |
| --- | --- |
| Bronchitis | Divination |
| Dyspepsia | Friendship, To Promote |
| Flatulence | Love, To Attract |
| | Luck, To Obtain |
| | Money, Riches, Treasures, Wealth |

| **Parts Used** | **Element** | **Planet** |
| --- | --- | --- |
| Fruit | Fire | Sun |
| Juice | | |
| Oil | | |
| Peel | | |

**Do Not Use**
Pregnancy ☐
Lactation ☐    **Male** ☑    **Female** ☐
Children ☐
Frail ☐

# *Cnicus benedictus*

## Blessed Thistle, Holy Thistle

**Family** Asteraceae            ☐ **Low Therapeutic Margin**

**Medicinal Uses**              **Magical Intentions**
Anorexia                        Hexes, To Break
Catarrh                         Protection
Dyspepsia                       Purification
Flatulence                      Sexual Potency, To Regain or maintain
Ulcer, skin
Wounds

**Parts Used**          **Element**          **Planet**
Aerial                  Fire                 Mars

**Do Not Use**
Pregnancy   ☐
Lactation   ☐            **Male** ☑            **Female** ☐
Children    ☐
Frail       ☐

**Cautions**
Strong tea acts as an emetic.

# *Cocos nucifera*

## Coconut

**Family** Araceae

☐ **Low Therapeutic Margin**

**Medicinal Uses**
Chapped Skin

**Magical Intentions**
Chastity, To Maintain
Protection
Purification

**Parts Used**
Fruit

**Element**
Water

**Planet**
Moon

**Do Not Use**
Pregnancy ☐
Lactation ☐
Children ☐
Frail ☐

**Male** ☐

**Female** ☑

# *Coix lachryma-jobi*

## Job's Tears

**Family** Poaceae

☐ **Low Therapeutic Margin**

**Medicinal Uses**
Abscess
Arthritis
Cancer
Catarrh
Dysentery
Fever

**Magical Intentions**
Healing, To Promote
Luck, To Obtain
Wishes, To Manifest

**Parts Used**
Seed

**Element**

**Planet**

**Do Not Use**
Pregnancy ☐
Lactation ☐
Children ☐
Frail ☐

**Male** ☐

**Female** ☐

# *Commiphora molmol*

# Myrrh

**Family** Burseraceae          ☐ **Low Therapeutic Margin**

**Medicinal Uses**          **Magical Intentions**
Abrasions                    Exorcism
Amenorrhea                   Healing, To Promote
Asthma                       Protection
Boils                        Spirituality, To Strengthen
Bronchitis
Cystitis
Gingivitis
Halitosis
Indigestion
Pharyngitis
Pyorrhea
Sinusitis
Thrush
Ulcer, mouth
Wounds

**Parts Used**          **Element**          **Planet**
Gum resin               Water                Moon

**Do Not Use**
Pregnancy  ☑
Lactation   ☑          **Male** ☐          **Female** ☑
Children   ☐
Frail      ☐

**Cautions**

Use of undiluted tincture in the mouth may give rise to a transient burning sensation & irritation of the palate. Theoretically, may interfere with existing antidiabetic therapy as hypoglycemic properties have been reported. Doses over 4gm may cause kidney irritation & diarrhea. Large amounts can affect the heart rate.

Topically, can cause dermatitis so use patch test.

**Notes**

Resin dissolves much more easily in alcohol than water, so tincture is preferred. If making infusion, ensure resin is well powdered.

# *Convallaria majalis*

# Lily of the Valley

**Family** Ruscaceae     ☑ **Low Therapeutic Margin**

**Medicinal Uses**
Congestive heart failure

**Magical Intentions**
Depression Management
Happiness, To Promote
Mental Powers, To Strengthen

**Parts Used**
Aerial

**Element**
Air

**Planet**
Mercury

**Do Not Use**
Pregnancy ☑
Lactation ☑     **Male** ☑     **Female** ☐
Children ☑
Frail ☑

**Cautions**
POISON

# *Cordyline spp.*

## Ti Plant

**Family** Liliaceae          ☐ **Low Therapeutic Margin**

**Medicinal Uses**          **Magical Intentions**
Asthma                    Healing, To Promote
Nervous tension           Protection

**Parts Used**          **Element**          **Planet**
Leaves                 Fire               Jupiter
Root

**Do Not Use**
Pregnancy   ☐
Lactation   ☐          **Male** ☐          **Female** ☑
Children   ☐
Frail      ☐

# *Coriandrum sativum*

## Coriander, Cilantro

**Family** Apiaceae     ☐ **Low Therapeutic Margin**

| **Medicinal Uses** | **Magical Intentions** |
|---|---|
| Bloating | Healing, To Promote |
| Flatulence | Health, To Maintain |
| Halitosis | Love, To Attract |

**Parts Used**     **Element**     **Planet**
Essential Oil     Fire     Mars
Leaves
Seed

**Do Not Use**
Pregnancy   ☐
Lactation   ☐          **Male** ☑          **Female** ☐
Children   ☐
Frail   ☐

**Cautions**
Do not take the essential oil internally.

# *Crataegus laevigata*

# Hawthorn

**Family** Rosaceae          ☐ **Low Therapeutic Margin**

| **Medicinal Uses** | **Magical Intentions** |
|---|---|
| Arrhythmia | Chastity, To Maintain |
| Circulation, poor | Depression Management |
| Congestive heart failure | Fertility, To Increase |
| | Happiness, To Promote |

| **Parts Used** | **Element** | **Planet** |
|---|---|---|
| Berries | Fire | Mars |
| Flowering Tops | | |
| Fruit | | |
| Leaves | | |

**Do Not Use**

Pregnancy ☑

Lactation ☑          **Male** ☑          **Female** ☐

Children ☑

Frail ☑

**Cautions**

Avoid using with other cardioactive herbs due to unpredictability of effects & adverse effects.

# *Crocus sativus*

## Saffron

**Family** Iridaceae          ☐ **Low Therapeutic Margin**

**Medicinal Uses**          **Magical Intentions**

Amenorrhea          Depression Management

Colic          Happiness, To Promote

Dysmenorrhea          Healing, To Promote

Indigestion          Love, To Attract

Lust, To Increase/Create

Psychic Powers, To Strengthen

Strength, To Instill

**Parts Used**          **Element**          **Planet**

Stigma          Fire          Sun

**Do Not Use**

Pregnancy  ☐

Lactation  ☐          **Male**  ☑          **Female**  ☐

Children  ☐

Frail  ☐

**Cautions**

In very large doses, may induce abortion. During pregnancy take only in amounts normally used during cooking.

# *Cryptanthus spp.*

## Bromeliad

**Family** Bromeliaceae         □ **Low Therapeutic Margin**

**Medicinal Uses**         **Magical Intentions**
None known         Money, Riches, Treasures, Wealth
         Protection

**Parts Used**         **Element**         **Planet**
Aerial         Air         Sun

**Do Not Use**
Pregnancy   □
Lactation   □         **Male** ☑         **Female** □
Children   □
Frail   □

# *Cucumis sativus*

## Cucumber

**Family** Cucurbitaceae    ☐ **Low Therapeutic Margin**

**Medicinal Uses**
Catarrh
Sunburn

**Magical Intentions**
Chastity, To Maintain
Fertility, To Increase
Healing, To Promote

**Parts Used**
Fruit

**Element**
Water

**Planet**
Moon

**Do Not Use**
Pregnancy ☐
Lactation ☐    **Male** ☐      **Female** ☑
Children ☐
Frail ☐

# *Cucurbita pepo*

## Pumpkin

**Family** Cucurbitaceae     ☐ **Low Therapeutic Margin**

**Medicinal Uses**
Fluid Retention
Worms

**Magical Intentions**
Protection

**Parts Used**
Seed

**Element**
Water

**Planet**
Moon

**Do Not Use**
Pregnancy ☐
Lactation ☐
Children ☐
Frail ☐

**Male** ☐        **Female** ☑

# *Cuminum cyminum*

## Cumin

**Family** Apiaceae          □ **Low Therapeutic Margin**

**Medicinal Uses**          **Magical Intentions**
Cancer                     Exorcism
Diabetes                   Fidelity, to Ensure
                           Protection

**Parts Used**          **Element**          **Planet**
Fruit                  Fire                 Mars

**Do Not Use**
Pregnancy  □
Lactation  □          **Male** ☑          **Female** □
Children  □
Frail  □

# *Cupressus sempervirens*

## Cypress

**Family** Cupressaceae

☐ **Low Therapeutic Margin**

**Medicinal Uses**
None known

**Magical Intentions**
Healing, To Promote
Longevity, To Attain
Protection

**Parts Used**
Essential Oil
Leaves

**Element**
Earth

**Planet**
Saturn

**Do Not Use**
Pregnancy ☐
Lactation ☐
Children ☐
Frail ☐

**Male** ☐

**Female** ☑

# *Curcuma longa*

## Turmeric

**Family** Zingiberaceae          ☐ **Low Therapeutic Margin**

**Medicinal Uses**          **Magical Intentions**
Arthritis                   Purification
Asthma
Athletes Foot
Cholesterol, High
Eczema
Gastritis
Jaundice
Nausea
Psoriasis

**Parts Used**          **Element**          **Planet**
Rhizome

**Do Not Use**
Pregnancy  ☐
Lactation   ☐          **Male** ☐          **Female** ☐
Children    ☐
Frail       ☐

**Cautions**
May cause skin rashes and can increase sensitivity to sunlight.

# *Cymbopogon citratus*

## Lemongrass

**Family** Poaceae

☐ **Low Therapeutic Margin**

**Medicinal Uses**
Candida

**Magical Intentions**
Lust, To Increase/Create
Psychic Powers, To Strengthen
Snakes, To Repel

**Parts Used**
Essential Oil
Leaves

**Element**
Air

**Planet**
Mercury

**Do Not Use**
Pregnancy ☐
Lactation ☐
Children ☐
Frail ☐

**Male** ☑       **Female** ☐

**Cautions**
Can cause sensitivity & oral use should be avoided, although amounts used in cookery are considered safe.

# *Cypripedium pubescens*

## Lady's Slipper (Yellow)

**Family** Orchidaceae    ☐ **Low Therapeutic Margin**

**Medicinal Uses**
Nervous tension
Neuralgia

**Magical Intentions**
Protection

**Parts Used**
Root, fresh

**Element**
Water

**Planet**
Saturn

**Do Not Use**
Pregnancy ☐
Lactation ☐    **Male** ☐      **Female** ☑
Children ☐
Frail ☐

**Notes**
ENDANGERED SPECIES

# *Cytisus scoparius*

## Broom

**Family** Fabaceae

☑ **Low Therapeutic Margin**

**Medicinal Uses**
None known

**Magical Intentions**
Divination
Protection
Purification

**Parts Used**
Flowering Tops

**Element**
Air

**Planet**
Mars

**Do Not Use**
Pregnancy ☑
Lactation ☑
Children ☑
Frail ☑

**Male** ☑

**Female** ☐

**Cautions**
POISON

# *Daemonorops draco*

## Dragon's Blood

**Family** Araceae      ☐ **Low Therapeutic Margin**

**Medicinal Uses**
None known

**Magical Intentions**
Exorcism
Love, To Attract
Protection

**Parts Used**
Gum resin

**Element**
Fire

**Planet**
Mars

**Do Not Use**
Pregnancy ☐
Lactation ☐      **Male** ☑      **Female** ☐
Children ☐
Frail ☐

**Notes**
Recent studies suggest Dragon's Blood may help stop memory loss.

# *Datura stramonium*

# Datura, Thornapple

**Family** Solanaceae          ☑ **Low Therapeutic Margin**

**Medicinal Uses**          **Magical Intentions**
Asthma                    Hexes, To Break
Cramp                     Protection
Pertussis                 Sleep

**Parts Used**          **Element**          **Planet**
Flowering Tops          Water               Saturn
Leaves
Seed

**Do Not Use**
Pregnancy   ☑
Lactation   ☑          **Male** ☐          **Female** ☑
Children    ☑
Frail       ☑

**Cautions**
Toxic at more than small doses. Use under professional supervision only.

# *Daucus carota*

## Wild Carrot, Queen Anne's Lace

**Family** Apiaceae  □ **Low Therapeutic Margin**

**Medicinal Uses**

Colic

Cystitis

Flatulence

Urinary tract infection

**Magical Intentions**

Fertility, To Increase

Lust, To Increase/Create

**Parts Used**

Aerial

Seed

**Element**

Fire

**Planet**

Mars

**Do Not Use**

Pregnancy  □

Lactation  □       **Male** ☑       **Female** □

Children  □

Frail  □

**Cautions**

Juice of fresh plant may cause photosensitivity.

# *Dianthus caryophyllus*

## Carnation, Gillyflower

**Family** Caryophyllaceae    ☐ **Low Therapeutic Margin**

**Medicinal Uses**          **Magical Intentions**
Nervous tension            Healing, To Promote
                           Protection
                           Strength, To Instill

**Parts Used**         **Element**         **Planet**
Aerial                 Fire                Sun

**Do Not Use**
Pregnancy  ☐
Lactation  ☐          **Male**  ☑          **Female**  ☐
Children   ☐
Frail      ☐

# *Digitalis purpurea*

## Foxglove

**Family** Scrophulariaceae      ☑ **Low Therapeutic Margin**

**Medicinal Uses**          **Magical Intentions**
Cardiac disease           Protection

**Parts Used**          **Element**          **Planet**
Leaves               Water               Venus

**Do Not Use**
Pregnancy   ☑
Lactation   ☑          **Male**  ☐                    **Female**  ☑
Children   ☑
Frail      ☑

**Cautions**
Potentially fatal. Use under professional supervision only.

# *Diospyros virginiana*

## Persimmon

**Family** Ebenaceae          ☐ **Low Therapeutic Margin**

**Medicinal Uses**          **Magical Intentions**
None known          Healing, To Promote
          Luck, To Obtain

**Parts Used**          **Element**          **Planet**
Fruit          Water          Venus

**Do Not Use**
Pregnancy  ☐
Lactation  ☐          **Male** ☐          **Female** ☑
Children  ☐
Frail  ☐

# *Dipteryx odorata*

## Tonka

**Family** Fabaceae

☑ **Low Therapeutic Margin**

**Medicinal Uses**

None known

**Magical Intentions**

Courage, To Attain

Friendship, To Promote

Love, To Attract

Money, Riches, Treasures, Wealth

Wishes, To Manifest

**Parts Used**

Seed

**Element**

Water

**Planet**

Venus

**Do Not Use**

Pregnancy ☑

Lactation ☑   **Male** ☐     **Female** ☑

Children ☑

Frail ☑

**Cautions**

Has cardiotoxic and anticoagulant effects.

# *Echinacea spp.*

## Echinacea

**Family** Asteraceae      ☐ **Low Therapeutic Margin**

**Medicinal Uses**      **Magical Intentions**

Colds      Strength, To Instill

Gingivitis

Laryngitis

Pyorrhea

Respiratory infection

Tonsillitis

Warts

| **Parts Used** | **Element** | **Planet** |
|---|---|---|
| Root | Earth | Jupiter |

**Do Not Use**

Pregnancy ☐

Lactation ☐      **Male** ☑      **Female** ☐

Children ☐

Frail ☐

**Cautions**

May cause allergic reaction in people sensitive to Asteraceae Family.
May interfere with immunosuppressant therapy.

# *Eletteria cardamomum*

# Cardamom

**Family** Zingiberaceae          □ **Low Therapeutic Margin**

**Medicinal Uses**          **Magical Intentions**

Anorexia                   Divination

Asthma                     Love, To Attract

Bronchitis                 Lust, To Increase/Create

Cramp

Debility

Gastritis

Indigestion

Kidney stones

**Parts Used**          **Element**          **Planet**

Seed                   Water               Venus

**Do Not Use**

Pregnancy   □

Lactation   □          **Male** □                    **Female** ☑

Children    □

Frail       □

**Cautions**

Do not take the essential oil internally.

# *Eleutherococcus senticosus*

## Siberian Ginseng

**Family** Araliaceae     ☐ **Low Therapeutic Margin**

**Medicinal Uses**
Angina
Blood pressure, high
Blood Pressure, low
Bronchitis
Cancer
Stress

**Magical Intentions**
None known

**Parts Used**
Root

**Element**

**Planet**

**Do Not Use**
Pregnancy ☐
Lactation ☐     **Male** ☐     **Female** ☐
Children ☐
Frail ☐

**Cautions**
May interfere with cardiac medications and hypoglycemic agents.
May also enhance some drug effects. In a clinical study, the herb
appeared to increase the efficacy of the antibiotics monomycin &
kanamycin.

# *Elymus repens*

## Couch Grass

**Family** Poaceae      ☐ **Low Therapeutic Margin**

**Medicinal Uses**
Cystitis
Kidney stones
Urethritis
Urinary tract infection

**Magical Intentions**
None known

**Parts Used**      **Element**      **Planet**
Rhizome

**Do Not Use**
Pregnancy   ☐
Lactation   ☐      **Male** ☐      **Female** ☐
Children   ☐
Frail   ☐

**Cautions**
Theoretical risk of potassium depletion when couch grass is used in combination with potassium- depleting diuretics.

# *Ephedra sinica*

## Ephedra, Ma Huang

**Family** Ephedraceae          ☐ **Low Therapeutic Margin**

**Medicinal Uses**          **Magical Intentions**
Asthma                     None known
Bronchitis
Sinusitis

**Parts Used**          **Element**          **Planet**
Stem

**Do Not Use**
Pregnancy   ☐
Lactation    ☐          **Male** ☐          **Female** ☐
Children    ☐
Frail       ☐

### Cautions

Should not be used in the presence of cardiovascular conditions, thyroid disease, diabetes, or by men experiencing difficulty urinating due to prostate enlargement.

Combined with cardiac glycosides or halothane, can produce cardiac arrhythmia. Combining ephedra with monoamine oxidase can significantly increase the sympathetic action of the alkaloid ephedrine in the herb, possibly causing fatal hypertension.

# *Equisetum arvense*

# Horsetail

**Family** Equisetaceae      ☐ **Low Therapeutic Margin**

**Medicinal Uses**          **Magical Intentions**
Bedwetting               Fertility, To Increase
Incontinence             Snakes, To Call
Wounds

**Parts Used**       **Element**       **Planet**
Stem               Earth            Saturn

**Do Not Use**
Pregnancy   ☐
Lactation   ☐      **Male** ☐               **Female** ☑
Children    ☐
Frail       ☐

# *Erica vulgaris*

## Heather

**Family** Ericaceae

☐ **Low Therapeutic Margin**

**Medicinal Uses**
Colds
Colic
Cough
Kidney stones
Urinary gravel
Urinary tract infection

**Magical Intentions**
Luck, To Obtain
Protection
Rain, To Cause To Fall

**Parts Used**
Aerial

**Element**
Water

**Planet**
Venus

**Do Not Use**
Pregnancy ☐
Lactation ☐
Children ☐
Frail ☐

**Male** ☐

**Female** ☑

# *Eriodictyon californicum*

## Yerba Santa

**Family** Hydrophyllaceae    ☐ **Low Therapeutic Margin**

**Medicinal Uses**          **Magical Intentions**
Asthma                      Beauty, To Attain
Bronchitis                  Healing, To Promote
                            Protection
                            Psychic Powers, To Strengthen

**Parts Used**        **Element**              **Planet**
Leaves

**Do Not Use**
Pregnancy  ☐
Lactation  ☐          **Male**  ☐              **Female**  ☑
Children  ☐
Frail  ☐

# *Eryngium spp.*

## Eryngo, Sea Holly

**Family** Umbelliferae      ☐ **Low Therapeutic Margin**

**Medicinal Uses**          **Magical Intentions**
Bronchial asthma           Love, To Attract
Bronchitis                 Lust, To Increase/Create
Jaundice                   Peace/Harmony, To Instill
                           Travelling, to Protect While

**Parts Used**        **Element**        **Planet**
Root                  Water              Venus

**Do Not Use**
Pregnancy  ☐
Lactation  ☐      **Male** ☐              **Female** ☑
Children   ☐
Frail      ☐

# *Erythraea centarium*

## Centaury

**Family** Gentianaceae          □ **Low Therapeutic Margin**

**Medicinal Uses**          **Magical Intentions**
Anemia                    Hexes, To Break
Anorexia                  Meditation, To Aid
Appetite Loss             Snakes, To Repel
Dyspepsia
Gallbladder problems
Hepatitis
Indigestion
Jaundice
Metrorrhagia
Nausea
Worms

**Parts Used**          **Element**          **Planet**
Aerial                  Fire                 Sun

**Do Not Use**
Pregnancy  □
Lactation  □          **Male**  ☑          **Female**  □
Children  □
Frail  □

**Cautions**
Caution for sensitive liver.
Excessive doses will cause mucous membrane irritation, nausea &
vomiting.

# *Eucalyptus globulus*

## Eucalyptus

**Family** Myrtaceae      ☐ **Low Therapeutic Margin**

**Medicinal Uses**      **Magical Intentions**
Asthma            Healing, To Promote
Bronchitis          Protection
Dyspepsia
Fever
Leukorrhea

**Parts Used**       **Element**        **Planet**
Essential Oil        Water           Moon
Leaves

**Do Not Use**
Pregnancy  ☐
Lactation   ☐      **Male** ☐            **Female** ☑
Children   ☐
Frail     ☐

# *Euonymus atropurpureus*

## Wahoo

**Family** Celastraceae          □ **Low Therapeutic Margin**

**Medicinal Uses**          **Magical Intentions**
Gallbladder problems          Courage, To Attain
Jaundice          Hexes, To Break
          Success, To Attain

**Parts Used**          **Element**          **Planet**
Root

**Do Not Use**
Pregnancy   □
Lactation   □          **Male**  □          **Female**  □
Children   □
Frail   □

**Cautions**
Contraindicated for people taking cardiac glycosides or other
cardioactive agents.

# *Eupatorium perfoliatum*

## Boneset

**Family** Asteraceae    ☐ **Low Therapeutic Margin**

**Medicinal Uses**    **Magical Intentions**
Dyspepsia          Exorcism
Flu                Protection

**Parts Used**    **Element**    **Planet**
Aerial        Water       Saturn

**Do Not Use**
Pregnancy ☐
Lactation ☐    **Male** ☐      **Female** ☑
Children ☐
Frail ☐

**Cautions**
May cause allergic reaction in people sensitive to Asteraceae Family.

# *Eupatorium purpureum*

## Joe Pye Weed, Gravel Root

**Family** Asteraceae          □ **Low Therapeutic Margin**

**Medicinal Uses**          **Magical Intentions**
Cystitis          Love, To Attract
Kidney stones
Urethritis

**Parts Used**          **Element**          **Planet**
Rhizome          Water          Saturn
Root

**Do Not Use**
Pregnancy  □
Lactation   □          **Male** □          **Female** □
Children   □
Frail      □

**Cautions**
May cause allergic reaction in people sensitive to Asteraceae Family

# *Euphrasia officinalis*

## Eyebright

**Family** Scrophulariaceae    ☐ **Low Therapeutic Margin**

**Medicinal Uses**
Eye inflammation
Sinusitis

**Magical Intentions**
Mental Powers, To Strengthen
Psychic Powers, To Strengthen

**Parts Used**
Aerial

**Element**
Air

**Planet**
Sun

**Do Not Use**
Pregnancy ☐
Lactation ☐
Children ☐
Frail ☐

**Male** ☑      **Female** ☐

# *Fagopyrum esculentum*

## Buckwheat

**Family** Polygonaceae    □ **Low Therapeutic Margin**

**Medicinal Uses**
Blood pressure, high
Bruises
Varicose veins

**Magical Intentions**
Money, Riches, Treasures, Wealth
Protection

**Parts Used**
Flowers
Leaves

**Element**
Earth

**Planet**
Venus

**Do Not Use**
Pregnancy   □
Lactation   □    **Male** □      **Female** ☑
Children   □
Frail    □

# *Fagus sylvatica*

## Beech

**Family** Fagaceae          ☐ **Low Therapeutic Margin**

**Medicinal Uses**          **Magical Intentions**
Bronchitis          Wishes, To Manifest

**Parts Used**          **Element**          **Planet**
Gum resin          Saturn

**Do Not Use**
Pregnancy  ☐
Lactation  ☐          **Male**  ☐          **Female**  ☑
Children  ☐
Frail      ☐

# *Ferula assa-foetida*

## Asafoetida

**Family** Apiaceae                □ **Low Therapeutic Margin**

**Medicinal Uses**          **Magical Intentions**
Blood pressure, high      Exorcism
Bronchitis                      Protection
Constipation                  Purification
Indigestion
Pertussis

**Parts Used**          **Element**          **Planet**
Gum resin               Fire                    Mars

**Do Not Use**
Pregnancy   □
Lactation   □          **Male** ☑          **Female** □
Children   □
Frail      □

# *Ficus carica*

## Fig

**Family** Moraceae    ☐ **Low Therapeutic Margin**

**Medicinal Uses**      **Magical Intentions**
Constipation          Divination
Cough               Fertility, To Increase
Inflammation        Love, To Attract

**Parts used**      **Element**      **Planet**
Fruit             Fire            Jupiter

**Do Not Use**
Pregnancy ☐
Lactation ☐     **Male** ☑       **Female** ☐
Children ☐
Frail ☐

# *Filipendula ulmaria*

## Meadowsweet

**Family** Rosaceae     ☐ **Low Therapeutic Margin**

**Medicinal Uses**

Gastritis

Heartburn

Nausea

Ulcer, peptic

**Magical Intentions**

Divination

Happiness, To Promote

Love, To Attract

Peace/Harmony, To Instill

**Parts Used**     **Element**     **Planet**

Aerial     Air     Jupiter

**Do Not Use**

Pregnancy ☐

Lactation ☐     **Male** ☑     **Female** ☐

Children ☐

Frail ☐

**Cautions**

Should be avoided by people with salicylate sensitivity.

# *Foeniculum vulgare*

## Fennel

**Family** Apiaceae

☐ **Low Therapeutic Margin**

**Medicinal Uses**
Bronchitis
Colic
Conjunctivitis
Digestion, sluggish
Flatulence

**Magical Intentions**
Divination
Healing, To Promote
Protection
Purification

**Parts Used**
Seed

**Element**
Fire

**Planet**
Mercury

**Do Not Use**
Pregnancy ☐
Lactation ☐
Children ☐
Frail ☐

**Male** ☑

**Female** ☐

# *Fragaria vesca*

## Strawberry

**Family** Apocynaceae          ☐ **Low Therapeutic Margin**

**Medicinal Uses**          **Magical Intentions**
Acne                      Love, To Attract
Diarrhea                  Luck, To Obtain
Dysentery
Eczema

**Parts Used**          **Element**          **Planet**
Fruit                    Water                Venus
Leaves
Seed

**Do Not Use**
Pregnancy  ☐
Lactation   ☐          **Male** ☐          **Female** ☑
Children   ☐
Frail      ☐

# *Fraxinus exelsior*

## Ash

**Family** Oleaceae     □ **Low Therapeutic Margin**

**Medicinal Uses**     **Magical Intentions**
Arthritis               Health, To Maintain
Constipation       Prosperity, To Obtain
                          Protection

**Parts Used**     **Element**     **Planet**
Bark              Fire           Sun
Leaves

**Do Not Use**
Pregnancy □
Lactation □     **Male** ☑     **Female** □
Children □
Frail □

# *Fucus vesiculosus*

## Bladderwrack, Kelp

**Family** Fucaceae

□ **Low Therapeutic Margin**

**Medicinal Uses**
Goiter

**Magical Intentions**
Money, Riches, Treasures, Wealth
Protection
Psychic Powers, To Strengthen

| **Parts Used** | **Element** | **Planet** |
|---|---|---|
| Whole Plant | Water | Moon |

**Do Not Use**
Pregnancy ☑
Lactation ☑      **Male** □     **Female** ☑
Children □
Frail □

**Cautions**

Iodine content may cause hyper- or hypothyroidism; may interfere with existing treatment for abnormal thyroid function. Prolonged ingestion may reduce gastrointestinal iron absorption; may affect absorption of sodium & potassium and cause diarrhea.

# *Fumaria officinalis*

## Fumitory

**Family** Fumariaceae       ☐ **Low Therapeutic Margin**

**Medicinal Uses**          **Magical Intentions**
Acne                        Exorcism
Conjunctivitis              Money, Riches, Treasures, Wealth
Eczema

**Parts Used**      **Element**         **Planet**
Aerial              Earth               Saturn

**Do Not Use**
Pregnancy   ☐
Lactation   ☐       **Male** ☐                    **Female** ☑
Children    ☐
Frail       ☐

# *Galega officinalis*

## Goat's Rue

**Family** Fabaceae     ☑ **Low Therapeutic Margin**

**Medicinal Uses**
Diabetes

**Magical Intentions**
Healing, To Promote
Health, To Maintain

**Parts Used**
Aerial

**Element**
Air

**Planet**
Mercury

**Do Not Use**
Pregnancy ☐
Lactation ☐     **Male** ☑     **Female** ☐
Children ☐
Frail ☐

**Cautions**
Use only under professional supervision.

# *Galium aparine*

## Cleavers

**Family** Rubiaceae        ☐ **Low Therapeutic Margin**

**Medicinal Uses**          **Magical Intentions**
Blood pressure, high        Friendship, To Promote
Burns                       Love, To Attract
Colds                       Protection
Cystitis
Diarrhea
Fluid Retention
Gall stones
Insomnia
Kidney stones
Psoriasis
Sores
Sunburn
Wounds

| **Parts Used** | **Element** | **Planet** |
|----------------|-------------|------------|
| Aerial | Fire | Saturn |

**Do Not Use**
Pregnancy  ☑
Lactation  ☑          **Male** ☐              **Female** ☑
Children  ☐
Frail  ☐

**Cautions**
Powerful diuretic: should be not used when there is a tendency toward diabetes as it can increase amount of sugar in the urine.

# *Galium odoratum*

## Woodruff

**Family** Rubiaceae

☐ **Low Therapeutic Margin**

**Medicinal Uses**
None known

**Magical Intentions**
Money, Riches, Treasures, Wealth
Protection
Success, To Attain

**Parts Used**
Aerial

**Element**
Fire

**Planet**
Mars

**Do Not Use**
Pregnancy ☐
Lactation ☐          **Male** ☑          **Female** ☐
Children ☐
Frail ☐

# *Gardenia jasminoides*

## Gardenia

**Family** Rubiaceae          ☐ **Low Therapeutic Margin**

**Medicinal Uses**          **Magical Intentions**
None known               Healing, To Promote
                         Love, To Attract
                         Peace/Harmony, To Instill
                         Spirituality, To Strengthen

**Parts Used**          **Element**          **Planet**
                        Water                Moon

**Do Not Use**
Pregnancy ☐
Lactation ☐          **Male** ☐          **Female** ☑
Children ☐
Frail ☐

# *Gaultheria procumbens*

## Wintergreen

**Family** Betulaceae     ☐ **Low Therapeutic Margin**

**Medicinal Uses**
Arthritis
Arthritis, rheumatoid
Neuralgia
Sciatica
Sprain

**Magical Intentions**
Healing, To Promote
Hexes, To Break
Protection

| **Parts Used** | **Element** | **Planet** |
|---|---|---|
| Leaves | Water | Moon |
| Oil | | |

**Do Not Use**
Pregnancy ☐
Lactation ☐    **Male** ☐      **Female** ☑
Children ☐
Frail ☐

**Cautions**
Pure oil can cause irritation.

# *Gentiana lutea*

## Gentian

**Family** Gentianaceae

☐ **Low Therapeutic Margin**

**Medicinal Uses**
Amenorrhea
Anorexia
Appetite Loss
Arthritis, rheumatoid
Digestion, sluggish
Dyspepsia
Flatulence
Indigestion
Jaundice
Liver congestion
Sinusitis
Vomiting
Worms

**Magical Intentions**
Love, To Attract
Power, To Obtain
Theft, To Prevent

**Parts Used**
Bark
Rhizome
Root

**Element**
Fire

**Planet**
Mars

**Do Not Use**
Pregnancy ☑
Lactation ☐
Children ☐
Frail ☐

**Male** ☑

**Female** ☐

**Cautions**

In predisposed people, may cause headaches. Contraindicated for gastric or duodenal ulcers & where gastric irritation & inflammation are present. Using tea, not tincture, minimizes irritation.

# *Geranium maculatum*

## Cranesbill

**Family** Gentianaceae       □ **Low Therapeutic Margin**

**Medicinal Uses**          **Magical Intentions**
Catarrh                  None known
Diarrhea
Thrush
Tooth extraction
Ulcer, duodenal
Ulcer, mouth
Ulcer, skin

**Parts Used**          **Element**          **Planet**
Leaves
Root

**Do Not Use**
Pregnancy  □
Lactation  □          **Male** □          **Female** □
Children  □
Frail    □

**Cautions**
High tannin content could cause liver damage.

# *Geum urbanum*

## Avens

**Family** Rosaceae              ☐ **Low Therapeutic Margin**

**Medicinal Uses**              **Magical Intentions**
Diarrhea                         Exorcism
Dysentery                        Love, To Attract
Hemorrhoids                      Purification
Irritable bowel syndrome
Leukorrhea
Throat infection
Ulcer, peptic

**Parts Used**              **Element**              **Planet**
Aerial                       Fire                     Jupiter
Root

**Do Not Use**
Pregnancy   ☐
Lactation   ☐          **Male** ☑          **Female** ☐
Children   ☐
Frail      ☐

# *Gingko biloba*

## Gingko

**Family** Gingkoaceae          ☐ **Low Therapeutic Margin**

**Medicinal Uses**          **Magical Intentions**
ADHD                       None known
Alzheimers
Dizziness
Memory Loss
Tinnitus
Vertigo

**Parts Used**          **Element**          **Planet**
Leaves
Seed

**Do Not Use**
Pregnancy  ☐
Lactation  ☐          **Male** ☐          **Female** ☐
Children  ☐
Frail  ☐

**Cautions**
May have an additive effect when used with other antiplatelet agents.
May potentiate the effects of papaverine used to treat male impotence.
Occasional side effects such as headaches & upset stomach have been
reported. Spontaneous bleeding is one concerning potential side
effects.
Cease taking gingko at least 2 & preferably 4 weeks before surgery.
May inhibit fertilization. Not demonstrated in humans, but avoid use
where couples are trying to conceive.
Raw fruits are reported toxic. Seeds contain a neurotoxin in larger

amounts than leaves. Boiling seeds seems to reduce toxin to safe levels. However, best if seeds are not used long term.

# *Glycyrrhiza glabra*

## Licorice

**Family** Fabaceae      ☐ **Low Therapeutic Margin**

**Medicinal Uses**
Arthritis, rheumatoid
Bronchitis
Constipation
Cough
Gastritis
Hepatitis
Respiratory infection
Sore throat
Ulcer, duodenal
Ulcer, gastric

**Magical Intentions**
Fidelity, to Ensure
Love, To Attract
Lust, To Increase/Create

| **Parts Used** | **Element** | **Planet** |
|---|---|---|
| Rhizome | Water | Venus |
| Root | | |

**Do Not Use**

| Pregnancy ☐ | | |
|---|---|---|
| Lactation ☐ | **Male** ☐ | **Female** ☑ |
| Children ☐ | | |
| Frail ☐ | | |

**Cautions**
Excessive doses can deplete the body of potassium and cause
retention of sodium. More effective when taken before food.
Contraindicated for diabetes, hypertension, liver disorders, severe
kidney insufficiency, cardiovascular disease, hypo- or hyperglycemia.
May interfere with existing hormonal therapy.

# *Gossypium herbaceum*

## Cotton

**Family** Malvaceae

☐ **Low Therapeutic Margin**

**Medicinal Uses**
Dysmenorrhea

**Magical Intentions**
Healing, To Promote
Luck, To Obtain
Protection
Rain, To Cause To Fall

**Parts Used**
Bark
Root
Seed

**Element**
Earth

**Planet**
Moon

**Do Not Use**
Pregnancy ☑
Lactation ☑          **Male** ☐          **Female** ☑
Children ☐
Frail ☐

**Cautions**
May cause low sperm count. Could possibly induce abortions.

# *Hamamelis virginiana*

# Witch Hazel

**Family** Hamamelidaceae      ☐ **Low Therapeutic Margin**

| **Medicinal Uses** | **Magical Intentions** |
|---|---|
| Bruises | Chastity, To Maintain |
| Burns | Protection |
| Colitis | |
| Diarrhea | |
| Hemorrhoids | |
| Insect bites | |
| Menopause | |
| Miscarriage, threatened | |
| Nosebleed | |
| Varicose ulcers | |
| Varicose veins | |

| **Parts Used** | **Element** | **Planet** |
|---|---|---|
| Bark | Fire | Sun |
| Leaves | | |
| Twigs | | |

**Do Not Use**

| | | |
|---|---|---|
| Pregnancy ☐ | | |
| Lactation ☐ | **Male** ☑ | **Female** ☐ |
| Children ☐ | | |
| Frail ☐ | | |

**Cautions**

Tannins may cause liver damage.

# *Hedera helix*

## Ivy

**Family** Araliaceae    □ **Low Therapeutic Margin**

**Medicinal Uses**

Bronchitis

Catarrh

**Magical Intentions**

Healing, To Promote

Protection

**Parts Used**

Berries

Leaves

**Element**

Water

**Planet**

Saturn

**Do Not Use**

Pregnancy □

Lactation □    **Male** □      **Female** ☑

Children □

Frail □

# *Helianthus annuus*

## Sunflower

**Family** Asteraceae          □ **Low Therapeutic Margin**

**Medicinal Uses**          **Magical Intentions**
Colds          Fertility, To Increase
Cough          Friendship, To Promote
          Healing, To Promote
          Wisdom, To Promote
          Wishes, To Manifest

**Parts Used**          **Element**          **Planet**
Flowers          Fire          Sun
Oil
Seed

**Do Not Use**
Pregnancy   □
Lactation   □          **Male** ☑          **Female** □
Children   □
Frail   □

**Cautions**
May cause allergic reaction in those sensitive to Asteraceae Family.

# *Hibiscus sabdariffa*

## Hibiscus

**Family** Malvaceae     ☐ **Low Therapeutic Margin**

**Medicinal Uses**
Blood pressure, high
Dysmenorrhea

**Magical Intentions**
Divination
Love, To Attract
Lust, To Increase/Create

**Parts Used**
Flowers

**Element**
Water

**Planet**
Venus

**Do Not Use**
Pregnancy ☐
Lactation ☐     **Male** ☐       **Female** ☑
Children ☐
Frail ☐

**Notes**
Usually used as a flavoring agent in teas; recent studies suggest it
could have an anti-obesity effect.

# *Hordeum distichon*

## Barley

**Family** Graminaceae          ☐ **Low Therapeutic Margin**

**Medicinal Uses**          **Magical Intentions**

Appetite Loss          Healing, To Promote

Diarrhea          Love, To Attract

Sore throat          Protection

Sores

Urinary tract infection

| **Parts Used** | **Element** | **Planet** |
|---|---|---|
| Seed | Earth | Venus |

**Do Not Use**

Pregnancy ☐

Lactation ☐          **Male** ☐          **Female** ☑

Children ☐

Frail ☐

**Notes**

Research in the 1990's suggests barley may help treat hepatitis, control diabetes and that barley bran may lower cholesterol and prevent bowel cancer.

# *Humulus lupulus*

# Hops

**Family** Cannabaceae          □ **Low Therapeutic Margin**

**Medicinal Uses**          **Magical Intentions**
Anxiety                    Healing, To Promote
Dyspepsia                  Sleep
Headache, Tension          Stress Management
Indigestion
Insomnia
Nervous tension
Neuralgia
Tension
Ulcer, skin

**Parts Used**          **Element**          **Planet**
Flowers                 Air                  Mars

**Do Not Use**
Pregnancy   □
Lactation   □          **Male** ☑          **Female** □
Children    □
Frail       □

**Cautions**
Do not used in patients with marked depression as the sedative effects
may accentuate symptoms.
May also potentiate the effects of alcohol or existing sedative therapy.

# *Hyacinthus orientalis*

## Hyacinth

**Family** Hyacinthaceae      ☑ **Low Therapeutic Margin**

**Medicinal Uses**      **Magical Intentions**
None known      Depression Management
Happiness, To Promote
Love, To Attract
Protection

| **Parts Used** | **Element** | **Planet** |
|---|---|---|
| Flowers | Water | Venus |

**Do Not Use**
Pregnancy ☑
Lactation ☑      **Male** ☐      **Female** ☑
Children ☑
Frail ☑

**Cautions**
DO NOT TAKE INTERNALLY.

# *Hydrastis canadensis*

## Goldenseal

**Family** Ranunculaceae          ☐ **Low Therapeutic Margin**

**Medicinal Uses**          **Magical Intentions**
Appetite Loss               Healing, To Promote
Colitis                     Money, Riches, Treasures, Wealth
Conjunctivitis
Dysmenorrhea
Earache
Eczema
Eye inflammation
Gallbladder problems
Ringworm
Sinusitis
Thrush
Ulcer, peptic
Vaginal infection

**Parts Used**          **Element**          **Planet**
Rhizome                  Fire                 Sun
Root

**Do Not Use**
Pregnancy   ☑
Lactation   ☑          **Male** ☑          **Female** ☐
Children    ☑
Frail       ☐

**Cautions**

Contraindicated for individuals with elevated blood pressure.

Prolonged use may decrease Vitamin B absorption.

Use 2-4 weeks only. Can accumulate in the system and produce toxic symptoms. If used in a preventative role for long periods, may cause what it originally cured. Can cause symptoms of hypoglycemia if used over long periods.

# *Hypericum perforatum*

## St. John's Wort

**Family** Clusiaceae     ☐ **Low Therapeutic Margin**

| **Medicinal Uses** | **Magical Intentions** |
|---|---|
| Anxiety | Divination |
| Herpes simplex | Fertility, To Increase |
| Herpes zoster | Happiness, To Promote |
| Myalgia | Health, To Maintain |
| Neuralgia | Love, Divination Of |
| Sciatica | Power, To Obtain |
| Sunburn | Protection |
| Tension | Strength, To Instill |
| Ulcer, duodenal | Stress Management |
| Ulcer, gastric | |
| Wounds | |

| **Parts** | **Element** | **Planet** |
|---|---|---|
| Aerial | Fire | Sun |

**Do Not Use**
Pregnancy ☐
Lactation ☐     **Male** ☑     **Female** ☐
Children ☐
Frail ☐

**Cautions**
Could reduce the activity of simultaneously administered drugs that are known substrates of the isozyme CYP3A4, including nonsedating antihistamines, oral contraceptives, certain antiretroviral agents, antiepileptic medications, calcium channel blockers, some chemotherapeutic drugs, macrolide antibiotics and selected antifungals.

Hypericin has shown to increase photosensitivity.

# *Hyssopus officinalis*

## Hyssop

**Family** Lamiaceae          ☐ **Low Therapeutic Margin**

**Medicinal Uses**          **Magical Intentions**
Asthma          Protection
Bronchitis          Purification
Bruises
Catarrh
Chickenpox
Cough
Fever
Indigestion
Kidney stones
Sore throat
Worms
Wounds

**Parts Used**          **Element**          **Planet**
Flowering Herb          Fire          Jupiter

**Do Not Use**
Pregnancy  ☑
Lactation   ☑          **Male** ☑          **Female** ☐
Children   ☐
Frail      ☐

# *Ilex aquifolium*

# Holly

**Family** Aquifoliaceae    ☑ **Low Therapeutic Margin**

**Medicinal Uses**      **Magical Intentions**
Arthritis, rheumatoid      Luck, To Obtain
Fever      Protection
Jaundice

**Parts Used**      **Element**      **Planet**
Berries      Fire      Mars
Leaves

**Do Not Use**
Pregnancy ☑
Lactation ☑      **Male** ☑      **Female** ☐
Children ☑
Frail ☑

# *Ilex paraguariensis*

## Yerba Mate

**Family** Aquifoliaceae    ☐ **Low Therapeutic Margin**

**Medicinal Uses**
Cancer
Depression

**Magical Intentions**
Fidelity, to Ensure
Love, To Attract
Lust, To Increase/Create

**Parts Used**      **Element**      **Planet**
Leaves
Twigs

**Do Not Use**
Pregnancy ☐
Lactation ☐      **Male** ☑      **Female** ☐
Children ☐
Frail ☐

**Cautions**
Contains pyrrolizidine alkaloids so may cause cancer as well as cure some types.

# *Illicium verum*

## Star Anise

**Family** Illiciaceae      □ **Low Therapeutic Margin**

**Medicinal Uses**       **Magical Intentions**
Arthritis, rheumatoid    Luck, To Obtain
Colic                    Psychic Powers, To Strengthen
Flatulence
Indigestion

**Parts Used**       **Element**       **Planet**
Fruit                Air               Jupiter

**Do Not Use**
Pregnancy  □
Lactation  □      **Male** ☑       **Female** □
Children   □
Frail      □

**Notes**
Use as an infusion - safe enough even for children.

# *Imperatoria ostruthium*

## Masterwort

**Family** Apiaceae                    ☐ **Low Therapeutic Margin**

**Medicinal Uses**           **Magical Intentions**
None known                   Courage, To Attain
                             Protection
                             Strength, To Instill

**Parts Used**               **Element**               **Planet**
Leaves                       Fire                      Mars

**Do Not Use**
Pregnancy   ☐
Lactation   ☐            **Male**  ☑            **Female**  ☐
Children    ☐
Frail       ☐

**Notes**
No currently known medicinal uses

# *Inula conyza*

## Spikenard

**Family** Asteraceae

☐ **Low Therapeutic Margin**

**Medicinal Uses**
Bruises
Wounds

**Magical Intentions**
Love, To Attract

**Parts Used**
Aerial

**Element**
Water

**Planet**
Venus

**Do Not Use**
Pregnancy ☐
Lactation ☐
Children ☐
Frail ☐

**Male** ☐

**Female** ☑

# *Inula helenium*

## Elecampane

**Family** Asteraceae          □**Low Therapeutic Margin**

**Medicinal Uses**          **Magical Intentions**
Asthma                     Anger Management
Bronchitis                 Love, To Attract
Cough                      Protection
Inflammation               Psychic Powers, To Strengthen
Metrorrhagia
Neuralgia
Pertussis
Sciatica
Tuberculosis
Water retention
Worms
Wounds

**Parts Used**          **Element**          **Planet**
Rhizome                 Air                  Mercury
Root

**Do Not Use**
Pregnancy  ☑
Lactation  ☑          **Male** ☑          **Female** □
Children   □
Frail      □

**Cautions**
May cause allergic reaction in people sensitive to Asteraceae Family.
May cause contact dermatitis.
May infere with hypoglycemic and antihypertensive treatments.

# *Ipomoea purga*

## High John the Conqueror, Jalap

**Family** Convolvulaceae     ☑ **Low Therapeutic Margin**

**Medicinal Uses**          **Magical Intentions**
None known               Happiness, To Promote
                         Legal Matters, To Assist In
                         Love, To Attract
                         Money, Riches, Treasures, Wealth
                         Success, To Attain

**Parts Used**     **Element**          **Planet**
Root           Fire               Mars

**Do Not Use**
Pregnancy  ☐
Lactation  ☐          **Male**  ☑          **Female**  ☐
Children  ☐
Frail  ☐

**Cautions**
Even in moderate doses, stimulates the elimination of profuse watery stools and can cause vomiting.

# *Iris germanica var. florentina*

## Orris

**Family** Iridaceae      □ **Low Therapeutic Margin**

**Medicinal Uses**          **Magical Intentions**
Bronchitis                 Divination
Colic                      Love, To Attract
Cough                      Protection
Liver congestion
Sore throat
Water retention

**Parts Used**      **Element**      **Planet**
Rhizome             Water            Venus
Root

**Do Not Use**
Pregnancy   □
Lactation   □        **Male**  □                **Female**  ☑
Children    □
Frail       □

# *Iris versicolor*

# Blue Flag

**Family** Iridaceae

☐**Low Therapeutic Margin**

**Medicinal Uses**
Eczema
Hepatitis
Herpes simplex
Psoriasis
Uterine fibroids

**Magical Intentions**
Money, Riches, Treasures, Wealth

**Parts Used**
Rhizome

**Element**
Water

**Planet**
Venus

**Do Not Use**
Pregnancy  ☐
Lactation  ☐
Children  ☐
Frail  ☐

**Male** ☐

**Female** ☑

# *Jasminum officinale*

## Jasmine

**Family** Oleaceae

☐ **Low Therapeutic Margin**

**Medicinal Uses**
Anxiety
Irritability
Nervous tension

**Magical Intentions**
Love, To Attract
Mental Powers, To Strengthen
Money, Riches, Treasures, Wealth
Prophetic Dreams, To Cause

**Parts Used**
Essential Oil
Flowers

**Element**
Water

**Planet**
Moon

**Do Not Use**
Pregnancy ☐
Lactation ☐
Children ☐
Frail ☐

**Male** ☐

**Female** ☑

# *Juglans nigra*

## Walnut (Black)

**Family** Juglandaceae   ☐ **Low Therapeutic Margin**

**Medicinal Uses**
Acne
Athletes Foot
Bleeding
Boils
Cold sores
Colic
Constipation
Diabetes
Eczema
Fever
Hemorrhoids
Infection
Liver congestion
Psoriasis
Ringworm
Sore throat
Tonsillitis
Ulcer, duodenal
Ulcer, gastric
Ulcer, mouth
Ulcer, peptic
Ulcer, skin
Varicose veins
Worms

**Magical Intentions**
Health, To Maintain
Infertility, To Create
Mental Powers, To Strengthen
Wishes, To Manifest

| Parts Used | Element | Planet |
|---|---|---|
| Fruit | Fire | Sun |
| Inner bark | | |
| Leaves | | |

**Do Not Use**

| | | | | |
|---|---|---|---|---|
| Pregnancy | ☑ | | | |
| Lactation | ☑ | **Male** ☑ | **Female** ☐ |
| Children | ☐ | | | |
| Frail | ☐ | | | |

**Cautions**

Contains high percentage of tannins; might cause precipitation of some other herbs or drugs.

**Notes**

Most important part is green hulls.

# *Juniperus communis*

## Juniper

**Family** Cupressaceae          ☐ **Low Therapeutic Margin**

| **Medicinal Uses** | **Magical Intentions** |
|---|---|
| Arthritis | Divination |
| Bladder inflammation | Exorcism |
| Cough | Healing, To Promote |
| Flatulence | Health, To Maintain |
| Fluid Retention | Love, To Attract |
| Glaucoma | Protection |
| Gout | Theft, To Prevent |
| Indigestion | |
| Leukorrhea | |
| Sciatica | |
| Thrush | |
| Wounds | |

| **Parts Used** | **Element** | **Planet** |
|---|---|---|
| Bark | Fire | Sun |
| Berries | | |
| Essential Oil | | |
| Leaves | | |

**Do Not Use**

Pregnancy ☑

Lactation ☑          **Male** ☑          **Female** ☐

Children ☐

Frail ☐

**Cautions**

Reported abortifacient and affects the menstrual cycle. Should not be used for more than 4-6 weeks without 2 week break. Contraindicated for inflammatory kidney disease. Prolonged use may lead to abnormally low potassium levels. May potentiate hypoglycemic and diuretic therapies.

# *Lactuca virosa*

# Wild Lettuce

**Family** Asteraceae    ☐ **Low Therapeutic Margin**

| **Medicinal Uses** | **Magical Intentions** |
|---|---|
| Dysmenorrhea | Chastity, To Maintain |
| Insomnia | Divination |
| Pertussis | Love, Divination Of |
| | Protection |
| | Sleep |

| **Parts Used** | **Element** | **Planet** |
|---|---|---|
| Leaves | Water | Moon |

**Do Not Use**

Pregnancy ☐

Lactation ☐          **Male** ☐                    **Female** ☑

Children ☐

Frail ☐

**Cautions**

May cause allergic reaction in people sensitive to Asteraceae Family.

# *Laurus nobilis*

## Bay

**Family** Lauraceae        □ **Low Therapeutic Margin**

**Medicinal Uses**          **Magical Intentions**
Arthritis, rheumatoid        Employment, To Attain/Maintain
Dandruff                     Healing, To Promote
                             Protection
                             Psychic Powers, To Strengthen
                             Purification
                             Strength, To Instill

**Parts Used**          **Element**          **Planet**
Essential Oil           Fire                 Sun
Leaves

**Do Not Use**
Pregnancy  □
Lactation   □          **Male** ☑          **Female** □
Children    □
Frail       □

**Notes**
Essential oil used externally for rheumatism & in hair dressing for
dandruff.

# *Lavandula angustifolia*

## Lavender

**Family** Lamiaceae      ☐ **Low Therapeutic Margin**

**Medicinal Uses**

Depression

Headache, Tension

**Magical Intentions**

Anger Management

Chastity, To Maintain

Happiness, To Promote

Longevity, To Attain

Love, To Attract

Peace/Harmony, To Instill

Protection

Purification

Sleep

Stress Management

Travelling, to Protect While

**Parts Used**

Essential Oil

Flowers

**Element**

Air

**Planet**

Mercury

**Do Not Use**

Pregnancy ☐

Lactation ☐        **Male** ☑                **Female** ☐

Children ☐

Frail ☐

**Notes**

Can be used interchangeably with *Lavandula officinalis*

# *Leonurus cardiaca*

# Motherwort

**Family** Lamiaceae    ☐ **Low Therapeutic Margin**

**Medicinal Uses**    **Magical Intentions**

Anxiety    Hexes, To Break

Metrorrhagia    Love, To Attract

PMS    Protection

Tachycardia

Tension

**Parts Used**    **Element**    **Planet**

Aerial        Venus

**Do Not Use**

Pregnancy  ☐

Lactation  ☐    **Male**  ☐    **Female**  ☑

Children  ☐

Frail  ☐

**Cautions**

Excessive use may interfere with other cardiovascular treatments.

# *Levisticum officinale*

## Lovage

**Family** Apiaceae

☐ **Low Therapeutic Margin**

**Medicinal Uses**
Amenorrhea
Bronchitis
Colic
Dysmenorrhea
Flatulence
Indigestion
Urinary tract infection

**Magical Intentions**
Love, To Attract

**Parts Used**
Leaves
Root
Seed

**Element**
Fire

**Planet**
Sun

**Do Not Use**
Pregnancy ☑
Lactation ☐
Children ☐
Frail ☐

**Male** ☑

**Female** ☐

**Cautions**
Do not take if you have kidney disease.

# *Linum usitatissimum*

## Flax

**Family** Linaceae

☐ **Low Therapeutic Margin**

**Medicinal Uses**
Constipation
Digestion, sluggish

**Magical Intentions**
Beauty, To Attain
Healing, To Promote
Money, Riches, Treasures, Wealth
Protection
Psychic Powers, To Strengthen

**Parts Used**
Seed

**Element**
Fire

**Planet**
Mercury

**Do Not Use**
Pregnancy ☐
Lactation ☐
Children ☐
Frail ☐

**Male** ☑

**Female** ☐

**Cautions**
Can affect absorption of drugs.

# *Lippia citriodora*

## Lemon Verbena

**Family** Verbenaceae         ☐ **Low Therapeutic Margin**

**Medicinal Uses**          **Magical Intentions**
Dyspepsia            Love, To Attract
Flatulence           Purification
Indigestion

**Parts Used**          **Element**          **Planet**
Leaves              Air               Mercury

**Do Not Use**
Pregnancy   ☐
Lactation   ☐          **Male** ☑          **Female** ☐
Children   ☐
Frail      ☐

# *Liquidambar styraciflua*

## Sweetgum, Liquidamber

**Family** Hamamelidaceae       ☐ **Low Therapeutic Margin**

**Medicinal Uses**          **Magical Intentions**
Diarrhea                Protection
Fever
Metrorrhagia
Ulcer, skin

**Parts Used**          **Element**          **Planet**
Gum resin              Fire               Sun
Inner bark
Leaves

**Do Not Use**
Pregnancy   ☐
Lactation    ☐      **Male** ☑          **Female** ☐
Children     ☐
Frail        ☐

**Notes**

Resin & inner bark used in cough syrups, small lumps of resin may be chewed to treat sore throat pain. Decoction of bark and leaf settles stomach & relieves lung congestion. Bark decocted in milk stops diarrhea. Salve made with resin heals wounds & skin rashes.

# *Lobelia inflata*

## Lobelia

**Family** Campanulaceae    ☑ **Low Therapeutic Margin**

**Medicinal Uses**
Asthma
Bronchial asthma
Bronchitis
Epilepsy
Pertussis

**Magical Intentions**
Love, To Attract

| **Parts Used** | **Element** | **Planet** |
|---|---|---|
| Aerial | Water | Saturn |

**Do Not Use**
Pregnancy ☑
Lactation ☑    **Male** ☐    **Female** ☑
Children ☐
Frail ☐

**Cautions**
Side effects are similar to those of nicotine & tobacco and include nausea, vomiting, diarrhea, coughing, tremors & dizziness. Symptoms of overdose include profuse diaphoresis, tachycardia, convulsions, hypothermia, hypotension & coma.

# *Lonicera caprifolium*

## Honeysuckle

**Family** Caprifoliaceae　　□**Low Therapeutic Margin**

**Medicinal Uses**　　**Magical Intentions**
None known　　Depression Management
Money, Riches, Treasures, Wealth
Protection
Psychic Powers, To Strengthen

| **Parts Used** | **Element** | **Planet** |
|---|---|---|
| Flowers | Earth | Jupiter |
| Leaves | | |

**Do Not Use**
Pregnancy □
Lactation □　　**Male** ☑　　　**Female** □
Children □
Frail □

**Notes**
Rarely used medicinally; *L. japonica* widely used in Traditional
Chinese Medicine for fever, inflammation, dysentery & abscess.

# *Lycopodium clavatum*

# Club Moss

**Family** Lycopodiaceae    ☑ **Low Therapeutic Margin**

**Medicinal Uses**           **Magical Intentions**
Gastritis                    Power, To Obtain
Indigestion                  Protection
Kidney stones

**Parts Used**          **Element**      **Planet**
Whole plant except root  Water           Moon

**Do Not Use**
Pregnancy   ☐
Lactation   ☐          **Male** ☐              **Female** ☑
Children    ☐
Frail       ☐

**Cautions**
Potentially toxic. Use only under professional supervision.

# *Lythrum salicaria*

## Loosestrife

**Family** Lythraceae          ☐ **Low Therapeutic Margin**

**Medicinal Uses**          **Magical Intentions**
Diarrhea                   Peace/Harmony, To Instill
Dysentery                  Protection
Leukorrhea
Metrorrhagia
Ulcer, skin
Wounds

**Parts Used**          **Element**          **Planet**
Aerial                  Earth                Moon

**Do Not Use**
Pregnancy   ☐
Lactation   ☐          **Male** ☐                    **Female** ☑
Children    ☐
Frail       ☐

**Notes**
Use as an infusion. Mild enough for people of all ages.

# *Mahonia aquifolium*

## Oregon Grape

**Family** Berberidaceae     ☐ **Low Therapeutic Margin**

**Medicinal Uses**          **Magical Intentions**
Constipation             Money, Riches, Treasures, Wealth
Eczema                   Prosperity, To Obtain
Psoriasis

**Parts Used**          **Element**          **Planet**
Rhizome               Earth
Root

**Do Not Use**
Pregnancy   ☐
Lactation    ☐          **Male** ☐                **Female** ☑
Children     ☐
Frail        ☐

# *Malva sylvestris*

## Mallow

**Family** Malvaceae

☐ **Low Therapeutic Margin**

**Medicinal Uses**
Cough
Swelling

**Magical Intentions**
Exorcism
Love, To Attract
Protection

**Parts Used**
Flowers
Leaves
Root

**Element**
Water

**Planet**
Moon

**Do Not Use**
Pregnancy ☐
Lactation ☐
Children ☐
Frail ☐

**Male** ☐

**Female** ☑

# *Mandragora officinarum*

## Mandrake

**Family** Solanaceae          ☑ **Low Therapeutic Margin**

**Medicinal Uses**          **Magical Intentions**
Arthritis                  Fertility, To Increase
Arthritis, rheumatoid      Health, To Maintain
Ulcer, skin                Money, Riches, Treasures, Wealth
                           Protection

**Parts Used**          **Element**          **Planet**
Root                    Fire                 Mercury

**Do Not Use**
Pregnancy  ☐
Lactation  ☐          **Male** ☑          **Female** ☐
Children   ☐
Frail      ☐

**Cautions**
Do not take internally.

# *Marrubium vulgare*

# Horehound (White)

**Family** Lamiaceae     □ **Low Therapeutic Margin**

**Medicinal Uses**

Amenorrhea

Appetite Loss

Asthma

Bronchitis

Catarrh

Colds

Constipation

Pertussis

Sore throat

Worms

Wounds

**Magical Intentions**

Exorcism

Healing, To Promote

Mental Powers, To Strengthen

Protection

| **Parts Used** | **Element** | **Planet** |
|---|---|---|
| Flowering Tops | Air | Mercury |
| Leaves | | |

**Do Not Use**

Pregnancy ☑

Lactation ☑     **Male** ☑     **Female** □

Children □

Frail □

**Cautions**

The plant juice can cause contact dermatitis.

Excessive doses will cause nausea & diarrhea, may cause arrhythmia

# *Matricaria recutita*

## German Chamomile

**Family** Asteraceae

**Medicinal Uses**

Abscess
Anxiety
Appetite Loss
Arthritis
Colds
Colic
Conjunctivitis
Depression
Diarrhea
Dyspepsia
Flu
Insomnia
Migraine
Motion sickness
Muscle strain
Neuralgia
Sinusitis
Teething, babies
Ulcer, gastric
Vertigo

☐ **Low Therapeutic Margin**

**Magical Intentions**

Anger Management
Legal Matters, To Assist In
Love, To Attract
Money, Riches, Treasures, Wealth
Purification
Sleep
Stress Management

**Parts Used**

Essential Oil
Flowering Tops

**Element**

Water

**Planet**

Sun

**Do Not Use**
Pregnancy ☐
Lactation ☐          **Male** ☑                    **Female** ☐
Children ☐
Frail ☐

**Cautions**
May cause allergic reaction in people sensitive to Asteraceae Family.
The coumarin constituent may interfere with anticoagulant therapy if
used in excessive doses.
Recommend avoiding excessive use during pregnancy & lactation due
to reputed effects on the menstrual cycle & uterotonic activity.

# *Medicago sativa*

# Alfalfa

**Family** Fabaceae     ☐ **Low Therapeutic Margin**

| **Medicinal Uses** | **Magical Intentions** |
|---|---|
| Appetite Loss | Anti-Hunger |
| Candida | Money, Riches, Treasures, Wealth |
| Ulcer, peptic | Prosperity, To Obtain |
| Water retention | |

| **Parts Used** | **Element** | **Planet** |
|---|---|---|
| Aerial | Earth | Venus |

**Do Not Use**

| | | | |
|---|---|---|---|
| Pregnancy ☐ | | | |
| Lactation ☐ | **Male** ☐ | | **Female** ☑ |
| Children ☐ | | | |
| Frail ☐ | | | |

**Cautions**

Excessive intake not recommended due to estrogenic effects & can produce a lupus-like syndrome; can also exacerbate SLE.

# *Melaleuca alternifolia*

## Tea Tree

**Family** Myrtaceae      ☐ **Low Therapeutic Margin**

**Medicinal Uses**          **Magical Intentions**
Athletes Foot              None known
Boils
Colds
Cough
Herpes simplex
Insect bites
Laryngitis
Psoriasis
Sinusitis
Thrush

**Parts Used**          **Element**          **Planet**
Essential Oil

**Do Not Use**
Pregnancy   ☐
Lactation   ☐          **Male** ☐          **Female** ☐
Children   ☐
Frail   ☐

**Cautions**
For External use. People with sensitive skin should dilute first with a
fixed carrier oil.

# *Melissa officinalis*

## Lemon Balm

**Family** Lamiaceae      ☐ **Low Therapeutic Margin**

**Medicinal Uses**

Dyspepsia

Flatulence

Herpes simplex

Neuralgia

**Magical Intentions**

Anger Management

Depression Management

Healing, To Promote

Love, To Attract

Success, To Attain

| **Parts Used** | **Element** | **Planet** |
|---|---|---|
| Aerial | Water | Moon |

**Do Not Use**

Pregnancy ☐

Lactation ☐      **Male** ☐      **Female** ☑

Children ☐

Frail ☐

**Cautions**

May interfere with the action of thyroid hormones.

# *Mentha pulegium*

## Pennyroyal

**Family** Lamiaceae          ☐ **Low Therapeutic Margin**

**Medicinal Uses**          **Magical Intentions**
Flatulence                 Peace/Harmony, To Instill
Metrorrhagia               Protection
                           Strength, To Instill

**Parts Used**          **Element**          **Planet**
Aerial                  Fire                 Mars

**Do Not Use**
Pregnancy  ☐
Lactation  ☐          **Male** ☑          **Female** ☐
Children   ☐
Frail      ☐

# *Mentha spicata*

# Spearmint

**Family** Lamiaceae

☐ **Low Therapeutic Margin**

**Medicinal Uses**
Colic
Fever
Flatulence
Fluid Retention
Hemorrhoids
Hiccoughs
Indigestion
Morning sickness
Nausea
Suppressed urine
Vomiting

**Magical Intentions**
Anger Management
Healing, To Promote
Love, To Attract
Mental Powers, To Strengthen
Protection

**Parts Used**
Essential Oil
Flowering Tops
Leaves

**Element**
Water

**Planet**
Venus

**Do Not Use**
Pregnancy ☐
Lactation ☐
Children ☐
Frail ☐

**Male** ☐

**Female** ☑

**Cautions**

Essential oil is potent & doses in excess of recommended amounts can cause gastrointestinal irritation & depression of the Central Nervous System.

Possible effect on the male reproductive system - decreased testosterone levels in rates, developmental effects on sperm. If couples are having fertility problems, might be better for the male not to drink mint tea.

# *Mentha x piperita*

# Peppermint

**Family** Lamiaceae

☐ **Low Therapeutic Margin**

| **Medicinal Uses** | **Magical Intentions** |
|---|---|
| Appetite Loss | Anger Management |
| Colds | Healing, To Promote |
| Colic | Love, To Attract |
| Dyspepsia | Psychic Powers, To Strengthen |
| Fever | Purification |
| Flatulence | Sleep |
| Flu | |
| Headache, Tension | |
| Insomnia | |
| Measles | |
| Morning sickness | |
| Nausea | |
| Teething, babies | |
| Toothache | |

| **Parts Used** | **Element** | **Planet** |
|---|---|---|
| Aerial | Fire | Mercury |
| Essential Oil | | |

**Do Not Use**

Pregnancy ☐

Lactation ☐          **Male** ☑          **Female** ☐

Children ☐

Frail ☐

**Cautions**

Excessive doses of oil can cause vomiting & drowsiness. Orally, oil can cause heartburn, nausea & vomiting, and allergic reactions, including flushing & headaches.

Topically, oil can cause skin irritation & contact dermatitis. Always use in a 1% solution.

Contraindicated with occlusion of bile ducts, gallbladder inflammation & severe liver damage.

Other preliminary research suggests that peppermint may lower testosterone levels & decrease spermatogenesis in male animals. It is not known whether this occurs in humans, although anecdotal reports suggest reduced libido in men consuming 4 cups + per day of peppermint tea.

There are some drug interactions - be sure to check.

# *Monarda fistulosa*

## Bee Balm, Oswego Tea, Horsemint

**Family** Labiatae          ☐ **Low Therapeutic Margin**

**Medicinal Uses**          **Magical Intentions**
Cancer                     Mental Powers, To Strengthen

**Parts Used**          **Element**          **Planet**
Leaves                  Air

**Do Not Use**
Pregnancy   ☐
Lactation   ☐          **Male** ☐          **Female** ☑
Children    ☐
Frail       ☐

# *Morus spp.*

# Mulberry

**Family** Moraceae      ☐ **Low Therapeutic Margin**

**Medicinal Uses**

Cough

Dizziness

Eye inflammation

Eye Strain

Fever

Fluid Retention

Headache, Tension

Sore throat

Toothache

Vertigo

**Magical Intentions**

Protection

Strength, To Instill

| **Parts Used** | **Element** | **Planet** |
|---|---|---|
| Fruit | Air | Mercury |
| Leaves | | |
| Root Bark | | |
| Twigs | | |

**Do Not Use**

Pregnancy ☐

Lactation ☐      **Male** ☑      **Female** ☐

Children ☐

Frail ☐

# *Musa sapientum*

## Banana

**Family** Musaceae

☐ **Low Therapeutic Margin**

**Medicinal Uses**
Bronchitis
Cough
Diarrhea
Ulcer, gastric

**Magical Intentions**
Fertility, To Increase
Prosperity, To Obtain

**Parts Used**
Fruit
Leaves
Root

**Element**
Water

**Planet**
Venus

**Do Not Use**
Pregnancy ☐
Lactation ☐
Children ☐
Frail ☐

**Male** ☐

**Female** ☑

# *Myrica cerifera*

## Bayberry, Wax Myrtle

**Family** Myricaceae          ☐ **Low Therapeutic Margin**

**Medicinal Uses**          **Magical Intentions**
Boils          Employment, To Attain/Maintain
Chills
Colds
Colitis
Diarrhea
Flu
Leukorrhea
Menorrhagia
Sore throat
Thrush
Ulcer, mouth
Wounds

**Parts Used**          **Element**          **Planet**
Bark
Leaves
Root
Wax

**Do Not Use**
Pregnancy ☑
Lactation ☑          **Male** ☐          **Female** ☐
Children ☐
Frail ☐

**Cautions**

Large doses may interfere with existing hypertensive, hypotensive or steroid therapy.

# *Myristica fragrans*

## Nutmeg, Mace

**Family** Myristicaceae    ☐ **Low Therapeutic Margin**

**Medicinal Uses**

Appetite Loss

Arthritis

Arthritis, rheumatoid

Diarrhea

Digestion, sluggish

Eczema

Gastritis

Nausea

Vomiting

**Magical Intentions**

Health, To Maintain

Luck, To Obtain

Mental Powers, To Strengthen

Money, Riches, Treasures, Wealth

Psychic Powers, To Strengthen

**Parts Used**

Oil

Seed

**Element**

Fire

**Planet**

Jupiter

**Do Not Use**

Pregnancy ☑

Lactation ☐    **Male** ☑    **Female** ☐

Children ☐

Frail ☐

**Cautions**

In excessive doses, nutmeg & mace are strongly stimulant, hallucinogenic & toxic. Do not take more than 3g of either herb daily.

**Notes**

Mace is the aril surrounding the seed casing. Nutmeg is the seed kernel.

# *Myrtus communis*

## Myrtle

**Family** Myrtaceae

☐ **Low Therapeutic Margin**

**Medicinal Uses**
Herpes simplex
Urinary tract infection

**Magical Intentions**
Fertility, To Increase
Love, To Attract
Money, Riches, Treasures, Wealth
Peace/Harmony, To Instill
Youth, To Maintain or Regain

**Parts Used**
Fruit
Leaves

**Element**
Water

**Planet**
Venus

**Do Not Use**
Pregnancy ☐
Lactation ☐
Children ☐
Frail ☐

**Male** ☐

**Female** ☑

# *Narcissus spp.*

## Daffodil, Narcissus

**Family** Amaryllidaceae | ☑ **Low Therapeutic Margin**

**Medicinal Uses**
None known

**Magical Intentions**
Fertility, To Increase
Love, Divination Of
Luck, To Obtain

**Parts Used**
Bulb
Flowers
Leaves

**Element**
Water

**Planet**
Venus

**Do Not Use**
Pregnancy ☑
Lactation ☑ **Male** ☐ **Female** ☑
Children ☑
Frail ☑

**Cautions**
POISON

# *Nepeta cataria*

## Catnip

**Family** Lamiaceae     ☐ **Low Therapeutic Margin**

**Medicinal Uses**
Bronchitis
Colds
Colic
Diarrhea
Dyspepsia
Fever
Flatulence
Flu
Gallbladder problems
Headache, Tension
Hiccoughs
Insomnia
Pertussis

**Magical Intentions**
Anger Management
Beauty, To Attain
Depression Management
Fertility, To Increase
Happiness, To Promote
Love, To Attract

**Parts Used**
Flowering Tops
Leaves

**Element**
Water

**Planet**
Venus

**Do Not Use**
Pregnancy ☑
Lactation ☑     **Male** ☐     **Female** ☑
Children ☐
Frail ☐

# *Nicotiana tabacum*

## Tobacco

**Family** Solanaceae    ☑ **Low Therapeutic Margin**

**Medicinal Uses**    **Magical Intentions**
None known    Healing, To Promote
Purification

**Parts Used**    **Element**    **Planet**
Leaves    Fire    Mars

**Do Not Use**
Pregnancy ☑
Lactation ☑    **Male** ☑    **Female** ☐
Children ☑
Frail ☑

**Cautions**
POISON

# *Ocimum basilicum*

## Basil (Sweet)

**Family** Lamiaceae

□ **Low Therapeutic Margin**

**Medicinal Uses**
Acne
Kidney stones

**Magical Intentions**
Exorcism
Love, To Attract
Money, Riches, Treasures, Wealth
Prophetic Dreams, To Cause
Protection

**Parts Used**
Aerial

**Element**
Fire

**Planet**
Mars

**Do Not Use**
Pregnancy □
Lactation □
Children ☑
Frail □

**Male** ☑

**Female** □

# *Olea europaea*

## Olive

**Family** Oleaceae

☐ **Low Therapeutic Margin**

**Medicinal Uses**
Bruises
Burns
Cholesterol, High
Constipation
Dandruff
Fever
Insect bites
Itching
Nervous tension
Sprain

**Magical Intentions**
Fertility, To Increase
Healing, To Promote
Lust, To Increase/Create
Peace/Harmony, To Instill
Protection

**Parts Used**
Leaves
Oil

**Element**
Fire

**Planet**
Sun

**Do Not Use**
Pregnancy ☐
Lactation ☐
Children ☐
Frail ☐

**Male** ☑

**Female** ☐

# *Orchis spp.*

## Adam & Eve

**Family** Orchidaceae    ☑ **Low Therapeutic Margin**

**Medicinal Uses**    **Magical Intentions**
None known    Happiness, To Promote
Love, To Attract

**Parts Used**    **Element**    **Planet**
Root    Water    Venus

**Do Not Use**
Pregnancy ☑
Lactation ☑    **Male** ☐    **Female** ☐
Children ☑
Frail ☑

# *Origanum dictamnus*

## Dittany of Crete

**Family** Lamiaceae     ☐ **Low Therapeutic Margin**

**Medicinal Uses**     **Magical Intentions**
None known     Astral Projection, To Aid
Manifestations, To Aid

**Parts Used**     **Element**     **Planet**
Leaves     Water     Venus

**Do Not Use**
Pregnancy ☐
Lactation ☐     **Male** ☐     **Female** ☑
Children ☐
Frail ☐

**Notes**
Not in current medicinal use but possibly a vulnerary

# *Origanum vulgare*

## Marjoram

**Family** Lamiaceae        □ **Low Therapeutic Margin**

| **Medicinal Uses** | **Magical Intentions** |
|---|---|
| Colds | Depression Management |
| Cough | Happiness, To Promote |
| Digestion, sluggish | Healing, To Promote |
| Flu | Health, To Maintain |
| Headache, Tension | Love, To Attract |
| | Money, Riches, Treasures, Wealth |
| | Protection |

**Parts Used**        **Element**        **Planet**
Leaves                 Air                Mercury

**Do Not Use**
Pregnancy ☑
Lactation □        **Male** ☑          **Female** □
Children □
Frail □

# *Oryza sativa*

## Rice

**Family** Poaceae

☐ **Low Therapeutic Margin**

**Medicinal Uses**
Arteriosclerosis
Cholesterol, High
Diarrhea

**Magical Intentions**
Fertility, To Increase
Money, Riches, Treasures, Wealth
Protection
Rain, To Cause To Fall

**Parts Used**
Oil
Seed

**Element**
Air

**Planet**
Sun

**Do Not Use**
Pregnancy ☐
Lactation ☐
Children ☐
Frail ☐

**Male** ☑

**Female** ☐

# *Paeonia officinalis*

## Peony

**Family** Paeoniaceae          ☐ **Low Therapeutic Margin**

**Medicinal Uses**          **Magical Intentions**

Nervous tension          Exorcism

Protection

**Parts Used**          **Element**          **Planet**

Root          Fire          Sun

**Do Not Use**

Pregnancy  ☐

Lactation   ☐          **Male**  ☑          **Female**  ☐

Children   ☐

Frail      ☐

# *Panax quinquefolius*

## American Ginseng

**Famil** Araliaceae

☐ **Low Therapeutic Margin**

**Medicinal Uses**
Debility

**Magical Intentions**
Healing, To Promote
Love, To Attract
Lust, To Increase/Create
Protection
Wishes, To Manifest

**Parts Used**
Root

**Element**
Fire

**Planet**
Sun

**Do Not Use**
Pregnancy ☑
Lactation ☑
Children ☐
Frail ☐

**Male** ☑

**Female** ☐

# *Papaver spp.*

## Poppy

**Family** Papaveraceae          □ **Low Therapeutic Margin**

**Medicinal Uses**          **Magical Intentions**
Nervous tension          Fertility, To Increase
Invisibility, To Attain
Love, To Attract
Luck, To Obtain
Money, Riches, Treasures, Wealth
Sleep

**Parts Used**          **Element**          **Planet**
Flowers          Water          Moon

**Do Not Use**
Pregnancy   □
Lactation   □          **Male**  □          **Female**  ☑
Children   □
Frail       □

# *Passiflora incarnata*

# Passionflower

**Family** Passifloraceae    ☐ **Low Therapeutic Margin**

**Medicinal Uses**

Blood pressure, high

Herpes simplex

Herpes zoster

**Magical Intentions**

Anger Management

Friendship, To Promote

Peace/Harmony, To Instill

Sleep

Stress Management

**Parts Used**

Leaves

Whole Plant

**Element**

Water

**Planet**

Venus

**Do Not Use**

Pregnancy    ☐

Lactation    ☐

Children    ☐

Frail    ☐

**Male** ☐

**Female** ☑

**Cautions**

Will potentiate the effects of sedative drugs. Theoretically, it is contraindicated for people taking MAOI inhibitors.

# *Pelargonium spp.*

## Geranium, Rose Geranium

**Family** Gentianaceae          ☐ **Low Therapeutic Margin**

**Medicinal Uses**          **Magical Intentions**

Chapped Skin          Fertility, To Increase

Health, To Maintain

Love, To Attract

Lust, To Increase/Create

Protection

Snakes, To Repel

**Parts Used**          **Element**          **Planet**

Essential Oil          Water          Venus

**Do Not Use**

Pregnancy   ☐

Lactation   ☐          **Male** ☐          **Female** ☑

Children   ☐

Frail   ☐

# *Persea americana*

## Avocado

**Family** Lauraceae

☐ **Low Therapeutic Margin**

**Medicinal Uses**
Cholesterol, High
Cough
Diabetes
Gout
Herpes simplex
Worms
Wounds

**Magical Intentions**
Beauty, To Attain
Love, To Attract
Lust, To Increase/Create

**Parts Used**
Bark
Fruit
Leaves
Seed

**Element**
Water

**Planet**
Venus

**Do Not Use**
Pregnancy  ☑
Lactation  ☐
Children  ☐
Frail  ☐

**Male** ☐

**Female** ☑

# *Petroselinum crispum*

## Parsley

**Family** Apiaceae          ☐ **Low Therapeutic Margin**

**Medicinal Uses**          **Magical Intentions**
Amenorrhea               Divination
Anemia                   Lust, To Increase/Create
Appetite Loss            Protection
Arthritis                Purification
Arthritis, rheumatoid
Asthma
Blood pressure, high
Colic
Conjunctivitis
Cough
Cystitis
Dandruff
Dysmenorrhea
Halitosis
Hepatitis
Insect bites
Jaundice
Kidney stones
Nephritis

| **Parts Used** | **Element** | **Planet** |
| --- | --- | --- |
| Essential Oil | Air | Mercury |
| Leaves | | |
| Root | | |
| Seed | | |

**Do Not Use**

Pregnancy ☑

Lactation ☑ **Male** ☑ **Female** ☐

Children ☐

Frail ☐

**Cautions**

Do not use where there is inflammatory kidney disease.

Essential oil must not be used in large doses. High levels of apiol & myristicin can cause deafness, giddiness, lowering of blood pressure, slowing of pulse, paralysis & fatty degeneration of liver & kidneys.

# *Phoenix dactylifera*

# Date Palm

**Family** Araceae          ☐ **Low Therapeutic Margin**

**Medicinal Uses**          **Magical Intentions**
Catarrh                    Fertility, To Increase
Colds
Fever
Sore throat

**Parts Used**          **Element**          **Planet**
Fruit                  Air                  Sun

**Do Not Use**
Pregnancy   ☐
Lactation   ☐          **Male**  ☑          **Female**  ☐
Children   ☐
Frail      ☐

# *Phytolacca americana*

# Poke

**Family** Phytolaccaeceae        ☐ **Low Therapeutic Margin**

**Medicinal Uses**            **Magical Intentions**
Catarrh                  Courage, To Attain
Laryngitis               Hexes, To Break
Lymphatic inflammation
Mastitis
Mumps
Sinusitis
Tonsillitis

**Parts Used**            **Element**            **Planet**
Root                  Fire                Mars

**Do Not Use**
Pregnancy  ☑
Lactation   ☑        **Male** ☑        **Female** ☐
Children   ☑
Frail      ☑

**Cautions**
In large doses, poke is a powerful emetic & purgative.

# *Pimenta dioica*

## Allspice, Pimento

**Family** Myrtaceae          □ **Low Therapeutic Margin**

**Medicinal Uses**          **Magical Intentions**
Diarrhea                   Healing, To Promote
Dyspepsia                  Love, To Attract
Flatulence                 Luck, To Obtain
                           Money, Riches, Treasures, Wealth

**Parts Used**          **Element**          **Planet**
Fruit                   Fire                 Mars

**Do Not Use**
Pregnancy   □
Lactation   □          **Male** ☑          **Female** □
Children   □
Frail   □

**Cautions**

# *Pimpinella anisum*

## Anise

**Family** Apiaceae

☐**Low Therapeutic Margin**

**Medicinal Uses**
Bronchitis
Colic
Flatulence
Pertussis

**Magical Intentions**
Divination
Love, To Attract
Protection
Purification
Youth, To Maintain or Regain

**Parts Used**
Seed

**Element**
Air

**Planet**
Jupiter

**Do Not Use**
Pregnancy ☐
Lactation ☐
Children ☐
Frail ☐

**Male** ☑

**Female** ☐

**Cautions**
May be allergenic & photosensitizing. May interfere with anticoagulant therapy.

# *Pinus spp.*

## Pine

**Family** Pinaceae          □ **Low Therapeutic Margin**

**Medicinal Uses**          **Magical Intentions**

Arthritis          Employment, To Attain/Maintain

Arthritis, rheumatoid          Exorcism

Colds          Fertility, To Increase

Cough          Healing, To Promote

Muscle strain          Money, Riches, Treasures, Wealth

          Protection

**Parts Used**          **Element**          **Planet**

Fruit          Air          Mars

Inner bark

Oil

**Do Not Use**

Pregnancy   □

Lactation   □          **Male** ☑          **Female** □

Children   □

Frail   □

# *Piper cubeba*

## Cubeb

**Family** Piperaceae          □ **Low Therapeutic Margin**

**Medicinal Uses**          **Magical Intentions**
Bronchitis               Love, To Attract
Flatulence
Urinary tract infection

**Parts Used**          **Element**          **Planet**
Fruit               Fire               Mars

**Do Not Use**
Pregnancy  □
Lactation  □          **Male** ☑          **Female** □
Children  □
Frail    □

**Cautions**
Do not use if suffering from inflammatory conditions of the digestive tract.

# *Piper methysticum*

## Kava Kava

**Family** Piperaceae          ☐ **Low Therapeutic Margin**

| **Medicinal Uses** | **Magical Intentions** |
|---|---|
| Anxiety | Luck, To Obtain |
| Depression | Protection |
| Headache, Tension | Visions, To Induce |

| **Parts Used** | **Element** | **Planet** |
|---|---|---|
| Root | Water | Saturn |

**Do Not Use**

Pregnancy  ☐

Lactation  ☐          **Male** ☐          **Female** ☑

Children  ☐

Frail  ☐

**Cautions**

A side effect of heavy kava consumption is "kava dermopathy", a skin rash. May potentiate the effects of substances that act on the Central Nervous System. Small number of hepatoxicity cases related to kava have been reported.

# *Piper nigrum*

## Pepper

**Family** Piperaceae          ☐ **Low Therapeutic Margin**

**Medicinal Uses**          **Magical Intentions**

Appetite Loss          Exorcism

Bloating          Protection

Constipation

Fever

Flatulence

Nausea

Toothache

**Parts Used**          **Element**          **Planet**

Essential Oil          Fire          Mars

Fruit

**Do Not Use**

Pregnancy  ☐

Lactation  ☐          **Male** ☑          **Female** ☐

Children  ☐

Frail  ☐

**Cautions**

Do not take essential oil internally.

**Notes**

Use liberally as a spice or make decoction of dried fruit. Essential oil can be diluted then massaged onto gums for toothache or into skin for rheumatic pain.

# *Pistacia lentiscus*

## Mastic

**Family** Anacardiaceae    ☐ **Low Therapeutic Margin**

**Medicinal Uses**
None known

**Magical Intentions**
Lust, To Increase/Create
Manifestations, To Aid
Psychic Powers, To Strengthen

**Parts Used**
Gum resin

**Element**
Air

**Planet**
Sun

**Do Not Use**
Pregnancy   ☐
Lactation   ☐     **Male** ☑       **Female** ☐
Children   ☐
Frail    ☐

**Notes**
Rarely used medicinally but could be employed as an expectorant for
bronchial troubles & coughs and to treat diarrhea.

# *Pistacia vera*

## Pistachio

**Family** Anacardiaceae

☐ **Low Therapeutic Margin**

**Medicinal Uses**
Cholesterol, High

**Magical Intentions**
Love Spells, To Break

**Parts Used**
Seed

**Element**
Air

**Planet**
Mercury

**Do Not Use**
Pregnancy ☐
Lactation ☐
Children ☐
Frail ☐

**Male** ☑

**Female** ☐

# *Plantago major*

## Broad-leafed Plantain

**Family** Plantaginaceae       □ **Low Therapeutic Margin**

**Medicinal Uses**
Bleeding
Boils
Burns
Cystitis
Diabetes
Eczema
Immune System
Infection
Inflammation
Insect bites
Leukorrhea
Lumbago
Mastitis
Ringworm
Scalds
Toothache
Water retention
Worms
Wounds

**Magical Intentions**
Healing, To Promote
Protection
Snakes, To Repel
Strength, To Instill

**Parts Used**
Flowering Tops
Leaves
Root
Seed

**Element**
Earth

**Planet**
Venus

**Do Not Use**

Pregnancy ☐

Lactation ☐      **Male** ☐      **Female** ☑

Children ☐

Frail ☐

**Cautions**

Reports of contact sensitization.

# *Pogostemon cablin*

## Patchouli

**Family** Lamiaceae          □ **Low Therapeutic Margin**

**Medicinal Uses**          **Magical Intentions**

None known

Fertility, To Increase

Lust, To Increase/Create

Money, Riches, Treasures, Wealth

Protection

**Parts Used**          **Element**          **Planet**

Leaves          Earth          Saturn

**Do Not Use**

Pregnancy   □

Lactation   □          **Male** □          **Female** ☑

Children   □

Frail   □

# *Polygala senega*

## Seneca Snakeroot

**Family** Polygalaceae          ☐ **Low Therapeutic Margin**

**Medicinal Uses**          **Magical Intentions**
Bronchial asthma          Luck, To Obtain
Laryngitis          Money, Riches, Treasures, Wealth
Pharyngitis          Protection

**Parts Used**          **Element**          **Planet**
Rhizome

**Do Not Use**
Pregnancy  ☐
Lactation  ☐          **Male**  ☐          **Female**  ☐
Children  ☐
Frail  ☐

**Cautions**
If too much is taken, may irritate lining of gut & cause vomiting.

## *Polygonatum multiflorum*

## Solomon's Seal

**Family** Liliaceae            □ **Low Therapeutic Margin**

**Medicinal Uses**        **Magical Intentions**
Bruises                  Exorcism
                         Protection

**Parts Used**           **Element**            **Planet**
Rhizome                  Water                  Saturn

**Do Not Use**
Pregnancy   □
Lactation   □        **Male** □              **Female** ☑
Children    □
Frail    □

**Cautions**
Do not take internally except under professional advice. The aerial parts are harmful if eaten.

# *Polygonum aviculare*

## Knotgrass, Knotweed

**Family** Polygonaceae          ☐ **Low Therapeutic Margin**

**Medicinal Uses**          **Magical Intentions**
Bleeding                  Health, To Maintain
Diarrhea
Hemorrhoids
Metrorrhagia
Worms

**Parts Used**          **Element**          **Planet**
Aerial                 Earth                Saturn

**Do Not Use**
Pregnancy   ☐
Lactation   ☐          **Male** ☐          **Female** ☑
Children   ☐
Frail      ☐

# *Polygonum bistorta*

## Bistort

**Family** Polygonaceae          ☐ **Low Therapeutic Margin**

**Medicinal Uses**            **Magical Intentions**
Burns                        Fertility, To Increase
Diarrhea                     Psychic Powers, To Strengthen
Dysentery
Hemorrhoids
Irritable bowel syndrome
Leukorrhea
Sore throat
Ulcer, mouth
Ulcer, peptic
Wounds

**Parts Used**          **Element**          **Planet**
Leaves                  Earth                Saturn
Rhizome

**Do Not Use**
Pregnancy   ☐
Lactation   ☐          **Male**  ☐                    **Female**  ☑
Children    ☐
Frail       ☐

**Cautions**
Use internally for no more than 3-4 weeks at a time.

**Notes**
One of the most astringent of all medicinal plants.

# *Populus candicans*

# Balm of Gilead

**Family** Salicaceae          □ **Low Therapeutic Margin**

**Medicinal Uses**          **Magical Intentions**
Bronchitis               None known
Cough
Eczema
Laryngitis
Psoriasis
Sore throat

**Parts Used**          **Element**          **Planet**
Unopened buds          Water               Saturn

**Do Not Use**
Pregnancy  □
Lactation  □          **Male**  □          **Female**  □
Children  □
Frail    □

# *Portulaca oleracea*

## Purslane

**Family** Portulacaceae    ☐ **Low Therapeutic Margin**

**Medicinal Uses**
Appendicitis
Boils
Diarrhea
Dysentery
Fever
Urethritis
Worms

**Magical Intentions**
Happiness, To Promote
Love, To Attract
Luck, To Obtain
Protection
Sleep

**Parts Used**
Aerial

**Element**
Water

**Planet**
Moon

**Do Not Use**
Pregnancy ☑
Lactation ☐
Children ☐
Frail ☐

**Male** ☐      **Female** ☑

# *Potentilla erecta*

# Cinquefoil, Tormentil

**Family** Rosaceae          ☐ **Low Therapeutic Margin**

**Medicinal Uses**          **Magical Intentions**

Burns                        Divination

Colitis                      Love, To Attract

Dysentery                    Money, Riches, Treasures, Wealth

Hemorrhoids                  Prophetic Dreams, To Cause

Irritable bowel syndrome     Protection

Pyorrhea                     Sleep

Throat infection

**Parts Used**          **Element**          **Planet**

Aerial                   Fire                 Jupiter

Root

**Do Not Use**

Pregnancy  ☐

Lactation  ☐          **Male** ☑          **Female** ☐

Children  ☐

Frail  ☐

378

# *Primula veris*

## Cowslip

**Family** Primulaceae          □ **Low Therapeutic Margin**

**Medicinal Uses**          **Magical Intentions**
Bleeding          Healing, To Promote
Bronchitis          Money, Riches, Treasures, Wealth
Cough          Youth, To Maintain or Regain

**Parts Used**          **Element**          **Planet**
Flowers          Water          Venus
Leaves
Root

**Do Not Use**
Pregnancy ☑
Lactation □          **Male** □          **Female** ☑
Children □
Frail □

**Cautions**
Do not take if allergic to aspirin or taking anticoagulant medication.
Excessive doses can cause vomiting & diarrhea.

# *Prunus amygdalus var dulcis*

## Almond (Sweet)

**Family** Rosaceae      ☐ **Low Therapeutic Margin**

| **Medicinal Uses** | **Magical Intentions** |
|---|---|
| Cholesterol, High | Anger Management |
| Diabetes | Immortality, To Attain |
| | Money, Riches, Treasures, Wealth |
| | Prosperity, To Obtain |
| | Wisdom, To Promote |

| **Parts Used** | **Element** | **Planet** |
|---|---|---|
| Oil | Water | Sun |
| Seed | | |

**Do Not Use**

| | | |
|---|---|---|
| Pregnancy ☐ | | |
| Lactation ☐ | **Male** ☑ | **Female** ☐ |
| Children ☐ | | |
| Frail ☐ | | |

**Cautions**

In large doses, oil is toxic, causing Central Nervous System depression & respiratory failure.

380

# *Prunus armeniaca*

## Apricot

**Family** Rosaceae    ☐ **Low Therapeutic Margin**

**Medicinal Uses**      **Magical Intentions**
Appetite Loss          Love, To Attract
Inflammation

**Parts Used**      **Element**      **Planet**
Bark             Water         Venus
Fruit
Seed

**Do Not Use**
Pregnancy ☐
Lactation ☐      **Male** ☐        **Female** ☑
Children ☐
Frail ☐

**Cautions**
Apricot kernels are highly toxic and should not be consumed.

# *Prunus avium*

# Sweet Cherry

**Family** Rosaceae     □ **Low Therapeutic Margin**

| **Medicinal Uses** | **Magical Intentions** |
| --- | --- |
| Arthritis | Divination |
| Cystitis | Love, To Attract |
| Gout | |

| **Parts Used** | **Element** | **Planet** |
| --- | --- | --- |
| Fruit | Water | Venus |
| Stem | | |

**Do Not Use**

Pregnancy  □

Lactation  □      **Male** □        **Female** ☑

Children  □

Frail   □

**Cautions**

Seeds are toxic and should not be consumed.

# *Prunus domestica*

## Plum

**Family** Rosaceae      □ **Low Therapeutic Margin**

**Medicinal Uses**      **Magical Intentions**
Constipation      Healing, To Promote

**Parts Used**      **Element**      **Planet**
Fruit      Water      Venus

**Do Not Use**
Pregnancy   □
Lactation   □      **Male** □      **Female** ☑
Children   □
Frail   □

**Notes**
When dried known as "prune"

# *Prunus persica*

## Peach

**Family** Rosaceae

☐ **Low Therapeutic Margin**

**Medicinal Uses**
Bronchitis
Cough
Pertussis

**Magical Intentions**
Exorcism
Protection

**Parts Used**
Bark
Flowers
Leaves

**Element**
Fire

**Planet**
Sun

**Do Not Use**
Pregnancy ☐
Lactation ☐
Children ☐
Frail ☐

**Male** ☑

**Female** ☐

# *Prunus serotina*

## Wild Cherry, Black Cherry

**Family** Rosaceae

☐ **Low Therapeutic Margin**

**Medicinal Uses**
Bronchitis
Cough
Digestion, sluggish
Eye inflammation
Pertussis

**Magical Intentions**
None known

**Parts Used**
Bark

**Element**
Water

**Planet**
Venus

**Do Not Use**
Pregnancy ☐
Lactation ☐       **Male** ☐       **Female** ☐
Children ☐
Frail ☐

# *Pterocarpus santalinus*

## Red Sandalwood, Sanderswood

**Family** Caesalpiniaceae          ☐ **Low Therapeutic Margin**

**Medicinal Uses**          **Magical Intentions**

Diabetes          Divination

Exorcism

Healing, To Promote

Love, To Attract

Meditation, To Aid

Protection

Spirituality, To Strengthen

**Parts Used**          **Element**          **Planet**

Bark          Water          Venus

**Do Not Use**

Pregnancy   ☐

Lactation   ☐          **Male** ☐                    **Female** ☑

Children   ☐

Frail      ☐

# *Pulsatilla vulgaris*

## Pasqueflower

**Family** Ranunculaceae          ☐**Low Therapeutic Margin**

**Medicinal Uses**          **Magical Intentions**
Asthma                    Healing, To Promote
Boils                     Health, To Maintain
Dysmenorrhea              Protection
Earache
Headache, Tension
Insomnia
Respiratory infection

**Parts Used**          **Element**          **Planet**
Aerial                 Fire                 Mars

**Do Not Use**
Pregnancy  ☐
Lactation  ☐          **Male** ☑          **Female** ☐
Children  ☐
Frail  ☐

**Cautions**
Fresh pulsatilla is poisonous & should not be ingested. External
contact with fresh plant should also be avoided. Toxic principles
rapidly degrade during drying.

# *Punica granatum*

# Pomegranate

**Family** Lythraceae                    ☐ **Low Therapeutic Margin**

**Medicinal Uses**          **Magical Intentions**
Flatulence                  Divination
Indigestion                 Fertility, To Increase
Worms                       Luck, To Obtain
                            Money, Riches, Treasures, Wealth
                            Wishes, To Manifest

**Parts Used**          **Element**              **Planet**
Bark                    Fire                     Mercury
Fruit
Peel

**Do Not Use**
Pregnancy   ☐
Lactation   ☐          **Male** ☑              **Female** ☐
Children    ☐
Frail       ☐

**Cautions**

Do not use the rind or bark medicinally unless under professional supervision.

# *Pyrus malus*

## Apple

**Family** Rosaceae

☐ **Low Therapeutic Margin**

**Medicinal Uses**
Constipation
Eye inflammation
Fever

**Magical Intentions**
Healing, To Promote
Immortality, To Attain
Love, Divination Of

**Parts Used**
Fruit
Juice

**Element**
Water

**Planet**
Venus

**Do Not Use**
Pregnancy ☐
Lactation ☐
Children ☐
Frail ☐

**Male** ☐

**Female** ☑

**Cautions**
Seeds are poisonous in large amounts.

# *Quercus alba*

## Oak

**Family** Fagaceae

☐ **Low Therapeutic Margin**

**Medicinal Uses**

Diarrhea

Dysentery

Hemorrhoids

Laryngitis

Leukorrhea

Pharyngitis

Tonsillitis

**Magical Intentions**

Fertility, To Increase

Healing, To Promote

Health, To Maintain

Luck, To Obtain

Money, Riches, Treasures, Wealth

Protection

**Parts Used**

Bark

**Element**

Fire

**Planet**

Sun

**Do Not Use**

Pregnancy ☐

Lactation ☐

Children ☐

Frail ☐

**Male** ☑

**Female** ☐

**Cautions**

Do not use when constipation is present.

# *Raphanus sativus*

## Radish

**Family** Brassicaceae    ☐ **Low Therapeutic Margin**

**Medicinal Uses**
Kidney stones

**Magical Intentions**
Lust, To Increase/Create
Protection

**Parts Used**
Fruit
Root

**Element**
Fire

**Planet**
Mars

**Do Not Use**
Pregnancy  ☐
Lactation  ☐     **Male** ☑      **Female** ☐
Children  ☐
Frail   ☐

# *Rhamnus frangula*

## Buckthorn

**Family** Rhamnaceae    ☐ **Low Therapeutic Margin**

**Medicinal Uses**

Constipation

**Magical Intentions**

Exorcism

Legal Matters, To Assist In

Protection

Wishes, To Manifest

| **Parts Used** | **Element** | **Planet** |
|---|---|---|
| Bark | Water | Saturn |

**Do Not Use**

Pregnancy ☐

Lactation ☐    **Male** ☐      **Female** ☑

Children ☐

Frail ☐

**Cautions**

Use only the dried bark that has been stored for at least one year.
Fresh bark is violently purgative.

# *Rhamnus purshiana*

## Cascara Sagrada

**Family** Rhamnaceae     ☐ **Low Therapeutic Margin**

**Medicinal Uses**     **Magical Intentions**
Constipation     Legal Matters, To Assist In
Hemorrhoids     Money, Riches, Treasures, Wealth
Lice     Protection

**Parts Used**     **Element**     **Planet**
Bark

**Do Not Use**
Pregnancy ☑
Lactation ☐     **Male** ☐     **Female** ☐
Children ☐
Frail ☐

**Cautions**
Contraindicated for spastic bowel conditions.
Excessive intake may lead to hypokalemia, nausea, vomiting,
cramping & excessive diarrhea.
Should be used with carminatives. Bark must be at least 1 year old or
it is too harsh.

# *Rheum officinale*

## Turkey Rhubarb

**Family** Polygonaceae      ☐ **Low Therapeutic Margin**

**Medicinal Uses**          **Magical Intentions**
Appetite Loss              Protection
Constipation
Digestion, sluggish
Hemorrhoids

**Parts Used**        **Element**        **Planet**
Rhizome              Earth              Venus
Root

**Do Not Use**
Pregnancy  ☑
Lactation  ☐        **Male** ☐              **Female** ☑
Children   ☑
Frail      ☐

**Cautions**
Do not use with intestinal obstructions, abdominal pain of unknown origin, or any inflammatory condition of the intestines such as appendicitis, colitis, Crohn's disease or IBS.
Should be used with caution if you have a history of kidney stones.
Excessive doses will cause griping & severe diarrhea.

# *Rheum palmatum*

## Chinese Rhubarb

**Family** Polygonaceae      ☐ **Low Therapeutic Margin**

**Medicinal Uses**

Constipation

Diarrhea

Dysentery

Dyspepsia

**Magical Intentions**

Protection

**Parts**

Rhizome

**Element**

Earth

**Planet**

Venus

**Do Not Use**

Pregnancy ☐

Lactation ☐     **Male** ☐     **Female** ☑

Children ☐

Frail ☐

**Cautions**

May cause increased effectiveness & toxic effects of cardiac glycosides and an effect on the action of antiarrhythmic drugs because it causes a loss of potassium. May reduce the absorption time of orally administered drugs. May color the urine red or yellow.

# *Rhodymenia palmata*

## Dulse

**Family** Palmariaceae        □ **Low Therapeutic Margin**

**Medicinal Uses**        **Magical Intentions**
None known        Lust, To Increase/Create

**Parts Used**        **Element**        **Planet**
Whole Plant        Water        Moon

**Do Not Use**
Pregnancy □
Lactation □        **Male** □        **Female** ☑
Children □
Frail □

**Notes**
Red Algae: full of vitamins & minerals

# *Rosa spp.*

## Rose

**Family** Rosaceae

☐ **Low Therapeutic Margin**

**Medicinal Uses**
Cramp
Dizziness
Earache
Headache, Tension
Toothache

**Magical Intentions**
Anger Management
Divination
Healing, To Promote
Love, Divination Of
Love, To Attract
Luck, To Obtain
Protection
Psychic Powers, To Strengthen

**Parts Used**
Flowers
Essential Oil

**Element**
Water

**Planet**
Venus

**Do Not Use**
Pregnancy ☐
Lactation ☐
Children ☐
Frail ☐

**Male** ☐

**Female** ☑

# *Rosmarinus officinalis*

## Rosemary

**Family** Lamiaceae ☐ **Low Therapeutic Margin**

| **Medicinal Uses** | **Magical Intentions** |
|---|---|
| Alopecia | Exorcism |
| Blood Pressure, low | Healing, To Promote |
| Circulation, poor | Love, To Attract |
| Digestion, sluggish | Lust, To Increase/Create |
| Dyspepsia | Mental Powers, To Strengthen |
| Headache, Tension | Protection |
| Migraine | Purification |
| Neuralgia | Sleep |
| Sciatica | Theft, To Prevent |
| | Youth, To Maintain or Regain |

**Parts Used**     **Element**     **Planet**
Leaves           Fire           Sun
Twigs

**Do Not Use**
Pregnancy  ☐
Lactation  ☐          **Male** ☑          **Female** ☐
Children  ☐
Frail  ☐

# *Rubus idaeus*

# Raspberry (Red)

**Family** Rosaceae          □ **Low Therapeutic Margin**

**Medicinal Uses**          **Magical Intentions**
Blood pressure, high          Love, To Attract
Catarrh          Protection
Childbirth
Constipation
Diarrhea
Fever
Hyperglycemia
Menorrhagia
Nausea
Sore throat

**Parts Used**          **Element**          **Planet**
Bark          Water          Venus
Fruit
Leaves
Stem

**Do Not Use**
Pregnancy  □
Lactation  □          **Male** □          **Female** ☑
Children  □
Frail  □

**Cautions**
Do not use where there's a history of miscarriage.

# *Rubus villosus*

## Blackberry

**Family** Rosaceae          ☐ **Low Therapeutic Margin**

**Medicinal Uses**          **Magical Intentions**

Burns                    Healing, To Promote

Diarrhea                 Money, Riches, Treasures, Wealth

Dysentery                Protection

Leukorrhea

**Parts Used**          **Element**          **Planet**

Root Bark              Water                Venus

**Do Not Use**

Pregnancy  ☐

Lactation   ☐          **Male** ☐                **Female** ☑

Children   ☐

Frail      ☐

# *Rumex crispus*

# Yellow Dock

**Family** Polygonaceae

☐ **Low Therapeutic Margin**

**Medicinal Uses**
Acne
Anemia
Arthritis, rheumatoid
Catarrh
Constipation
Cough
Cradle cap
Dermatitis
Diarrhea
Eczema
Fever
Gallbladder problems
Jaundice
Lymphatic inflammation
Psoriasis
Ringworm
Sores
Swelling
Tumors

**Magical Intentions**
Fertility, To Increase
Healing, To Promote
Money, Riches, Treasures, Wealth

**Parts Used**
Leaves
Root
Seed

**Element**
Air

**Planet**
Jupiter

**Do Not Use**

Pregnancy ☑

Lactation ☐       **Male** ☑       **Female** ☐

Children ☐

Frail ☐

**Cautions**

Individuals with a history of kidney stones should use Yellow Dock cautiously. A stimulant laxative, it should not be taken when there is a history of intestinal obstruction.

# *Ruta graveolens*

# Rue

**Family** Rutaceae          ☐ **Low Therapeutic Margin**

**Medicinal Uses**          **Magical Intentions**
Blood pressure, high          Exorcism
Headache, Tension          Gossip, To Halt
Metrorrhagia          Healing, To Promote
          Health, To Maintain
          Love, To Attract
          Mental Powers, To Strengthen
          Protection

**Parts Used**          **Element**          **Planet**
Aerial          Fire          Mars

**Do Not Use**
Pregnancy  ☑
Lactation  ☐          **Male** ☑          **Female** ☐
Children  ☐
Frail  ☐

**Cautions**
Rue essential oil is a powerful abortifacient and should be avoided at all times.

# *Saccharum officinarum*

## Sugar Cane

**Family** Poaceae     ☐ **Low Therapeutic Margin**

**Medicinal Uses**
Arthritis
Boils
Cancer
Colds
Cough
Diarrhea
Dysentery
Fever
Hiccoughs
Inflammation
Laryngitis
Pertussis
Sore throat
Wounds

**Magical Intentions**
Love, To Attract
Lust, To Increase/Create

**Parts Used**
Juice
Root

**Element**
Water

**Planet**
Venus

**Do Not Use**
Pregnancy ☐
Lactation ☐     **Male** ☐         **Female** ☑
Children ☐
Frail ☐

# *Salix alba*

# White Willow

**Family** Salicaceae
☐ **Low Therapeutic Margin**

**Medicinal Uses**
Arthritis, rheumatoid
Fever
Gout
Muscle strain

**Magical Intentions**
Divination
Healing, To Promote
Love, Divination Of
Love, To Attract
Protection

**Parts Used**
Bark

**Element**
Water

**Planet**
Moon

**Do Not Use**
Pregnancy  ☐
Lactation  ☐
Children  ☐
Frail  ☐

**Male**  ☐

**Female**  ☑

**Cautions**
Should be avoided by people with salicylate sensitivity.

# *Salvia officinalis*

## Sage

**Family** Lamiaceae     ☐ **Low Therapeutic Margin**

| **Medicinal Uses** | **Magical Intentions** |
|---|---|
| Amenorrhea | Immortality, To Attain |
| Bleeding | Longevity, To Attain |
| Cancer | Mental Powers, To Strengthen |
| Catarrh | Protection |
| Diabetes | Wisdom, To Promote |
| Dizziness | Wishes, To Manifest |
| Dysmenorrhea | |
| Fever | |
| Flatulence | |
| Indigestion | |
| Insect bites | |
| Laryngitis | |
| Nervous tension | |
| Respiratory infection | |
| Sore throat | |
| Tonsillitis | |
| Wounds | |

| **Parts Used** | **Element** | **Planet** |
|---|---|---|
| Essential Oil | Air | Jupiter |
| Leaves | | |

**Do Not Use**
Pregnancy ☑
Lactation ☑     **Male** ☑     **Female** ☐
Children ☐
Frail ☐

## Cautions

Do not use during lactation as it will dry up the milk supply. Because of this, it is useful for a mother who is weaning an older baby. Not for long term use and do not exceed recommended dosage.

Essential oil is reported to be a moderate skin irritant.

Contains thujone which is toxic in large doses.

# *Salvia officinalis var rubia*

## Red Sage

**Family** Lamiaceae          ☐ **Low Therapeutic Margin**

**Medicinal Uses**          **Magical Intentions**
Dyspepsia          Immortality, To Attain
Gingivitis          Longevity, To Attain
Laryngitis          Mental Powers, To Strengthen
Pharyngitis          Protection
Throat infection          Wisdom, To Promote
Tonsillitis          Wishes, To Manifest
Wounds

**Parts Used**          **Element**          **Planet**
Leaves

**Do Not Use**
Pregnancy  ☑
Lactation   ☑          **Male**  ☐          **Female**  ☐
Children   ☐
Frail      ☐

**Cautions**
Adverse reactions are likely only with overdoses or prolonged use.
The thujone causes symptoms such as tachycardia, hot flashes, convulsions & dizziness.

# *Sambucus nigra*

## Black Elder

**Family** Caprifoliaceae ☐ **Low Therapeutic Margin**

**Medicinal Uses**
Bruises
Chillblains
Colds
Flu
Sinusitis
Sprain
Wounds

**Magical Intentions**
Exorcism
Healing, To Promote
Prosperity, To Obtain
Protection
Sleep
Theft, To Prevent

**Parts Used**
Berries
Flowers
Leaves

**Element**
Water

**Planet**
Venus

**Do Not Use**
Pregnancy ☐
Lactation ☐     **Male** ☐          **Female** ☑
Children ☐
Frail ☐

# *Sanguinaria canadensis*

## Bloodroot

**Family** Papaveraceae          ☐ **Low Therapeutic Margin**

**Medicinal Uses**          **Magical Intentions**
Asthma                     Love, To Attract
Bronchitis                 Protection
Emphysema                  Purification
Laryngitis

**Parts Used**          **Element**          **Planet**
Root                    Fire                 Mars

**Do Not Use**
Pregnancy  ☑
Lactation  ☐          **Male**  ☑          **Female**  ☐
Children   ☐
Frail      ☐

**Cautions**
Although there are no published reports of human toxicity, at high doses the herb may cause nausea, vomiting, a sensation of burning in all contacted mucous membranes, bradycardia & hypertension.

# *Santalum album*

# White Sandalwood

**Family** Santalaceae      ☐ **Low Therapeutic Margin**

**Medicinal Uses**       **Magical Intentions**
Bronchitis            Exorcism
Cystitis             Healing, To Promote
Urinary tract infection      Protection
                Spirituality, To Strengthen

**Parts Used**       **Element**        **Planet**
Bark            Water          Moon
Oil

**Do Not Use**
Pregnancy   ☐
Lactation   ☐      **Male** ☐         **Female** ☑
Children   ☐
Frail     ☐

# *Satureja hortensis*

## Savory

**Family** Lamiaceae

☐ **Low Therapeutic Margin**

**Medicinal Uses**
None known

**Magical Intentions**
Mental Powers, To Strengthen
Sexual Potency, To Regain or maintain

**Parts Used**
Whole Plant

**Element**
Air

**Planet**
Mercury

**Do Not Use**
Pregnancy ☐
Lactation ☐
Children ☐
Frail ☐

**Male** ☑

**Female** ☐

# *Scrophularia nodosa*

## Figwort

**Family** Scrophulariaceae    ☐ **Low Therapeutic Margin**

**Medicinal Uses**
Constipation
Eczema
Psoriasis

**Magical Intentions**
Health, To Maintain
Protection

**Parts Used**
Aerial

**Element**
Water

**Planet**
Venus

**Do Not Use**
Pregnancy  ☐
Lactation  ☐    **Male** ☐    **Female** ☑
Children  ☐
Frail  ☐

**Cautions**
Because it is a heart stimulant, it should be avoided by people with tachycardia.

# *Scutellaria lateriflora*

## Scullcap

**Family** Lamiaceae          ☐ **Low Therapeutic Margin**

**Medicinal Uses**          **Magical Intentions**
Blood pressure, high          Fidelity, to Ensure
Digestion, sluggish          Love, To Attract
Drug Withdrawal          Peace/Harmony, To Instill
Epilepsy          Stress Management
Headache, Tension
Hiccoughs
Hysteria
Insomnia
Migraine
Nervous tension
Seizures
Spasm
Tremors

**Parts Used**          **Element**          **Planet**
Aerial          Water          Saturn

**Do Not Use**
Pregnancy   ☐
Lactation   ☐          **Male** ☐          **Female** ☑
Children   ☐
Frail   ☐

**Cautions**
Can potentiate the effects of sedative medications.

# *Senecio vulgaris*

## Groundsel

**Family** Asteraceae      ☑ **Low Therapeutic Margin**

**Medicinal Uses**      **Magical Intentions**
Kidney stones      Healing, To Promote
Health, To Maintain

**Parts Used**      **Element**      **Planet**
Root      Water      Venus

**Do Not Use**
Pregnancy  ☐
Lactation  ☐      **Male** ☐      **Female** ☑
Children  ☐
Frail  ☐

# *Senna alexandrina*

## Senna

**Family** Fabaceae      □ **Low Therapeutic Margin**

| **Medicinal Uses** | **Magical Intentions** |
|---|---|
| Constipation | Love, To Attract |
| Halitosis | |
| Worms | |

**Parts Used**      **Element**      **Planet**

Leaves           Air            Mercury

Seed

**Do Not Use**

Pregnancy  □

Lactation  □        **Male ☑**           **Female □**

Children  □

Frail    □

**Cautions**

Should not be used by anyone with inflammation of the alimentary tract, irritable bowel disorder, hemorrhoids, or prolapse, as its action can be too severe. Should be used in small doses. Use cold decoctions or infusions as they are less likely to cause nausea.

Also contraindicated for intestinal obstruction, abdominal pain of unknown origin, inflammatory conditions of the intestines including appendicitis, colitis, Crohn's disease and irritable bowel.

Excessive use of Senna can cause excessive potassium loss.

# *Silybum marianum*

# Milk Thistle

**Family** Asteraceae    ☐ **Low Therapeutic Margin**

**Medicinal Uses**    **Magical Intentions**
Cirrhosis, liver    Snakes, To Enrage
Hepatitis

**Parts Used**    **Element**    **Planet**
Seed    Fire    Mars

**Do Not Use**
Pregnancy ☐
Lactation ☐    **Male** ☑    **Female** ☐
Children ☐
Frail ☐

# *Smilax spp.*

# Sarsaparilla

**Family** Liliaceae      ☐ **Low Therapeutic Margin**

**Medicinal Uses**

Psoriasis

**Magical Intentions**

Love, To Attract

Money, Riches, Treasures, Wealth

| **Parts Used** | **Element** | **Planet** |
|---|---|---|
| Rhizome | Fire | Jupiter |
| Root | | |

**Do Not Use**

Pregnancy ☐

Lactation ☐      **Male** ☑      **Female** ☐

Children ☐

Frail ☐

**Cautions**

May increase the absorption of digitalis glycosides.

# *Solanum lycopersicum*

## Tomato

**Family** Solanaceae

☐ **Low Therapeutic Margin**

**Medicinal Uses**
Cancer

**Magical Intentions**
Love, To Attract
Prosperity, To Obtain
Protection

**Parts Used**
Fruit

**Element**
Water

**Planet**
Venus

**Do Not Use**
Pregnancy ☐
Lactation ☐
Children ☐
Frail ☐

**Male** ☐

**Female** ☑

**Notes**

Recent research suggests the lycopenes in tomatoes could help with prostate cancer.

# *Solanum tuberosum*

## Potato

**Family** Solanaceae      □ **Low Therapeutic Margin**

**Medicinal Uses**          **Magical Intentions**
Burns                      Healing, To Promote
Headache, Tension
Hemorrhoids
Ulcer, peptic

**Parts Used**          **Element**          **Planet**
Fruit                   Earth                Moon

**Do Not Use**
Pregnancy  □
Lactation   □          **Male**  □          **Female**  ☑
Children   □
Frail      □

**Cautions**
Do not drink the juice of more than one large potato per day.

# *Solidago virgaurea*

## Goldenrod

**Family** Asteraceae      ☐ **Low Therapeutic Margin**

**Medicinal Uses**

Cystitis

Dyspepsia

Flu

Laryngitis

Pharyngitis

Urethritis

Urinary tract infection

Wounds

**Magical Intentions**

Divination

Money, Riches, Treasures, Wealth

| **Parts Used** | **Element** | **Planet** |
|---|---|---|
| Aerial | Air | Venus |

**Do Not Use**

Pregnancy ☐

Lactation ☐      **Male** ☐             **Female** ☑

Children ☐

Frail ☐

**Cautions**

May cause allergic reactions in people sensitive to Asteraceae Family.

# *Stachys officinalis*

## Wood Betony, Bishop's Wort

**Family** Lamiaceae          □ **Low Therapeutic Margin**

**Medicinal Uses**          **Magical Intentions**
Headache, Tension          Love, To Attract
Nervous tension          Protection
Nosebleed          Purification
PMS

**Parts Used**          **Element**          **Planet**
Aerial          Fire          Jupiter

**Do Not Use**
Pregnancy  ☑
Lactation  □          **Male**  ☑          **Female**  □
Children  □
Frail  □

# *Stellaria media*

# Chickweed

**Family** Caryophyllaceae    ☐ **Low Therapeutic Margin**

| **Medicinal Uses** | **Magical Intentions** |
|---|---|
| Arthritis, rheumatoid | Fertility, To Increase |
| Chapped Skin | Love, To Attract |
| Conjunctivitis | |
| Cracked skin | |
| Dermatitis | |
| Eczema | |
| Psoriasis | |

| **Parts Used** | **Element** | **Planet** |
|---|---|---|
| Flowering Herb | Water | Moon |

**Do Not Use**

Pregnancy ☐

Lactation ☐    **Male** ☐        **Female** ☑

Children ☐

Frail ☐

**Notes**

Herb should be used fresh or in the form of a water extract.

# *Styrax benzoin*

## Benzoin, Styrax

**Family** Styraceae        ☐ **Low Therapeutic Margin**

**Medicinal Uses**         **Magical Intentions**
Bronchitis              Astral Projection, To Aid
Cold sores              Meditation, To Aid
Colds                Mental Powers, To Strengthen
Cough                Prosperity, To Obtain
                   Purification

**Parts Used**       **Element**        **Planet**
Essential Oil        Air            Mars
Gum resin

**Do Not Use**
Pregnancy   ☐
Lactation   ☐      **Male** ☑            **Female** ☐
Children   ☐
Frail    ☐

**Notes**
Usually used as a preservative agent but can be used similarly to
Myrrh for antibacterial action.

## *Succisa pratensis*

## Devil's Bit

**Family** Dipsacaceae          ☐ **Low Therapeutic Margin**

**Medicinal Uses**          **Magical Intentions**
Cough                               Exorcism
Fever                               Luck, To Obtain
                                    Lust, To Increase/Create
                                    Protection

**Parts Used**          **Element**                    **Planet**
Aerial

**Do Not Use**
Pregnancy   ☐
Lactation   ☐          **Male**  ☑          **Female**  ☐
Children    ☐
Frail       ☐

# *Symphytum officinale*

## Comfrey

**Family** Boraginaceae     □ **Low Therapeutic Margin**

**Medicinal Uses**

Broken bones

Colds

Cough

Muscle strain

Sprain

Wounds

**Magical Intentions**

Money, Riches, Treasures, Wealth

Stress Management

Travelling, to Protect While

**Parts Used**

Leaves

Rhizome

Root

**Element**

Water

**Planet**

Saturn

**Do Not Use**

Pregnancy □

Lactation □

Children □

Frail □

**Male** □      **Female** ☑

**Cautions**

Especially root, contains pyrrolizidine alkaloids & N-oxides – potential hepatoxicity.

426

# *Symplocarpus foetidus*

## Skunk Cabbage

**Family** Araceae             ☐ **Low Therapeutic Margin**

**Medicinal Uses**          **Magical Intentions**
Asthma                      Legal Matters, To Assist In
Bronchitis
Fever
Pertussis

**Parts Used**          **Element**          **Planet**
Rhizome                 Water                Saturn
Root

**Do Not Use**
Pregnancy   ☐
Lactation   ☐          **Male**  ☐               **Female**  ☑
Children    ☐
Frail       ☐

# *Syringa vulgaris*

## Lilac

**Family** Oleaceae

☐ **Low Therapeutic Margin**

**Medicinal Uses**
Fever
Malaria

**Magical Intentions**
Beauty, To Attain
Exorcism
Protection

**Parts Used**
Fruit
Leaves

**Element**
Water

**Planet**
Venus

**Do Not Use**
Pregnancy ☐
Lactation ☐
Children ☐
Frail ☐

**Male** ☐

**Female** ☑

# *Syzgium aromaticum*

## Cloves

**Family** Myrtaceae     ☐ **Low Therapeutic Margin**

**Medicinal Uses**

Asthma

Bronchial asthma

Bronchitis

Diarrhea

Flatulence

Worms

**Magical Intentions**

Divination

Exorcism

Gossip, To Halt

Love, To Attract

Money, Riches, Treasures, Wealth

Protection

| **Parts Used** | **Element** | **Planet** |
| --- | --- | --- |
| Essential Oil | Fire | Jupiter |
| Flowers | | |

**Do Not Use**

Pregnancy ☐

Lactation ☐     **Male** ☑       **Female** ☐

Children ☐

Frail ☐

# *Tamarindus indicus*

## Tamarind

**Family** Caesalpiniaceae      ☐ **Low Therapeutic Margin**

**Medicinal Uses**       **Magical Intentions**
Morning sickness        Love, To Attract

**Parts Used**       **Element**       **Planet**
Bark                 Water             Saturn
Fruit
Leaves

**Do Not Use**
Pregnancy  ☐
Lactation  ☐       **Male** ☐            **Female** ☑
Children   ☐
Frail      ☐

# *Tanacetum parthenium*

## Feverfew

**Family** Asteraceae                    ☐ **Low Therapeutic Margin**

**Medicinal Uses**              **Magical Intentions**
Dizziness                       Protection
Metrorrhagia
Migraine
Tinnitus

**Parts Used**              **Element**              **Planet**
Leaves                      Water                   Venus

**Do Not Use**
Pregnancy ☑
Lactation ☐              **Male** ☑              **Female** ☐
Children ☐
Frail ☐

**Cautions**

May cause allergic reactions in people sensitive to Asteraceae Family.
Fresh leaves may cause mouth ulcers in susceptible people. May
interfere with aspirin & other anticoagulant medications.

# *Tanacetum vulgare*

## Tansy

**Family** Asteraceae    ☑ **Low Therapeutic Margin**

**Medicinal Uses**
Amenorrhea
Nausea
Scabies
Worms

**Magical Intentions**
Health, To Maintain
Longevity, To Attain

**Parts Used**
Aerial

**Element**
Water

**Planet**
Venus

**Do Not Use**
Pregnancy ☑
Lactation ☑
Children ☐
Frail ☐

**Male** ☐

**Female** ☑

**Cautions**
Overdose of oil or tea can be fatal.

# *Taraxacum officinale*

# Dandelion

**Family** Asteraceae

☐ **Low Therapeutic Margin**

**Medicinal Uses**
Arthritis, rheumatoid
Jaundice
Water retention

**Magical Intentions**
Divination
Spirits, To Call
Wishes, To Manifest

**Parts Used**
Leaves
Root

**Element**
Air

**Planet**
Jupiter

**Do Not Use**
Pregnancy ☐
Lactation ☐       **Male** ☑       **Female** ☐
Children ☐
Frail ☐

**Cautions**
May cause allergic reactions in people sensitive to Asteraceae Family.
Rare reports of contact dermatitis in people coming in contact with
latex found in stems

# *Thalictrum spp.*

## Meadow Rue

**Family** Ranunculaceae    ☐ **Low Therapeutic Margin**

**Medicinal Uses**
None known

**Magical Intentions**
Divination

**Parts Used**
Leaves

**Element**

**Planet**

**Do Not Use**
Pregnancy ☐
Lactation ☐    **Male** ☐    **Female** ☐
Children ☐
Frail ☐

# *Thymus vulgaris*

# Thyme

**Family** Lamiaceae          ☐ **Low Therapeutic Margin**

**Medicinal Uses**            **Magical Intentions**
Amenorrhea                    Courage, To Attain
Arthritis, rheumatoid        Healing, To Promote
Asthma                        Health, To Maintain
Bedwetting                    Love, To Attract
Bronchitis                    Psychic Powers, To Strengthen
Burns                         Purification
Candida                       Sleep
Chillblains
Colic
Conjunctivitis
Cough
Cramp
Diarrhea
Digestion, sluggish
Dysmenorrhea
Eczema
Fever
Flatulence
Halitosis
Headache, Tension
Laryngitis
Pertussis
Psoriasis
Ringworm
Sore throat
Spasm
Toothache

Ulcer, peptic
Worms
Wounds

**Parts Used**            **Element**            **Planet**
Essential Oil             Water                  Venus
Flowering Tops
Leaves

**Do Not Use**
Pregnancy  ☐
Lactation  ☐            **Male**  ☐            **Female**  ☑
Children  ☐
Frail  ☐

**Cautions**
While generally recognized as safe, traditionally reputed to affect the
menstrual cycle therefore amounts greater than usually used in food
should not be taken during pregnancy or lactation. Thyme essential oil
is a dermal and mucous membrane irritant, has a low therapeutic
margin and should never be used orally or topically without dilution.

# *Tilia platyphyllos*

## Linden, Lime (Tree)

**Family** Tiliaceae          ☐ **Low Therapeutic Margin**

**Medicinal Uses**          **Magical Intentions**
Blood pressure, high          Immortality, To Attain
Colds          Love, To Attract
Flu          Luck, To Obtain
Migraine          Protection
          Sleep

**Parts Used**          **Element**          **Planet**
Flowers          Air          Jupiter

**Do Not Use**
Pregnancy   ☐
Lactation   ☐          **Male**  ☑          **Female**  ☐
Children   ☐
Frail      ☐

# *Trifolium pratense*

## Red Clover

**Family** Fabaceae      ☐ **Low Therapeutic Margin**

**Medicinal Uses**
Acne
Anemia
Bronchitis
Burns
Cancer
Cough
Eczema
Herpes zoster
Infection
Lactation, promote milk
Nervous tension
Pertussis
Psoriasis
Sores
Wounds

**Magical Intentions**
Exorcism
Fidelity, to Ensure
Love, To Attract
Luck, To Obtain
Money, Riches, Treasures, Wealth
Protection
Success, To Attain

**Parts Used**
Flowering Tops

**Element**
Air

**Planet**
Mercury

**Do Not Use**
Pregnancy ☑
Lactation ☑    **Male** ☑    **Female** ☐
Children ☐
Frail ☐

**Cautions**

Potential herb/drug interactions. Pharmaceuticals that use this pathway include antiretrovirals & oral contraceptives.

**Notes**

When using for medicinal purposes, make a decoction of the flowers rather than an infusion.

# *Trigonella foenum-graecum*

## Fenugreek

**Family** Fabaceae

☐ **Low Therapeutic Margin**

**Medicinal Uses**

Anorexia

Appetite Loss

Cholesterol, High

Fever

Gastritis

Halitosis

Leukorrhea

Ulcer, gastric

**Magical Intentions**

Money, Riches, Treasures, Wealth

**Parts Used**

Seed

**Element**

Air

**Planet**

Mercury

**Do Not Use**

Pregnancy ☑

Lactation ☐

Children ☐

Frail ☐

**Male** ☑

**Female** ☐

# *Trilisa odoratissima*

## Deer's Tongue

**Family** Asteraceae

□ **Low Therapeutic Margin**

**Medicinal Uses**
None known

**Magical Intentions**
Gossip, To Halt
Lust, To Increase/Create
Psychic Powers, To Strengthen

**Parts Used**
Aerial

**Element**
Fire

**Planet**
Mars

**Do Not Use**
Pregnancy □
Lactation □
Children □
Frail □

**Male** ☑

**Female** □

# *Triticum spp*

## Wheat

**Family** Poaceae

☐ **Low Therapeutic Margin**

**Medicinal Uses**
Cancer
Constipation
Cough
Sore throat

**Magical Intentions**
Fertility, To Increase
Money, Riches, Treasures, Wealth

**Parts Used**
Seed
Whole Plant

**Element**
Earth

**Planet**
Venus

**Do Not Use**
Pregnancy ☐
Lactation ☐
Children ☐
Frail ☐

**Male** ☐

**Female** ☑

# *Turnera diffusa*

## Damiana

**Family** Turneraceae    ☐ **Low Therapeutic Margin**

**Medicinal Uses**
Depression
Dyspepsia
Impotence

**Magical Intentions**
Love, To Attract
Lust, To Increase/Create
Visions, To Induce

**Parts Used**
Leaves
Stem

**Element**
Fire

**Planet**
Mars

**Do Not Use**
Pregnancy ☐
Lactation ☐
Children ☐
Frail ☐

**Male** ☑      **Female** ☐

# *Tussilago farfara*

## Coltsfoot

**Family** Asteraceae     ☐ **Low Therapeutic Margin**

**Medicinal Uses**     **Magical Intentions**

Asthma             Love, To Attract

Bronchitis       Peace/Harmony, To Instill

Cystitis         Visions, To Induce

Emphysema

Pertussis

**Parts Used**     **Element**     **Planet**

Flowers        Water       Venus

Leaves

**Do Not Use**

Pregnancy ☐

Lactation ☐     **Male** ☐         **Female** ☑

Children ☐

Frail ☐

**Cautions**

Has cancer-causing agents but no danger of acute poisoning when herb is used as prescribed. Do not use for prolonged periods.

# *Ulmus campestris*

## Elm

**Family** Urticaceae          ☐ **Low Therapeutic Margin**

**Medicinal Uses**          **Magical Intentions**
None known          Love, To Attract

**Parts Used**          **Element**          **Planet**
Inner bark          Water          Saturn

**Do Not Use**
Pregnancy  ☐
Lactation   ☐          **Male**  ☐          **Female**  ☑
Children   ☐
Frail       ☐

# *Ulmus fulva*

# Slippery Elm

**Family** Ulmaceae        ☐ **Low Therapeutic Margin**

**Medicinal Uses**            **Magical Intentions**
Asthma                       Gossip, To Halt
Bronchitis
Burns
Childbirth
Constipation
Cough
Dermatitis
Diarrhea
Eczema
Gastritis
Hiatal hernia
Insomnia
Pneumonia
Psoriasis
Sore throat
Stress
Sunburn
Thrush
Vaginal infection

**Parts Used**          **Element**          **Planet**
Inner bark              Air                  Saturn

**Do Not Use**
Pregnancy  ☐
Lactation  ☐            **Male**  ☐              **Female**  ☑
Children   ☐
Frail      ☐

# *Urginea scilla*

## Squill

**Family** Liliaceae

☐ **Low Therapeutic Margin**

**Medicinal Uses**
Bronchitis
Pertussis

**Magical Intentions**
Hexes, To Break
Money, Riches, Treasures, Wealth
Protection

**Parts Used**
Root

**Element**
Fire

**Planet**
Mars

**Do Not Use**
Pregnancy  ☐
Lactation  ☐
Children  ☐
Frail  ☐

**Male**  ☑

**Female**  ☐

**Cautions**
May cause nausea and vomiting even in therapeutic doses.
Large amounts can be toxic

# *Urtica dioica*

# Nettle, Stinging Nettle

**Family** Urticaceae        ☐ **Low Therapeutic Margin**

**Medicinal Uses**

Arthritis, rheumatoid

Eczema

Gall stones

Myalgia

**Magical Intentions**

Exorcism

Gossip, To Halt

Healing, To Promote

Hexes, To Break

Lust, To Increase/Create

Protection

Stress Management

**Parts Used**

Aerial

Root

**Element**

Fire

**Planet**

Mars

**Do Not Use**

Pregnancy ☐

Lactation ☐

Children ☐

Frail ☐

**Male** ☑

**Female** ☐

**Cautions**

Fresh nettle causes urticaria if applied topically. Internal use may theoretically decrease the efficacy of anticoagulant drugs.

# *Vaccinium myrtillus*

## Blueberry; Huckleberry; Bilberry

**Family** Ericaceae          ☐ **Low Therapeutic Margin**

**Medicinal Uses**          **Magical Intentions**
Diabetes                     Hexes, To Break
Diarrhea                     Luck, To Obtain
Fluid Retention              Protection
Hemorrhoids

**Parts Used**          **Element**          **Planet**
Fruit                    Water                Venus
Leaves

**Do Not Use**
Pregnancy   ☐
Lactation   ☐          **Male** ☐          **Female** ☑
Children   ☐
Frail      ☐

# *Valeriana officinalis*

# Valerian

**Family** Valerianaceae          □ **Low Therapeutic Margin**

| **Medicinal Uses** | **Magical Intentions** |
|---|---|
| Anxiety | Divination |
| Blood pressure, high | Love, To Attract |
| Indigestion | Protection |
| Insomnia | Purification |
| Tension | Sleep |

| **Parts Used** | **Element** | **Planet** |
|---|---|---|
| Rhizome | Water | Venus |
| Root | | |
| Stem | | |

**Do Not Use**

Pregnancy  □
Lactation  □          **Male** □                    **Female** ☑
Children  □
Frail  □

**Cautions**

May potentiate the effects of sedative drugs. A characteristic
paradoxical reaction occurs in a few people, producing an unpleasant
stimulant response.

# *Vanilla spp.*

## Vanilla

**Family** Orchidaceae

☐ **Low Therapeutic Margin**

**Medicinal Uses**
None known

**Magical Intentions**
Friendship, To Promote
Love, To Attract
Lust, To Increase/Create
Mental Powers, To Strengthen

**Parts Used**
Seed

**Element**
Water

**Planet**
Venus

**Do Not Use**
Pregnancy ☐
Lactation ☐
Children ☐
Frail ☐

**Male** ☐

**Female** ☑

# *Verbascum thapsus*

## Mullein

**Family** Scrophulariaceae    ☐ **Low Therapeutic Margin**

| **Medicinal Uses** | **Magical Intentions** |
|---|---|
| Asthma | Courage, To Attain |
| Bronchitis | Divination |
| Cough | Exorcism |
| Cramp | Health, To Maintain |
| Digestion, sluggish | Love, To Attract |
| Dysentery | Protection |
| Earache | |
| Hayfever | |
| Hemorrhoids | |
| Insomnia | |
| Mastitis | |
| Pertussis | |
| Sores | |
| Sprain | |
| Toothache | |
| Wounds | |

| **Parts Used** | **Element** | **Planet** |
|---|---|---|
| Flowers | Fire | Saturn |
| Fruit | | |
| Leaves | | |
| Root | | |

**Do Not Use**
Pregnancy ☐
Lactation ☐    **Male** ☐      **Female** ☑
Children ☐
Frail ☐

# *Verbena officinalis*

## Vervain

**Family** Verbenaceae       ☐ **Low Therapeutic Margin**

**Medicinal Uses**         **Magical Intentions**
Colds                Anger Management
Cough                Chastity, To Maintain
Jaundice              Healing, To Promote
                  Love, To Attract
                  Luck, To Obtain
                  Money, Riches, Treasures, Wealth
                  Peace/Harmony, To Instill
                  Protection
                  Purification
                  Sleep
                  Youth, To Maintain or Regain

**Parts Used**         **Element**        **Planet**
Aerial               Earth           Venus

**Do Not Use**
Pregnancy  ☐
Lactation   ☐        **Male**  ☐          **Female**  ☑
Children   ☐
Frail      ☐

# *Vinca minor*

# Periwinkle

**Family** Apocynaceae

☐ **Low Therapeutic Margin**

**Medicinal Uses**
Colitis
Diarrhea
Menorrhagia
Metrorrhagia
Nosebleed

**Magical Intentions**
Love, To Attract
Lust, To Increase/Create
Mental Powers, To Strengthen
Money, Riches, Treasures, Wealth
Protection

**Parts Used**
Aerial

**Element**
Water

**Planet**
Venus

**Do Not Use**
Pregnancy ☐
Lactation ☐
Children ☐
Frail ☐

**Male** ☐

**Female** ☑

# *Viola odorata*

## Sweet Violet

**Family** Violaceae          ☐ **Low Therapeutic Margin**

**Medicinal Uses**          **Magical Intentions**
Arthritis, rheumatoid          Divination
Bronchitis          Healing, To Promote
Eczema          Love, To Attract
Urinary tract infection          Luck, To Obtain
          Lust, To Increase/Create
          Peace/Harmony, To Instill
          Protection
          Wishes, To Manifest

**Parts Used**          **Element**          **Planet**
Flowers          Water          Venus
Leaves

**Do Not Use**
Pregnancy   ☐
Lactation   ☐          **Male** ☐          **Female** ☑
Children   ☐
Frail      ☐

# *Viola tricolor*

# Heartsease, Pansy

**Family** Violaceae     ☐ **Low Therapeutic Margin**

**Medicinal Uses**     **Magical Intentions**

Acne     Divination

Bronchitis     Love, Divination Of

Cradle cap     Love, To Attract

Cystitis     Rain, To Cause To Fall

Edema

Pertussis

Psoriasis

**Parts Used**     **Element**     **Planet**

Aerial     Water     Saturn

**Do Not Use**

Pregnancy ☐

Lactation ☐     **Male** ☐     **Female** ☑

Children ☐

Frail ☐

# *Viscum album*

## Mistletoe

**Family** Lorantheaceae

☑ **Low Therapeutic Margin**

**Medicinal Uses**
Blood pressure, high
Cancer

**Magical Intentions**
Exorcism
Fertility, To Increase
Healing, To Promote
Health, To Maintain
Hunting, To Aid
Love, To Attract
Protection

**Parts Used**
Twigs

**Element**
Air

**Planet**
Sun

**Do Not Use**
Pregnancy ☐
Lactation ☐
Children ☐
Frail ☐

**Male** ☑

**Female** ☐

# *Vitex agnus-castus*

## Vitex, Chasteberry

**Family** Verbenaceae          ☐ **Low Therapeutic Margin**

**Medicinal Uses**          **Magical Intentions**
Dysmenorrhea          None known
Menopause
PMS

**Parts Used**          **Element**          **Planet**
Fruit               Moon

**Do Not Use**
Pregnancy   ☐
Lactation   ☐          **Male** ☐          **Female** ☑
Children   ☐
Frail   ☐

**Cautions**
Theoretically possible that the herb may interact with dopamine antagonists and dopamine-receptor-blocking agents.

# *Vitis vinifera*

## Grape

**Family** Vitaceae ☐ **Low Therapeutic Margin**

**Medicinal Uses** | **Magical Intentions**

Cough — Fertility, To Increase

Diabetes — Mental Powers, To Strengthen

Leukorrhea — Money, Riches, Treasures, Wealth

Metrorrhagia

**Parts Used** | **Element** | **Planet**

Fruit | Water | Moon

Leaves

**Do Not Use**

Pregnancy ☐

Lactation ☐   **Male** ☐        **Female** ☑

Children ☐

Frail ☐

# *Yucca spp.*

## Yucca

**Family** Agavaceae     ☐ **Low Therapeutic Margin**

**Medicinal Uses**     **Magical Intentions**
Blood pressure, high     Protection
Cholesterol, High     Purification
Diabetes

**Parts Used**     **Element**     **Planet**
Leaves     Fire     Mars

**Do Not Use**
Pregnancy ☐
Lactation ☐     **Male** ☑     **Female** ☐
Children ☐
Frail ☐

# *Zanthoxylum americanum*

## Prickly Ash

**Family** Rutaceae          ☐ **Low Therapeutic Margin**

**Medicinal Uses**          **Magical Intentions**
Arthritis, rheumatoid          Love, To Attract
Chillblains
Varicose ulcers
Varicose veins

**Parts Used**          **Element**          **Planet**
Bark          Fire          Mars
Berries

**Do Not Use**
Pregnancy ☐
Lactation ☐          **Male** ☑          **Female** ☐
Children ☐
Frail ☐

**Cautions**
May interfere with anticoagulant therapy

# *Zea mays*

## Corn

**Family** Poaceae □ **Low Therapeutic Margin**

**Medicinal Uses**
Bladder inflammation
Cystitis
Kidney stones
Urethritis

**Magical Intentions**
Divination
Luck, To Obtain
Protection

**Parts Used**
Silk

**Element**
Earth

**Planet**
Venus

**Do Not Use**
Pregnancy □
Lactation □
Children □
Frail □

**Male** □

**Female** ☑

# *Zingiber officinale*

## Ginger

**Family** Zingiberaceae    ☐ **Low Therapeutic Margin**

**Medicinal Uses**
Amenorrhea
Appetite Loss
Chillblains
Cholesterol, High
Cramp
Dysmenorrhea
Dyspepsia
Flatulence
Inflammation
Motion sickness
Nausea
Sore throat
Worms

**Magical Intentions**
Love, To Attract
Money, Riches, Treasures, Wealth
Power, To Obtain
Success, To Attain

**Parts Used**
Rhizome
Root

**Element**
Fire

**Planet**
Mars

**Do Not Use**
Pregnancy ☐
Lactation ☐
Children ☐
Frail ☐

**Male** ☑      **Female** ☐

**Cautions**

Do not use if gallstones present.

May influence bleeding times and immunological parameters because it inhibits thromboxane synthase & acts as a prostacyclin agent. Large doses (12-14mg) may enhance the effect of anticoagulant drugs. Could have potential interaction with antidiabetes drugs & even cause hypoglycemia. Has hypotensive & calcium blocking effects and may potentially interact with calcium channel blockers.

Weigh risks if using during pregnancy for morning sickness.

# BOOKS

O is a symbol of the world, of oneness and unity. In different cultures it also means the "eye," symbolizing knowledge and insight. We aim to publish books that are accessible, constructive and that challenge accepted opinion, both that of academia and the "moral majority."

Our books are available in all good English language bookstores worldwide. If you don't see the book on the shelves ask the bookstore to order it for you, quoting the ISBN number and title. Alternatively you can order online (all major online retail sites carry our titles) or contact the distributor in the relevant country, listed on the copyright page.

See our website **www.o-books.net** for a full list of over 500 titles, growing by 100 a year.

And tune in to myspiritradio.com for our book review radio show, hosted by June-Elleni Laine, where you can listen to the authors discussing their books.

mySpiritRadio